Using

WordPerfect 6.0

for Windows

▐ More Software Application Tutorials from McGraw-Hill

Using

WordPerfect 6.0
for Windows

Gwynne Larsen
Marcia Hydrusko

 McGRAW-HILL

New York St. Louis San Francisco Auckland Bogotá Caracas
Lisbon London Madrid Mexico Milan Montreal New Delhi Paris
San Juan Singapore Sydney Tokyo Toronto

MCGRAW-HILL
San Francisco, CA 94133

Using WordPerfect 6.0 for Windows

2 3 4 5 6 7 8 9 0 SEM SEM 9 0 9 8 7 6 5

ISBN 0-07-036602-0

Sponsoring editor: Roger Howell
Editorial assistant: Rhonda Sands
Technical reviewers: Shari Cohen and Sheila Sprenkel
Production supervisor: Leslie Austin
Project manager: Jane Granoff
Interior designer: Wendy Calmenson
Cover designer: Tom Trujillo
Composition: Cecelia Morales
Printer and binder: Semline, Inc.

Library of Congress Card Catalog No. 93-78737

Contents

Preface

Using WordPerfect 6.0 for Windows assumes no prior computer experience. The step-by-step, hands-on tutorial approach teaches novice users the basic to advanced features of WordPerfect 6.0 for Windows. In addition, the general concepts and capabilities of word processing are explained. This book can be used in an exclusively self-paced environment, the classroom, or as a reference.

Approach and Organization

The first lesson introduces the user to the Windows environment. Users then progress into WordPerfect 6.0 for Windows. Each feature is described, then demonstrated with hands-on exercises, multiple screen displays, and interesting examples. Numerous exercises emphasize how to effectively integrate Windows' multi-tasking capabilities with WordPerfect 6.0 for Windows.

Each lesson begins with a list of objectives. Separate sections then describe the different program features, beginning with a description of the function and the procedures necessary to use it, followed by exercises that lead the user through practical applications. "Notes" and "Caution" sections throughout alert the user to possible problems or errors. Each lesson concludes with a review of commands, a self-test, and additional exercises to reinforce the user's learning.

Distinguishing Features

As you review this book, you will note the following:

- **Comprehensive coverage**—Basic-to-advanced word processing concepts, including desktop publishing features, are presented in a building-block approach.

- **Step-by-step, hands-on approach**—Knowing when to use a command is not left to chance. Each exercise is written in a step-by-step, tutorial style that is easy to read and understand.

- **Mouse, keyboard, shortcut keys**—Mouse actions comprise the primary method of command presentation. Shortcut keyboard commands are also included when available.

- **Conceptual base**—In addition to presenting the commands, the theory behind each feature is described, including when, where, and how to use it.

- **Real-world scenario**—Lessons are built on examples using a publishing company to provide the user with opportunities to learn WordPerfect features within the context of a real business.
- **Screen displays and sample documents**—Graphic representations of menus, dialog boxes, and practice files throughout the book clarify concepts and help monitor user progress.
- **On Your Own**—At the end of each lesson, a review of commands, review questions, and assignments of varying levels of difficulty give users a thorough review of the material covered within the lesson.
- **Ready reference appendix**—Command summary of features, menu selection, and shortcut keys for Windows and WordPerfect 6.0 for Windows are presented at the end of the text.

Supporting Materials

- **3 ½" Student Data Disk**—Packaged with the Instructor's Manual, it contains documents for completing the hands-on exercises in the tutorials and the end-of chapter exercises beginning with Lesson 10.
- **Instructor's Manual**—Includes, for each lesson, answers to the Review of Commands and Lesson Review, completed examples of the Assignments, teaching tips, and a variety of test questions.

Hardware and Software Requirements

To run WordPerfect 6.0 for Windows effectively, an IBM, or compatible, microcomputer with at least a 386DX microprocessor, 6-8 MB of memory, and graphics capability is needed. Windows 3.1 and WordPerfect 6.0 for Windows are the software applications necessary for the course.

Acknowledgments

We would like to thank our families for their continued support and Roger Howell, Rhonda Sands, and Leslie Austin at McGraw-Hill, Ryan Stuart at Graphics West, and Jane Granoff for helping us produce the text in a timely manner. Also, many thanks to our reviewers, especially Sheila Spangler at Colby Community College, for their excellent feedback.

1 Introducing Windows

Objectives

After completing this lesson, you will be able to:

- Define a Local Area Network
- Explain the difference between a Text Based Interface and a Graphical User Interface
- Identify, describe, and use the Program Manager
- Identify application and document windows and their components
- Select and cancel menu options
- Manipulate and close windows and icons
- Describe the File Manager
- Edit, save, and print a file using the Paintbrush, Notepad, and Write accessories
- Use Object Linking and Embedding to update a figure in an application

Local Area Networks

The microcomputers in many school labs are part of a **Local Area Network** (LAN). A LAN connects microcomputers, printers, and other peripherals via cable to a larger microcomputer called a **file server**. The file server stores all the software used on the network. The network's operating environment might be a **Text Based Interface** (TBI), such as DOS (the Disk Operating System used on IBM and IBM-compatibles), or a **Graphical User Interface** (GUI), such as Windows. Although Windows is considered an operating *environment*, not an operating *system*, it does control your access to the software programs stored on the file server. The GUI command structure is composed of **icons** (symbols or pictures representing programs, accessories, and files) and **pull-down menus** (a list of command options that drops down from the top of the screen). Both icons and menus are accessed via the mouse.

1

▌ DOS

Although most file management functions can be performed through the File Manager in Windows or the File Manager in WordPerfect, there are some functions you might want to perform in DOS. The only DOS command we will cover here is how to **format** a disk (prepare the disk to accept data); copying, renaming, and deleting files will be covered in later chapters. A disk *must* be formatted to be usable. If the disk in your floppy drive is not formatted and you try to save to it, you will get an error message saying that the drive cannot be read. In addition to preparing the disk to accept data from your computer, formatting also deletes everything on the disk. Be sure that it's okay to lose all the data on the disk before formatting it.

You'll need to know the size and density of your disk before formatting it. Some computers display icons for you to select when formatting your disk, such as 5 ¼" high-density, 5 ¼" low-density, 3 ½" high-density, and 3 ½" low-density. If your disk is marked "double-density" it should be formatted for low-density.

NOTE: Steps preceded by a bullet are for your reference and are to be read only. They are not intended to be hands-on exercises.

- Double-click on the DOS icon.
- If you do not see a C:\DOS prompt, type CD\DOS and press (Enter).
- Type Format A: (or B: if your floppy disk is in the B drive) and press (Enter).

  CAUTION: Be sure to type A: or B:, or the C: drive will be erased along with all your programs and files on that drive. Also, in many computers, the Format command will automatically format the disk in the A drive to high-density, even if a low-density disk is in the drive.

- Follow the screen prompts, pressing (Enter) when asked for a label.
- When asked if you want to format another disk, answer Y or N depending on whether you have another disk to format.
- Press (Enter).

▌ Windows

Windows uses a lot of memory—six megabytes or more—and at least an 80386DX microprocessor to efficiently run several programs at once. WordPerfect for Windows will run on an 80386SX, but it is extremely slow. Still Windows offers many advantages over DOS.

A major advantage of Windows is that several programs can be simultaneously open and running, which is called **multitasking**. Another advantage is that you can often **cut** or **copy** data from one application and **paste** it into another application. (You will practice doing that.) Although Windows offers a complete line of useful applications, we will touch on only a few. Windows comes with a communications module, which allows you to communicate with another computer via modem. To use it, you would select Accessories, then Terminal, and follow the screen prompts. File Manager, Write, Recorder (which creates macros), Notepad, Calculator, Calendar, Cardfile, Clock, Media Player, and Sound Recorder are some of the other available tools you might want to explore.

*NOTE: Throughout this text, exercises that are to be completed by you (hands-on) are numbered, shown in a different color, and marked with a mouse icon. Text that you are to key in is shown in **boldface**.*

▌ Starting Windows

NOTE: You will not need a work disk for the first few exercises, as you will not save any data. Some computer labs, however, require that a formatted disk be in a floppy drive before you may start work.

If Windows is not already running on your computer:

1. Be sure your current drive is C (or wherever Windows resides)

2. Have the DOS prompt C:\ showing

3. Type **WIN**

4. Press (Enter)

When Windows is activated, the screen should be similar to the one shown in Figure 1-1, with the Program Manager and its icons displayed. However, don't be concerned if it is not exactly the same, because different software may be loaded or one icon may be a larger window. Windows' applications and documents are contained in areas called **windows**.

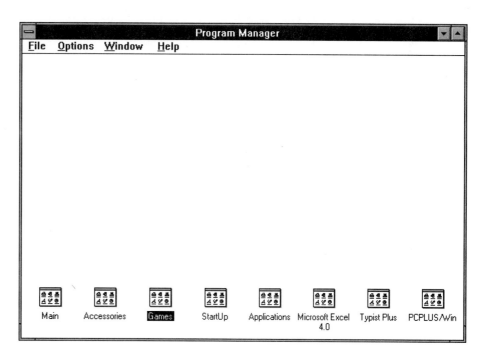

Figure 1-1

The Program Manager

The **Program Manager** is exactly what the name implies—a manager. The Program Manager directs and manages the flow of data, and tracks the software applications that are running and which documents belong in each window. It also controls the computer's hardware, such as the printers, the monitor, memory, and disk drives. When you exit the Program Manager, your Windows session is terminated.

Identifying Windows' Components

Notice that the Program Manager window has various parts or components. A number of important tasks can be performed by selecting one of those components (to select, use either the mouse or combinations of keystrokes). As you work with Windows, you will see that each window has the same basic components. Once you learn to execute a particular function in one window, you can use the same technique in other windows. Window components are identified in Figure 1-2 and described in the following text.

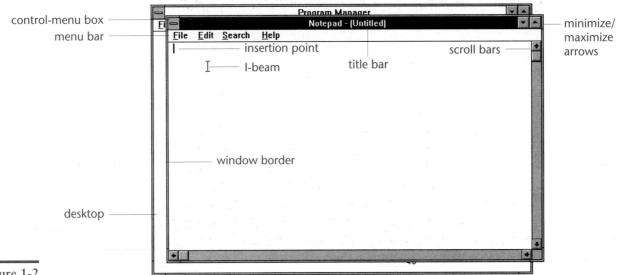

Figure 1-2

Desktop. The screen space that Windows covers is known as the **desktop**—think of it as the surface of a desk. You can move items (software and documents in the form of icons), add new ones, and delete old ones.

Window Borders. The outside edges of the window are called **borders.**

Title Bar. The first line across the top of the window—it identifies the name of the application and document—is called the **title bar.** If more than one window is open, the title bar for the active window is a different color than the other title bars (if you are using a color monitor).

Control-Menu Box. In the upper-left corner of each window is a small box with a dash inside called the **control-menu box.** This box's pull-down menu contains commands allowing you to control the size of the window, terminate the program, or close a document.

Sizing Buttons. Two arrows (one pointing down, one pointing up) called **sizing buttons** are in each window's upper-right corner. The down arrow is called the **minimize** button; when selected, it reduces a window into an icon at the bottom of the desktop. The up arrow is the **maximize** button; it expands the window to fill the screen.

Menu Bar. Directly below the title bar is the **menu bar,** which lists the primary commands of the application you are using. Most applications have at least File, Save, and Help menu options.

Icons. Icons are graphic symbols that represent documents and programs when not opened into a window.

Insertion Point. The **insertion point** is a flashing vertical bar that marks the place where the next action will occur, much as a cursor does in text-based applications. The insertion point will not move as you move the mouse itself; the mouse pointer, described next, moves with the mouse.

Mouse Pointer. The **mouse pointer** can have several different appearances: a single-headed arrow, a double-headed arrow, a quadruple-headed arrow, or an I-beam when in text. The mouse pointer helps move the insertion point by moving the pointer to the desired location and clicking the mouse button.

Program Groups

The Program Manager window is organized into **program groups** displayed as icons at the bottom of the window. Several individual programs can be included in one program group. When you open a program group into a window, additional icons display. These icons are called **program icons** and represent applications that you can run. Double-clicking on a program icon starts the application.

Windows comes with several predefined program groups: Main, Accessories, Games, Windows Applications, and Non-Windows Applications. Each program group contains several program icons. With sensible planning, you can easily organize your work and group your applications in a comprehensible way. As mentioned before, your Program Manager may appear different from the one shown in this text because of the different programs loaded. However, the process for using the Program Manager is the same.

Using the Mouse

Usually, the most efficient way to give Windows a command is to use the **mouse.** Move the mouse by sliding it across a flat surface (such as a desktop). As the mouse moves on the desktop, the mouse pointer (an arrow on the screen) moves in the corresponding direction. A slight movement of the mouse on the desktop will move the mouse pointer a great distance onscreen. If you run out of space on the desktop, simply pick up the mouse, set it back down elsewhere, and slide it again.

Mice come with two or three buttons. The left mouse button is the primary button that you will use. If your mouse has three buttons, you will not use the middle button. To select using the mouse, move the mouse pointer onto the desired item, then quickly press and release the left mouse button. This is referred to as **clicking,** or sometimes **point and click.** There are two additional terms that you need to be familiar with when using the mouse. **Double-clicking** means to rapidly press and release the left mouse button twice—the pressing should be done gently. **Dragging** means to hold the left mouse button down while moving the mouse.

In the following exercise, you will open a program group icon into a window.

1. Position the mouse pointer anywhere on the Accessories group icon

2. Click the left mouse button once

The icon menu appears as shown in Figure 1-3.

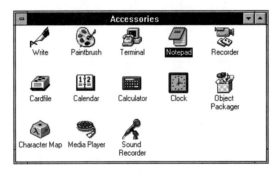

Figure 1-3

3. Position the mouse pointer on the <u>R</u>estore option

4. Click the left mouse button once

The Accessories window appears as shown in Figure 1-4.

Figure 1-4

Notice that the Accessories window has most of the same components as the Program Manager—title bar, control-menu box, minimize and maximize buttons, and icons.

The two kinds of windows that appear on your Windows desktop are known as **application windows** and **document windows**.

An application window contains a running application, such as WordPerfect. The name of the application, any associated document, and the application's menu bar appear at the top of the application window.

Document windows have the same components as application windows except for the menu bar. The document window shares the application window's menu bar. A document window may contain files or documents. Program Manager is an application window that allows you to open several document windows (called groups) in its application workspace. These windows share the application's menu bar, but have their own title bar. Notice that the Accessories window you have open does not have a menu bar. This window is a document window.

Leave the Accessories window open.

▌ Selecting and Canceling a Menu

There will be times when you inadvertently make the wrong menu choice. If you activate the wrong menu, just move the mouse pointer off the pull-down menu and click the left mouse button once.

1. Position the mouse pointer on the <u>W</u>indow menu option of the menu bar

2. Click the left mouse button once

A pull-down menu appears as shown in Figure 1-5.

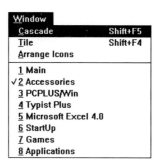

Figure 1-5

To cancel the pull-down menu:

3. Move the mouse pointer off the menu and click the left mouse button once

The Window pull-down menu closes.

4. Position the mouse pointer on <u>O</u>ptions in the menu bar

5. Click the left mouse button once

The Options menu shown in Figure 1-6 appears.

Figure 1-6

Note that there is a checkmark preceding "<u>S</u>ave Settings on Exit." A checkmark preceding a command denotes that the menu option is activated or turned on; to deactivate the option, click it. This option instructs Windows to save the arrangement of the Program Manager windows and icons when exiting.

NOTE: After your desktop is arranged as you like it, activate <u>S</u>ave Settings on Exit in the <u>O</u>ptions pull-down menu, then exit Windows. The next time you run Windows, deactivate <u>S</u>ave Settings on Exit in the <u>O</u>ptions pull-down menu; the original settings will remain regardless of the changes you make during future sessions.

If you are working in a computer lab, check with your instructor before doing the following exercise. Some labs will not want the original settings changed.

In this exercise you will turn off the <u>S</u>ave Settings on Exit feature.

1. Position the mouse pointer on the <u>S</u>ave Settings on Exit option

2. Click the left mouse button once

The pull-down menu closes. To ensure that the option is turned off:

3. Click the mouse pointer on Options in the menu bar and check to see that the checkmark is gone

4. Move the mouse pointer off the menu and click the left mouse button once to close the pull-down menu

Selecting a Menu via the Keyboard

You have been using the mouse to instruct Windows. Windows gives you an alternate method for selecting menu options—using the keyboard. Notice that each option on the menu bar has one underlined letter. To activate a menu option via keyboard, press the (Alt) key, then the underlined letter of the desired option. Once a pull-down menu is open, to select an option, type the underlined letter of the desired feature. If you open an incorrect menu, press (Esc) to cancel the menu option.

1. Press (Alt)

2. Type o (for Options)

   NOTE: Each option in a pull-down menu has one underlined letter. To activate the option, simply type the underlined letter. In this case you will type an "S" to activate the Save Settings on Exit option.

3. Type s

   The Options pull-down menu disappears.

   Open the Options pull-down menu to verify that the Save Settings on Exit option is turned on.

4. Press (Alt) + (O)

   To close the Options pull-down menu:

5. Press (Esc) twice

   You may use either the mouse or keyboard to activate an option from the menu bar or an option from a pull-down menu.

   To use the mouse, position the mouse pointer on the option and click the left mouse button once. To choose an option from the menu bar using the keyboard, press (Alt) + the underlined letter of the menu option. Once the pull-down menu is open, type the underlined letter of the desired option.

   NOTE: From this point forward, only the mouse approach for making selections will be part of the instructions. Keyboard shortcuts will be preceded by a checkmark.

▍ Opening a Program Group Window

As mentioned, the Program Manager contains several group icons. Each group icon contains several **application** icons, which are graphical representations of application programs that you may run. The easiest way to start an application is to open the group icon, then select the desired application icon. To open or restore a program group, position the mouse pointer on the icon and click the left mouse button once. A pop-up menu appears; click on its Restore option.

In this exercise, you will restore the Paintbrush icon to a window. You currently have the Accessories window open.

NOTE: Group icons and program icons may also be restored to a window by double-clicking on the icon. If you have difficulty double-clicking on the icon, click on the icon once to highlight the name of the icon, then press (Enter).

1. Double-click on the Paintbrush icon

The Paintbrush icon is restored and opens to a window.

▌ Moving a Window

When you have several windows open at the same time, they may stack on top of each other. You can easily move one of these windows.

- Position the mouse pointer in the title bar.
- Press and hold the left mouse button down while dragging the window to the desired position.
- Release the mouse button.

To cancel the move:

- Press (Esc) before releasing the mouse button.

Two windows are now open on your desktop. You will practice dragging a window to another position on the desktop.

1. Position the mouse pointer in the Paintbrush title bar

2. Press and hold the left mouse button; keeping the button depressed, drag the window to the upper left corner of the screen, then release the mouse button

▌ Changing a Window's Size

When working with multiple applications onscreen, you might want to reduce the size of a window (without minimizing it) or enlarge the window (without maximizing it). Windows gives you this capability.

You may have noticed in the previous exercises that the shape of the mouse pointer changed to a double-headed arrow when the pointer moved over a window border. The double-headed arrow is used to change a window's size.

When the mouse pointer changes to a double-headed arrow as you approach a border, press the left mouse button and drag the border until the window is the right size. You can see the border move as you drag it, but the window size is not actually changed until the left mouse button is released. With the pointer at a corner, the size of two borders can be changed at one time.

In this exercise, you will change the size of a window.

1. Move the mouse pointer slowly over the right border of the Paintbrush window until the shape changes to a double-headed arrow

2. Press and hold the left mouse button. Move the border in before releasing the mouse button

3. Move the mouse pointer slowly over the window's lower-right corner until the mouse pointer becomes a double-headed arrow

4. Press and hold the left mouse button. Drag the border toward the lower right before releasing the button

If you've minimized or maximized a window, when it is restored, the window will be the same size and in the same location as it was before being minimized or maximized.

▋ Activating a Window

Although Windows allows you to have several windows open at the same time, only one window may be active at any given time. When you open a new window, that window automatically becomes the **foreground** or **active** window. When several windows are open at the same time, the active window appears in front, and the title bar changes color to distinguish it from the other, inactive windows. To activate a window, move the mouse pointer anywhere within its borders and click the left mouse button once.

Background Windows

All windows that are open but not active are in the background. The **background** windows get a smaller share of the computer's processing time, so they run more slowly. For example, if the computer is searching a database in the background while you work on word processing in the active window, the search will take longer than it would if performed in the active window.

On your desktop, the Paintbrush window is the active window—it is in front of all other windows and the title bar is a different color.

NOTE: Sometimes it's not possible to see enough of a window to click on it. Press (Ctrl) + (Esc) *to activate* **Task List,** *an option box displaying active documents and programs, as shown in Figure 1-7. Highlight the program you want and click on Switch To to activate the desired window.*

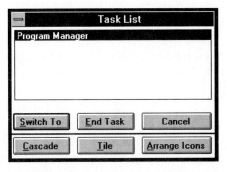

Figure 1-7

To activate the Accessories window:

1. Position the mouse pointer within the Accessories window (you may have to move the Paintbrush window or click on the maximize button in the upper-left corner)

2. Click the left mouse button once

The Accessories window is now the active, front window and its title bar is a different color. Now make the Paintbrush window current.

1. Position the mouse pointer within the Paintbrush window (you may have to move some windows)

2. Click the left mouse button once

The Paintbrush window is now the active window.

Closing a Program Group Window

When you no longer want a program group window open, you may reduce it to an icon by selecting Close in the control-menu box of the window to be closed. Another way to close a program group window is to double-click on its control-menu box. The control-menu box is the small box with the horizontal bar just to the left of the title bar.

 In this exercise, you will reduce the Paintbrush window to an icon.

1. Position the mouse pointer on the Paintbrush window's control-menu box (you may have to reposition the Paintbrush window to see the control-menu box)

2. Click the left mouse button once to display the Control menu

3. Click on Close

Launching a Program

As mentioned earlier, most icons in a program group window are graphical representations of application programs. To execute (launch) an application program, either double-click the mouse pointer on the icon or click on File in the menu bar, select the Run option, and type the name of the application.

 In this exercise, you will execute the Clock application by double-clicking on the icon. The Accessories window should still be restored to a window on your desktop.

1. Position the mouse pointer on the Clock icon

2. Double-click the left mouse button

An hourglass icon appears while the Clock program is being loaded. (The clock may display in Analog; it depends on the way it was last viewed).

Notice that the Clock window has the same components as the Program Manager—a title bar with the name of the application, a control-menu box, minimize and maximize buttons, and a menu bar. Because the Clock is an application, it has a menu bar.

3. Click on the Settings menu

4. Click on either Analog or Digital, whichever is not active

Maximizing a Window

Maximizing an application window expands the window to cover the entire desktop. When you begin working with applications such as WordPerfect for Windows, Calendar, and Cardfile, it is easier to view and edit documents using the full screen. There are two ways to maximize a window.

- Click on the control-menu box and choose the Maximize option.
- Click on the maximize button.

In this exercise, you will use the control-menu box to maximize the Clock window.

1. Position the mouse pointer on the Clock control-menu box

2. Click the left mouse button once

   The Control menu appears.

3. Click on the Maximize option

   The Clock window expands to fill the entire screen.

Restoring a Window

There are two ways to **restore** a window to its original size.

- Click on the control-menu box and select the Restore option.
- Click on the double-sided arrow in the upper-right corner of the screen. The maximize button has changed to a double-sided arrow to indicate that the window is maximized.

In this exercise, you will use the control-menu box to restore the Clock window to its original size.

1. Position the mouse pointer on the Clock window's control-menu box

2. Click the left mouse button once

   The Control menu appears.

3. Click on the Restore option

Minimizing a Program

To create more room on your desktop, Windows gives you the option to minimize a window. **Minimizing** a window shrinks it into an icon. When an application such as the Clock is minimized, the program is still running in the background and remains operational. All programs continue to operate until you close them. This is an advantage when you repeatedly need to look up information such as a date on your calendar, but you don't want those windows to be cluttering up your desktop.

There are two ways to minimize a window.

- Click on the control-menu box and select the Minimize option.
- Click on the minimize button.

In this exercise, you will use the control-menu box to minimize the Clock to an icon.

1. Position the mouse pointer on the Clock control-menu box

2. Click the left mouse button once

   The Control menu appears.

3. Click on the Mi<u>n</u>imize option

   The clock is now running as an icon near the bottom of the desktop.

Now you will close the Clock application.

1. Position the mouse pointer on the Clock icon

2. Double-click the left mouse button

   The Clock icon is now a window.

3. Position the mouse pointer on the Clock window's control-menu box

4. Double-click the left mouse button

   The Clock application is now closed.

   Notice that the Accessories group is still open. To close the Accessories group:

5. Position the mouse pointer on the Accessories group's control-menu box

6. Double-click the left mouse button

   The Accessories group is closed and the Program Manager window is the active window.

▌ File Manager

The File Manager program in Windows allows you to view and organize your files and directories. You can move, copy, rename, and delete files, create directories, and format disks. Because of the potential for destruction, some computer labs have deleted the File Manager from Windows. If available, it is an easy way to format a disk, done as described next.

- Double-click on File Manager.
- Click on Disk.
- Click on Format Disk.
- Select the appropriate disk drive.
- Select the appropriate capacity.
- Click on OK.

▌ Using Windows' Accessories

One of the accessories in the Windows package is the Notepad. **Notepad** is a text editor; it allows you to create, save, and print **ASCII** files (files that contain no formatting commands; also called DOS text files). Notepad can be used for writing short notes or memos, but it is most useful for creating and editing batch files. It has minimal word processing capabilities, such as word wrap, insert and delete, cut, copy, paste, change margins, find, and headers and footers. To keep the text from extending beyond the window, activate the word wrap option. (The .TXT extension is automatically assigned to Notepad files.)

Cut and Paste

It is possible to move or copy material from Notepad, Cardfile, or Paintbrush, among others. You must first **cut** (remove it from the original location) or **copy** (leave the original in place and make a copy) the text. Then open your destination program, such as Write, and **paste** it in.

Before cutting or copying text, **select** the text you want by **highlighting** it with the mouse or the (F8) key and arrow keys. Selected text is shown in reverse type; the type is white and the background black. When the mouse pointer is moved into text, it becomes an I-beam. There are several ways to select text: (1) Place the I-beam at the beginning of the text, click to activate the insertion point, hold down the mouse button, drag it to the end of the material, and release; (2) place the insertion point at the beginning of the text, press (F8) (for extend), and use the arrow keys to mark the text; or (3) place the insertion point at the beginning of the text, move the I-beam to the end of the text to be selected, press and hold the (Shift) key, and click the left mouse button. To paste text, open the destination program (or move to another area in the same program), position the insertion point, and select Edit ⇒ Paste.

Clipboard

Clipboard is a powerful Windows accessory that lets you store cut or copied information until it can be pasted. Material held in Clipboard remains there until a new selection is moved in, Clipboard is cleared, or the system is turned off. Thus, material can be pasted from Clipboard many times.

The DOS Print Screen command, which prints an exact copy of the material onscreen, is not accessible in Windows. However, you can copy the screen by pressing the Print Screen key ((PrtScrn), or possibly (Alt) + (PrtScrn), or (Ctrl) + (PrtScrn)), which automatically puts a copy of the screen in Clipboard. It is possible to view material in Clipboard by opening Clipboard viewer in Main. You can save it to a file by selecting File ⇒ Save As, and naming the file. You can also open another Windows application and paste Clipboard material into the document.

Saving a File

When a file is saved for the first time, or when you want to assign it a new name or new directory, select the File pull-down menu, then select Save, or Save As, and name the file. (Both Save and Save As respond the same when a file is saved for the first time.) After a file has been saved and named, and you are merely resaving the same file, select File ⇒ Save. The file will be saved without any further action from you. If you attempt to exit an application after you've changed the file, you will be asked whether to save the changes. If you select No, no changes since the last save will be saved; if you select Yes, all changes will be saved.

Printing a File

We are assuming that a printer is properly installed on your system. To check, you can click on File ⇒ Print Setup to see what printers have been installed and which printer is the default. To instruct Windows to print a file:

- Select File.
- Select Print.

The following exercise will show you how to create a file in Notepad, type text, select and copy text, save a file, print the file, and close Notepad.

Before you start, place a blank, formatted disk—a "work disk"—into one of the floppy drives to save the files you create. Because most labs do not allow students to save on the C: drive, our directions will refer to the A: drive. If you are saving to the B: drive or to any other drive, type the letter corresponding to your drive.

1. Double-click on Accessories

2. Double-click on Notepad

3. Select Edit

   The Edit menu displays as shown in Figure 1-8.

Edit	
Undo	Ctrl+Z
Cut	Ctrl+X
Copy	Ctrl+C
Paste	Ctrl+V
Delete	Del
Select All	
Time/Date	F5
Word Wrap	

Figure 1-8

4. Click on Word Wrap

5. Select Edit again

6. Click on Time/Date

7. Press (Enter) twice

8. Type the following:

   FEATURES TO CONSIDER WHEN CHOOSING A LAN

   You should consider several performance issues such as delay, throughput (the amount of data transmitted), reliability, and recoverability after a station failure when choosing a Local Area Network (LAN). You should also consider physical constraints such as raw data speed, maximum operating distance, and the maximum number of stations that can be used. Another issue is the environment in which the LAN will be installed--space allocated, electrical capacity, cable accessibility, and so on. If equipment and software are already in place, compatibility is a factor.

   To save it as a file named lansnpd:

9. Click on File

The File menu displays as shown in Figure 1-9.

Figure 1-9

10. Click on Save As

11. Type **A:lansnpd**

Notice that the .TXT extension is automatically added.

12. Click on OK or press (Enter)

To store it in Windows' Clipboard:

13. Select (highlight) the entire paragraph

14. Click on Edit ⇒ Copy

If you choose Cut, the material will be deleted from your file.

The text will be saved in Windows' Clipboard.

15. Click anywhere within Notepad to deselect the text

16. Close Notepad (double-click the control-menu box)

17. Answer **N** to Save Changes? dialog box

18. Double-click on the Write icon

Be sure the insertion point is at the top of the Write screen.

19. Click on Edit ⇒ Paste

Your text will appear in the Write program, where it can be saved as a file and printed.

20. Click on File ⇒ Save As

21. Type **A:Lanswp** to name the file

22. Click on OK or press (Enter)

23. To print it, click on File ⇒ Print

24. Click on File ⇒ Close

Object Linking and Embedding

Another powerful Windows tool is **Object Linking and Embedding** (OLE), a faster, more efficient way to create compound documents (documents containing several different elements, such as graphics, spreadsheets, drawings, and so on). OLE lets you create an object in one application document, called the **source** document, and insert it into a document in another application, called the **destination** document. If the object is only *embedded,* changes made in the second embedded document will have no effect on the original document. If the object is *linked*, changes made in the linked object will occur in the original object also. To make changes to the object while it is in the receiving document, select the object in the destination document and the source document will open, allowing you to make the changes. You save the time it would take to close a document, open another to make changes, close it, and open the original.

Many Windows applications now support OLE. You can have several documents linked to one source document. Thus, you can change the object from any of the linked documents; any change made will occur in all the documents. Before they can be linked, the source document must be saved. The following is an example of embedding an object created in Paintbrush into Write.

1. Open Paintbrush

2. Draw a figure

   You will see a small black dot on the screen. Hold down the left mouse button and draw any type of figure or picture. Artistic ability is not an issue here; witness our example in Figure 1-10.

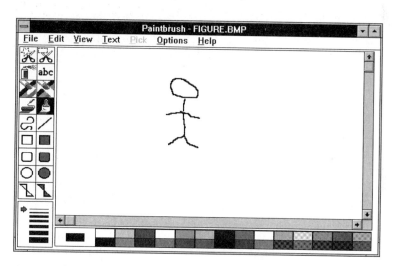

Figure 1-10

3. Save the document as a:figure

   The .bmp extension, which stands for "bit mapped," is automatically added.

4. Select the figure to be copied

   Move the mouse pointer to the scissors icon in the far left corner and click once. Move the pointer to the area outside the picture or figure and draw a circle around it. The circle will become a dotted line.

5. Click on Edit ⇒ Copy

6. Minimize Paintbrush

7. Open Write

8. Type the following paragraph:

```
I am going to insert a figure I drew in Paintbrush. I am
going to save the Write document, then make changes to
the figure. When I double-click on the figure in Write,
Paintbrush will open. I will make changes to the figure,
save the file, and exit Paintbrush. When I return to
Write, those changes will be made in my Write figure.
```

9. Save the file as figpaint

10. Move the insertion point to the end of the paragraph

11. Press (Enter) three times

12. Press (Tab) four times

13. Click on Edit ⇒ Paste Special

The Paste Special dialog box, as shown in Figure 1-11, opens.

Figure 1-11

14. Accept Paintbrush Picture Object

15. Press (Enter) to Paste

The figure is copied into Write.

16. Put the mouse pointer on the figure and double-click

Paintbrush opens with the source document open.

17. Make some changes to the drawing, such as those in Figure 1-12

Figure 1-12

18. Click on File ⇒ Update

19. Click on File ⇒ Exit & Return to figpaint.wri

Paintbrush is reduced to an icon.

The changes are made to the figure in your Write document, as shown in Figure 1-13, but your original figure in Paintbrush (figure.bmp) is not changed.

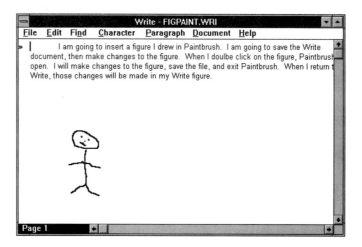

Figure 1-13

20. Close and Exit Paintbrush

21. Save and Exit Write

▌ Rearranging Windows

There are several possible arrangements of windows on your desktop: Cascade, Tile, and unorganized (random). In this exercise you will open several windows and arrange them.

1. The Accessories group should be open

2. Open the Games group (double-click on Games icon)

   NOTE: *If Games is not available on your computer, open one of the other group icons.*

3. Open the Main group icon

   Notice the disorganization of the windows on the desktop as shown in Figure 1-14.

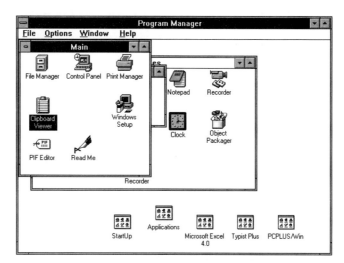

Figure 1-14

4. Click on <u>W</u>indow in the menu bar of the Program Manager

5. Choose <u>C</u>ascade

The windows are set up in layers onscreen as shown in Figure 1-15.

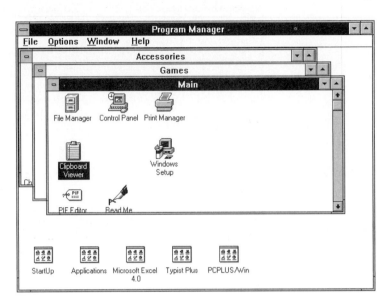

Figure 1-15

6. Select <u>W</u>indow ⇒ <u>T</u>ile

The groups will display onscreen in squares or rectangles with the title bars visible. See Figure 1-16.

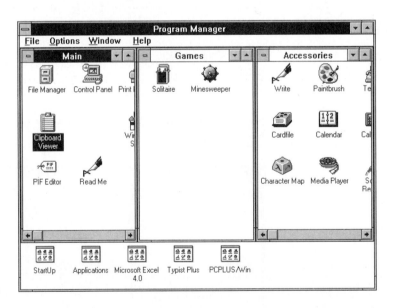

Figure 1-16

▌ **Closing a Program**

To exit or **close** an application program, choose the <u>C</u>lose option from the control-menu box. (A keyboard shortcut is to press (Alt) + (F4).) Remember that closing an application program is different from minimizing. A minimized program is running in the background and is instantly available. If a program has been closed, you must reactivate the program and in some instances load the desired file.

In this exercise, you will use the keyboard to close the Clock application.

1. Move the Accessories window so the Clock icon is visible

2. Position the mouse pointer on the Clock icon

3. Double-click the left mouse button

The Clock window is open.

4. Press (Alt) + (F4)

The application program is closed.

Exiting Windows

When you are finished using Windows, it is important that you return to the DOS prompt before turning off your computer. If there are any unsaved files, Windows will ask you if you want to save them. Before turning off the computer, check with your instructor. Computers in many labs are left on until the lab is closed.

There are three ways to exit Windows.

• Click on the File menu of the Program Manager and select the Exit Windows option.

• Click on the Program Manager's control-menu box and select Close (or double-click on the control-menu button).

• Press (Alt) + (F4) and click on OK.

If you inadvertently exit Windows, you may have to **reboot** (restart the computer without actually turning it off). Press the computer's Reset button or (Ctrl) + (Alt) + (Del) to reboot and type **win** at the C prompt.

Now close the open group windows: You will double-click on the control-menu boxes. Remember, double-clicking on a window's control-menu box is the same as selecting the Close option in the Control menu.

1. Position the mouse pointer on the Accessories window's control-menu box

2. Double-click the left mouse button

The Accessories program group window is reduced to an icon.

On your own, use the mouse or the keyboard to close the Games and Main windows.

On Your Own

Review of Commands

Description	Menu Commands	Function Keys
Start Windows		
Open a program		
Make a running program active		

Exit a program	_____	_____
Enlarge a window to fit the size of the desktop	_____	_____
Reduce a program to an icon	_____	_____
Return a window to its original size	_____	_____
Exit Windows	_____	_____
Copy text from one location to another	_____	_____
Save a Windows file for the first time	_____	_____
Arrange open programs in layers on the desktop	_____	_____
Arrange open programs in rectangles on the desktop	_____	_____

▌ Lesson Review

1. What is a Local Area Network (LAN)?

2. What is a Graphical User Interface (GUI)?

3. What term describes running several applications simultaneously?

4. What is an icon?

5. What is the term for pressing and releasing the mouse button?

6. What is the term for quickly pressing the mouse button twice?

7. What is the name of the command that expands the window to fill the desktop?

8. Explain the minimize command. How does it differ from closing a window?

9. How would you return an expanded window to its original size?

10. What is the term for moving text from one location to another?

11. What is Clipboard?

12. What is the difference between File ⇒ Save and File ⇒ Save As?

13. Name and describe three accessory programs available in Windows.

14. What is the difference between Object Linking and Object Embedding?

15. Describe one way to exit Windows.

▍ Assignments

1-1 Directions

Load Windows, then follow these steps.

1. Open the Accessories program group.

2. Activate the Clock application.

3. Maximize the Clock.

4. Display the Clock in Analog and Digital modes.

5. Minimize the Clock and move it to the upper right of the Desktop.

6. Close the Clock.

1-2 Directions

Load Windows, then follow these steps.

1. Open the Accessories program group.

2. Open Write.

3. Open Paintbrush.

4. Make Paintbrush the active program.

5. Draw a circle. Draw your initials freehand within the circle.

6. Save the file as Initial.bmp on your work disk.

7. Select the drawing by clicking on the scissors icon. Move the pointer to the area outside the figure and draw a rectangle around the figure. Release the mouse button; the rectangle will appear as a dotted line.

8. Copy the selected drawing to the Clipboard (select Edit ⇒ Copy).

9. Make Write the active Window.

10. Paste the Initial drawing in the upper left corner of the document (select Edit ⇒ Paste Special).

11. Save the file as Lettrhd.wri on your work disk.

12. Double-click on your drawing to bring up Paintbrush. Edit the picture until your monogram meets with your satisfaction.

13. Select File ⇒ Update. Then select File ⇒ Exit & Return to Lettrhd.wri.

14. Resave your document, close all applications, and exit Windows.

Getting Started

Objectives

After completing this lesson, you will be able to:

- Describe the components of the status bar
- Edit text using Backspace, Delete, Insert, and Typeover
- Describe WordPerfect's default settings
- Use WordPerfect's Help and Date features
- Type text using underline and boldface
- Describe hard and soft spaces, returns, and page breaks
- Save a document with both Save and Save As
- Move the insertion point through the document
- Display the Reveal Codes screen
- Spell check, print, and close a document
- Exit WordPerfect

Starting WordPerfect

Before you can start WordPerfect, Windows must be running with the Program Manager window open. The WordPerfect program group icon is located in the Program Manager window. To open the WordPerfect program group, double-click on that icon.

The WordPerfect program group window has six application icons: WordPerfect 6.0 (the main program), Speller, Thesaurus, Quick Finder/File Indexes, Kick Off, and Installation. Speller checks spelling; Thesaurus helps look for alternate words; Quick Finder/File Indexes and Kick Off let you set up indexes and directories to search for words or phrases in documents contained in the index; and Installation lets you modify the program from its original installation. To start WordPerfect, double-click on the WordPerfect 6.0 icon.

▌ Command Terminology

Because this text is covering a menu-based, mouse-oriented package, we will emphasize the use of the mouse on the pull-down menus and the command bars. However, because some users will already be familiar with WordPerfect and may prefer shortcut keys, those will also be presented. In a Windows environment, you work with a mouse pointer and an insertion point instead of the traditional cursor. When you are outside the work area, the mouse is shown as an arrow and when in text (even in command screens) it is an I-beam. When we say "position [or place or put] the insertion point," you must move the I-beam and click to move the insertion point.

The most efficient way to give commands is usually to use the mouse. The mouse is moved by sliding it across a flat surface. If you run out of space, pick up the mouse and set it down in a more spacious area. You may have a two- or three-button mouse. Most mouse commands are invoked with the left mouse button, but a few, such as the Quick Menus, are activated with the right button. Simply move the mouse pointer where you want it, and quickly press and release the button. This action is known as "clicking" or "point and click." Double-clicking is pressing and releasing the button twice quickly, and dragging is holding the button down as you move the mouse. Getting used to the mouse will take some practice for first-time users.

The insertion point marks where the text will begin and from what point on commands will take effect. As you type, text is inserted to the left of the insertion point. If you want to move the insertion point to another place in the document more speedily than using the arrow keys, move the mouse pointer to the desired location and click. The insertion point will move to that place. The terms *put*, *place*, and *position* all mean to move the mouse pointer or the insertion point to a specific location before clicking, double-clicking, or dragging.

CAUTION: when you use a command such as changing margins, tab stops, or line spacing, the command will take effect from the insertion point forward. If you are not careful, you might inadvertently move the insertion point before you use the command, thus inserting the command in an inappropriate place.

This text uses the standard WordPerfect for Windows keyboard, not the DOS-compatible keyboard.

Now you are ready to begin working with WordPerfect. Make sure the Program Manager window is open. Then follow these steps to start the program.

1. Double-click on the WordPerfect program group icon

The window shown in Figure 2-1 appears.

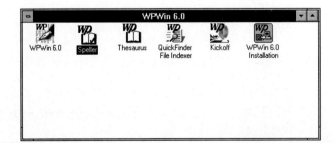

Figure 2-1

2. Double-click on the WordPerfect application icon

The WordPerfect Window

When WordPerfect is started, a new document window opens, maximized and ready for you to begin typing your document. The title bar reads "Document1-unmodified." This marks it as the first document opened, still unnamed, with no changes made since opening.

The WordPerfect window has all the basic components of a Windows window: a title bar; a menu bar; a control-menu box; minimize, maximize, and restore buttons; and scroll bars. The components of the WordPerfect window are labeled in Figure 2-2 with a button bar, the power bar, the ruler bar, and the status bar displayed. Only the power bar, button bar, and status bar display as defaults when you open a document. You must direct WordPerfect to display the others.

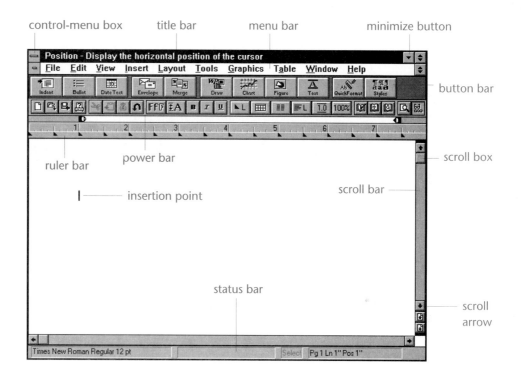

Figure 2-2

A single WordPerfect application window acts as a backdrop to the document windows (up to nine) that can be open at one time (if your computer has enough available memory). For example, in Figure 2-2 there are two control-menu boxes: one for the application and one for the open document. The *application's* control-menu box manages the WordPerfect application window, allowing you to minimize the window, close the application, restore a closed window, or switch to another Windows application.

In contrast, the *document's* control-menu box manages the active document window. For example, selecting the Close option in the document's control-menu box would close the document and give you a clear working window in which to create a new document. Similarly, the Minimize option would shrink the document into an icon displayed in the WordPerfect application window.

There are also two different Restore buttons: the top button controls the WordPerfect application window, and the bottom one affects the active document window.

The **workspace** is the area in which to create and edit a document. At the top of the workspace is the **insertion point** (the flashing vertical line). The text will appear to the left of the insertion point as you type. To move the insertion point, move the mouse pointer to the desired location and click. You cannot, however, move the insertion point beyond existing text. You must press (Enter) or (Spacebar) to create space to move the insertion point.

Using the Status Bar

At the bottom of the screen is the **status bar** as shown in Figure 2-3. The left end of the status bar indicates the **font** (the typeface and point size) that will be used for the current document. The right end of the status bar indicates the current position of the insertion point: the page number, line number, and position number. The line number (shown as "Ln") indicates the vertical position of the insertion point relative to the top of the page. The position number (shown as "Pos") indicates the horizontal position of the insertion point relative to the left edge of the page. The line number and position number are shown in inches. Note that the word "Select" is dimmed. When text is selected (highlighted) it will become black.

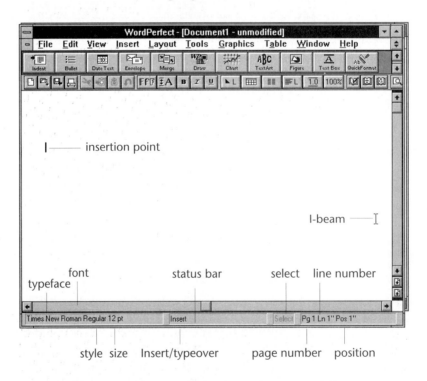

Figure 2-3

 To become familiar with the status bar, you will enter text. As you type, notice that the status bar changes to reflect the current position of the insertion point. Before you begin the exercise, look at the type size and style shown at the left end of the status bar.

1. Type `Interoffice Memorandum`

   As you type the text, the status bar indicates the position of the insertion point relative to the left edge of the page. Notice the position on the status bar.

2. Press (Enter) five times

   The (Backspace) key erases the character, a space, or a blank line to the left of the insertion point.

3. (Backspace) over the blank lines and "Interoffice Memorandum"

   Notice that the Pos number now shows 1".

   The (Del) key deletes text to the right of the insertion point.

4. Type computer

5. Position the I-beam to the left of the "l" and click once to activate the insertion point

6. Press the (Del) key once

   An easy way to delete a word is (Ctrl) + (Backspace)

7. Place the insertion point in "Computer"

8. Press (Ctrl) + (Backspace)

Default Settings

When you first open a WordPerfect window, all the formatting commands necessary to print a page are automatically set for you, such as top, bottom, left, and right margins; line spacing; and tab stops. These settings, called **default settings**, are as follows.

Left margin: 1"

Right margin: 1"

Top margin: 1"

Bottom margin: 1"

Line spacing: single

Tab stops: set every ½"

Justification: Left

Page length: 54 lines

Paper size: 8 ½" by 11"

Executing and Canceling Commands

You can use the mouse to execute a command in WordPerfect in the same way as in any other Windows application. Notice the menu bar located below the title bar. To select an option from the menu bar, position the mouse pointer on the menu name and click the left mouse button once. A pull-down menu appears for you to click on the desired option. If you select the wrong menu or option, simply position the mouse pointer off the menu and click the left mouse button once.

The keyboard can also be used to select an option on the menu bar. Press the (Alt) key, then press the underlined letter of the desired menu name. Once the pull-down menu appears, just type the underlined letter of the desired option. To close a menu without making a selection, press (Esc).

When you open a WordPerfect document, a set of command icons displays across the top of the screen in the **power bar**. These are frequently-used commands that can be selected by clicking on them with the mouse. In addition to the power bar, which is displayed in every document, twelve different **button bars** are available for specific functions, such as graphics, equations, and so on. Also, many of the features, such as Macro, Merge, Headers/Footers, Outline, and Footnotes have a **feature bar** that displays when you select that feature. Command buttons necessary to use that feature are contained on the feature bar. The commands on these bars can be accessed only via mouse.

WordPerfect also gives you **shortcut keys**, which may be either a single keystroke or a series of keystrokes. The templates (keystroke aids) provided with your WordPerfect software include many of the shortcut keys that can be used. Shortcut keys will be enclosed in parentheses in the text and marked by a checkmark (✓) in the exercises.

As you work with WordPerfect you will find that it is sometimes fastest to use the pull-down menus; if the feature is included on the button bar, that should be fastest, and sometimes the shortcut keys are fastest. Advanced users may prefer the shortcut keys, as you do not have to remove your hands from the keyboard. Beginners usually prefer the pull-down menus. You will soon discover which way works best for you.

Before going on, a few words about the arrangement of items and the conventions in this text may be helpful.

WordPerfect features will be in boldface type and defined at first mention. The steps to activate the feature will be listed with the menu and submenu names separated by an arrow, as "File ⇒ Save." Keyboard shortcuts (if any) to activate that feature will follow in parentheses. Numbered tutorials offer you the chance to practice what you've learned about these features.

The numbered steps (tutorials) give the menu commands, power bar icons, and shortcut keys necessary to carry out the given task. Words you are to type will be in boldface type. Shortcut keys will be preceded by a checkmark.

Because it is possible to use only the keyboard to access commands, the appropriate letter for each menu will be underlined. To activate commands via the keyboard, hold down the (Alt) key while pressing the underlined letter.

When you must press two keys at the same time, a plus sign will join the keys. For example, "Press (Ctrl) + (Home)" means to hold down the Control key and press the Home key.

The following exercise shows how to issue a command using both the mouse and shortcut keystrokes.

1. Click on <u>F</u>ile

   The pull-down menu shown in Figure 2-4 appears.

   Your file names after the Exit command may be different than those in Figure 2-4; it depends on the files you have been working with. Now close the menu:

2. Click anywhere in the workspace

   Now issue the same command using the shortcut keys.

3. Press (Alt) + (F)

   Now close the pull-down menu.

4. Press (Esc)

```
File
 New            Ctrl+N
 Template...    Ctrl+T
 Open...        Ctrl+O
 Close          Ctrl+F4

 Save           Ctrl+S
 Save As...     F3

 QuickFinder...
 Master Document      ▶
 Compare Document     ▶
 Document Summary...
 Document Info...

 Preferences...

 Print...       F5
 Select Printer...

 Exit           Alt+F4

 1 transpar.wks
 2 show.wpd
 3 outline.wpd
 4 new.wpd
```

Figure 2-4

Concepts and Keystrokes

The purpose of this text is to teach concepts along with keystrokes so that you can apply the knowledge learned to other word processing programs. In other words, once you know that you can move and copy text, create merge letters, columns, tables, graphics, and so on in WordPerfect, it is simply a matter of asking what commands will perform those functions in other programs. Because the text cannot cover all word processors' capabilities, you will want to explore other topics on your own.

▍ Getting Help

In addition to learning the features shown in this book, you can explore other features on your own. Using WordPerfect's Help feature is an ideal way to try out the other features. You can access WordPerfect's Help feature from the menu bar by choosing Help or by pressing (F1). Figure 2-5 shows the topics available. The following paragraphs describe the various Help features available.

```
    Help
 Contents...
 Search for Help On...
 How Do I...

 Macros...
 Coach...
 Tutorial...

 About WordPerfect...
```

Figure 2-5

Contents

If you select Contents from the Help menu as shown in Figure 2-6, items are listed with a short description to the right of each item. Select any of the items with the mouse pointer for additional information.

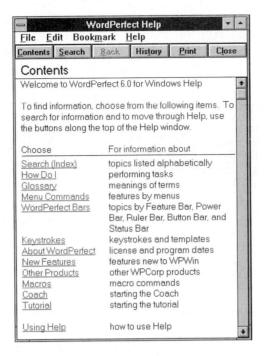

Figure 2-6

Search for Help On

The Search for Help On feature displays a search dialog box as shown in Figure 2-7. You can type a word or phrase in the text box, such as "graphics box," and select Show Topics. A list of topics relating to that feature is shown. Select one of the topics and select Go To for additional information. Press (Esc) to return to Contents and choose a different topic if desired.

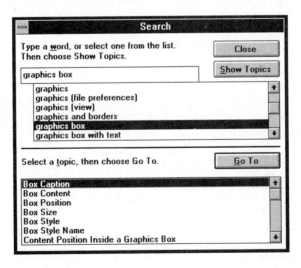

Figure 2-7

How Do I

Selecting How Do I displays a list of topics on the left side of the screen. Select a topic with the mouse pointer (which becomes a pointing finger) and the purpose of that feature, along with the steps to use it, are detailed on the right side of the screen as shown in Figure 2-8.

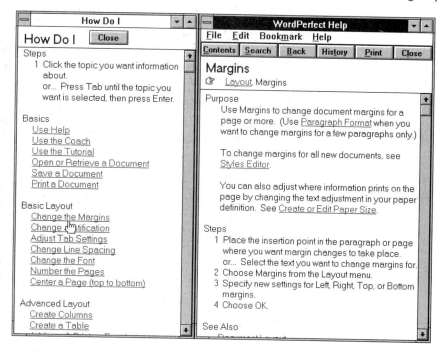

Figure 2-8

Coach

Coach is a wonderful new feature that leads you through a task step by step. Some of the possible choices are shown in Figure 2-9.

Figure 2-9

Tutorial

Figure 2-10 shows the opening screen of the Tutorial, which helps you learn some of the basic features of WordPerfect. Use this at any time for additional help.

As you are working through the book, if you want additional information about some of the topics covered or want to use a new feature, one of the many Help options available should show you what you need to know.

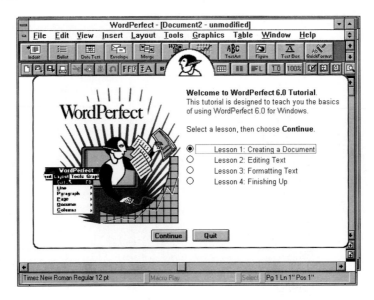

Figure 2-10

▐ Starting a New Document and Entering Text

When creating a new document, the default settings will take effect: 1" top, bottom, left, and right margins; single spacing; and aligned to the left margin. Of course, all defaults can be changed.

Other WordPerfect features automatically insert the current date, wrap words, indent, keep two words together on one line, boldface text, and check for spelling errors. The descriptions of these features will be followed by a bulleted list of usage instructions. These instructions are given for later reference when doing your exercises at the end of the chapters. Perform only numbered steps as you create the letter shown in Figure 2-11.

Inserting the Date

WordPerfect will automatically insert the current date (according to the computer's clock) into your document. There are two options to consider when using the Date feature: Text and Code. The Date Text feature inserts the date the document is created. However, if the document is printed or edited at a later date, the inserted date remains unchanged. *Remember, you are just to read the bulleted instructions, not perform them.* To insert the Date Text, from the menu bar:

- Choose Insert ⇒ Date ⇒ Date Text (Ctrl + D)

The Date Code feature also inserts the date. However, if the document is later printed or edited, the date is updated to reflect the current date. To insert the Date Code, from the menu bar:

- Choose Insert ⇒ Date ⇒ Date Code (Ctrl + Shift + D)

Using the Enter Key

As you type a document, you use the Enter key: (1) to end a short line such as with a date or inside address; (2) to create a blank line; (3) to end a paragraph; or (4) to create a new paragraph.

(today's date)

Dr. Doris L. Airsman
Wichita State College
3200 Arbor Street
Wichita, KS 67207

Dear Dr. Airsman:

YOur propectus, table of contents, and the first two chapters for <u>Using Access for Windows for the IBM</u> were recieved on November 20. We appreciate your submitting them to Bookworm Computer Publishing Company; however, we have already contracted with another author to write a Microsoft Access book for us.

We liked your style and approach **very much** and would be interested in discussing the the possibility of your writing another book forus. At this time we are looking for someone to write a beginning OS/2 book and an advanced <u>Paradox for Windows</u> book.

Pleae let us know if you are interested.

Sincerely yours,

(your name)
Editor

Figure 2-11

Word Wrap

When you are typing a paragraph and the insertion point approaches the right margin, do *not* press (Enter)—just keep typing. The words that cannot fit onto a line will be moved to the beginning of the next line. This feature is called **word wrap**.

Creating a New Paragraph

To create a new paragraph, simply position the insertion point in front of the character that is to be first in the new paragraph and press (Enter)—twice; once to terminate the line, and once to create a blank line.

Inserting Text

WordPerfect is automatically set to insert new text or characters. As you begin typing new text, all existing text from the insertion point forward moves over, making room for the new text. To insert new text, position the insertion point where the new text is to appear, and then begin typing the text. As the text is typed, the original text is pushed along and automatically reformatted.

▥ Using Typeover

The **Typeover** feature allows you to type over existing text. Press the insert key ((Ins)) to turn on Typeover. To turn off Typeover, simply press (Ins) again. A "Typeover" or "Insert" prompt displays in the center of the status bar to indicate the active mode.

▥ Underlining Text While Typing

Any quantity of text may be underlined while you are typing. To activate the Underline feature, from the menu bar:

- Choose Layout ⇒ Font.
- Mark Underline in the Appearance box.
- Click on OK.
- ((Ctrl) + (U)).

The type style and point size on the status bar are underlined to indicate that the Underline feature is active. Type the text to be underlined.
To deactivate the underline feature, repeat the steps.

▥ Boldfacing Text While Typing

As with underlining, you can **boldface** any quantity of text while typing. Bold-faced text is heavier than normal text, which gives it emphasis. To activate the Bold feature, from the menu bar:

- Choose Layout ⇒ Font ⇒ Bold ((Ctrl) + (B)).

The type style and point size on the status bar then appear bold to indicate that the Bold feature is active. Type the text you want to be in boldface; to deactivate the feature:

- Choose Layout ⇒ Font ⇒ Bold ((Ctrl) + (B)).

▥ Hard Spaces, Returns, and Page Breaks

Automatically inserted spaces, returns at the ends of lines, and page breaks at the ends of pages are called "soft." Those same spaces, returns, and page breaks entered by the writer are called "hard." Because it is incorrect to separate an initial from a name, a day from a month, and a.m. or p.m. from the time, it is good practice to insert hard spaces between numbers or words that should be kept together on a line.

Inserting a Hard Space

The Hard Space feature inserts a hard space between words instead of the regular space created using the (Spacebar). To insert a hard space, type the first word; then from the menu bar:

- Choose Layout ⇒ Line ⇒ Other Codes.
- Choose Hard Space.
- Choose Insert.
- ((Ctrl) + (Spacebar)).

▥ Saving a Document

Until documents are saved to disk, they are stored only in the computer's memory and will be lost if the computer is turned off. You have two choices when saving a file:

- <u>F</u>ile ⇒ Save <u>A</u>s ((F3)), or <u>F</u>ile ⇒ <u>S</u>ave ((Ctrl) + (S)).

Choosing either option displays the Save As dialog box when saving a document for the first time and you are prompted to name your document. These are the rules regarding file names: (1) A file name may be typed in uppercase or lowercase; (2) the name may not exceed eight characters, plus a three-letter extension; (3) the name may not contain any spaces; and (4) the name may contain the letters from A–Z, numbers from 0–9 and any of the following symbols: ~ ' ! @ # $ ^ & () _ =. File names should relate to the contents of the file and be something you're not likely to forget.

To update the disk with changes made after your initial save:

- Choose <u>F</u>ile ⇒ <u>S</u>ave ((Ctrl) + (S)).

WordPerfect automatically *replaces* the copy of the document on the disk, and you are *not* reminded that the original file on disk will be replaced with the version in memory (as in the DOS versions of WordPerfect). If, for any reason, you do not want to update the original file on disk with the one onscreen, close the file and do *not* save it.

The Save <u>A</u>s option in the <u>F</u>ile menu allows you to save the document in the active window with a new name. The original document remains unchanged on disk. To save a file with a new name:

- Choose <u>F</u>ile ⇒ Save <u>A</u>s ((F3)).

The Save As dialog box then appears. Type in the new file name. If you want the file to save to a different drive or directory, that information must precede the file name. For example, if you want an open file named contract.wpd saved on drive A with the new name report.wpd, type A:report.wpd in the Save As text box.

You will begin creating the letter shown in Figure 2-11 in the following exercises. You will first insert the current date using the Date Code feature. The insertion point should be at the top of your document, and the status bar should read "Pg 1 Ln 1" Pos 1"."

NOTE: You will begin using the command bars in Lesson 3.

1. Click on <u>I</u>nsert

The Insert menu shown in Figure 2-12 appears.

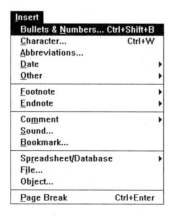

Figure 2-12

2. Click on <u>D</u>ate

The Code menu shown in Figure 2-13 displays.

Insert	
Bullets & **N**umbers...	Ctrl+Shift+B
Character...	Ctrl+W
Abbreviations...	
Date	▸ Date **T**ext Ctrl+D
Other	Date **C**ode Ctrl+Shift+D
	Date **F**ormat...
Footnote	
E**n**dnote	▸
Co**m**ment	▸
Sound...	
Bookmark...	
Sp**r**eadsheet/Database	▸
F**i**le...	
Objec**t**...	
Page Break	Ctrl+Enter

Figure 2-13

3. Click on Date **C**ode

   ✓ Press (Ctrl) + (Shift) + (D)

   The current date is inserted into your document.

The insertion point is currently positioned at the end of the date.

1. Press (Enter)

   Put blank lines between the date and the inside address.

2. Press (Enter) six times

   Type the inside address, pressing (Enter) at the end of each line. If you accidentally press the wrong key, delete the last character typed by pressing (Backspace).

3. Type:

   ```
   Dr. Doris L. Airsman
   Wichita State College
   3200 Arbor Street
   Wichita, KS 67207
   ```

4. Press (Enter) twice

   The first terminates the short line and the second creates a blank line.

5. Type `Dear Dr. Airsman:`

6. Press (Enter) twice

   Remember, as you type the following text, do not press (Enter) when the cursor approaches the right margin—use word wrap. Be sure to make the errors included in the exercise so that you can use the spell check program later in this lesson.

7. Type:

   ```
   YOur propectus, table of contents, and the first six
   chapters for
   ```

8. Press (Spacebar)

The title of Dr. Airsman's book must be underlined and you need to insert a hard space between the date and the day so that they stay together on the same line.

Turn on the underline feature.

1. Click on <u>L</u>ayout

The Layout pull-down menu appears as shown in Figure 2-14.

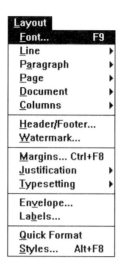

Figure 2-14

2. Click on F<u>o</u>nt

The Font option box displays as shown in Figure 2-15.

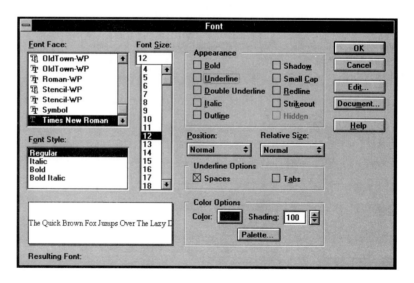

Figure 2-15

3. Click on <u>U</u>nderline (either in the box or on the name) to insert an "x"

   ✓ Press (Ctrl) + (U)

Notice that the type style and point size in the status bar are underlined: <u>Times New Roman Regular 12 pt</u>. The font may be different on your system.

4. Click on OK

5. Type <u>Using Access for Windows for the IBM</u>

   Turn off the Underline feature.

6. Click on <u>L</u>ayout ⇒ F<u>o</u>nt ⇒ <u>U</u>nderline

   ✓ Press (Ctrl) + (U)

7. Type ((Spacebar)) were recieved on November

   Don't press the (Spacebar) yet. Insert a hard space.

8. Click on <u>L</u>ayout ⇒ <u>L</u>ine

   The Line pull-down menu shown in Figure 2-16 appears.

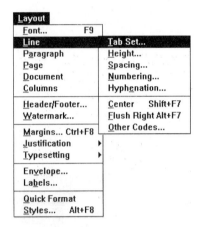

Figure 2-16

9. Click on <u>O</u>ther Codes

   The Other Codes option box appears as shown in Figure 2-17.

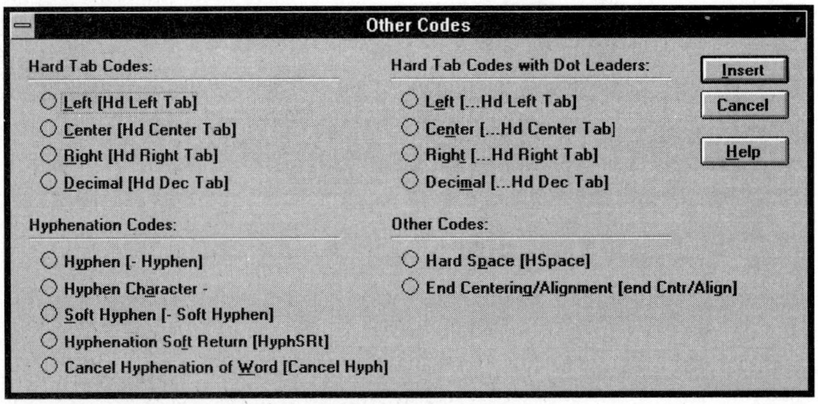

Figure 2-17

10. Click on the radio button beside Hard S<u>p</u>ace [HSpace]

11. Click on <u>I</u>nsert

    ✓ Press (Ctrl) + (Spacebar)

12. Type 20.

13. Put the I-beam in front of the "s" in "six" and click

14. Press the (Ins) key

    "Typeover" should display in the status bar.

15. Type **two**

    Move the insertion point after "November 20," press (Spacebar) twice, and finish typing the paragraph.

16. Type:

    `We appreciate your submitting them to Bookworm Computer Publishing Company; however, we have already contracted with an author to write a Microsoft Access book for us.`

17. Press (Enter) twice

    You decide to change "an" to "another."

18. Move the insertion point after the "n"

19. Press (Ins)

    "Insert" displays in the status bar.

20. Type **other**

    The text moves over to make room for the word.

 Save your letter to disk before continuing with the rest of the lesson.

1. Click on File ⇒ Save As

    ✓ Press (F3)

    The Save As dialog box appears as shown in Figure 2-18.

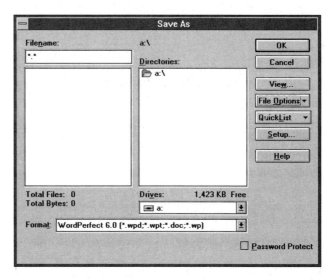

Figure 2-18

You are going to save your document as airsman. WordPerfect will add the three-letter extension ".wpd," which marks it as a document file. The insertion point is positioned in the Save As text box, ready for you to type a name. Notice that the Current Dir line shows where the document will be saved unless a different drive or directory is specified. (The directory will reflect the last place a document was saved.)

To save your file to a floppy disk in drive A or B as you did in Lesson 1, type a:airsman or b:airsman. Check with your instructor as to how to proceed. We will give only the file name and leave it up to you to add the appropriate drive letter.

2. Type `airsman`

3. Click on OK

▌ Moving Around in the Document

When you want to view a portion of your document not shown on the screen, you can click on the scroll bar on the right side of the screen to move the display up or down. However, only the display moves; the insertion point stays in its original position. You can also move the insertion point by placing the I-beam in the desired place and clicking the left mouse button once to reposition the insertion point.

Before you can insert or delete text, you must position the insertion point where the change is to be made. Several keystrokes are available for moving the insertion point, as shown in Table 2-1. The most time-saving keystrokes are (Home), (End), and (Ctrl) + (Home) and (Ctrl) + (End). Using them to get to the end of the line or end of the document is faster than using the arrow keys or scrolling.

Keystroke(s)	Action
(→)	Moves one character to the right
(←)	Moves one character to the left
(↑)	Moves one line up
(↓)	Moves one line down
(Ctrl) + (→)	Moves one word to the right
(Ctrl) + (←)	Moves one word to the left
(PgUp)	Moves to the top of the current screen
(PgDn)	Moves to the bottom of the current screen
(Home)	Moves to the beginning of a line
(End)	Moves to the end of a line
(Ctrl) + (↑)	Moves up one paragraph
(Ctrl) + (↓)	Moves down one paragraph
(Ctrl) + (Home)	Moves to the beginning of document
(Ctrl) + (End)	Moves to the end of document

Table 2-1

Moving in a Document

The insertion point will not move beyond the last keystroke of a document; press (Spacebar) or (Enter) to go beyond your current text.

Practice using both the scroll bars and some of the keystroke combinations to move the insertion point. First move the insertion point to the beginning of the document.

1. Press (Ctrl) + (Home)

2. Press (↓) six times

The insertion point is at the beginning of the line that reads "Dr. Doris L. Airsman." Move the insertion point to the end of that line.

3. Press (End)

Move the insertion point back to the beginning of the line.

4. Press (Home)

Move down one paragraph at a time.

5. Press (Ctrl) + (↓) five times

Remember, WordPerfect considers each line with a hard return to be a paragraph.

The insertion point is positioned on the first character of the first paragraph, which reads "YOur propectus, table of contents, . . ."

Now use the scroll bars to display a different part of your document.

6. Click twice on the scroll bar's down arrow

7. Click twice on the scroll bar's up arrow

Notice that the insertion point has not moved.

8. Press (Ctrl) + (Home)

The insertion point is positioned at the beginning of your document.

Using Reveal Codes

When you use a special feature such as underlining or a hard space, a formatting code is inserted for the feature. For example, when you instructed WordPerfect to turn on underlining, an Und box code was placed before and after the underlined text. When the hard space was inserted, WordPerfect placed a HSpace code there. However, these codes are hidden until a special screen called Reveal Codes is used. The Reveal Codes screen displays below the normal workspace screen.

To display the Reveal Codes screen, from the menu bar:

• Choose View ⇒ Reveal Codes ((Alt) + (F3)).

The insertion point displays in both screens. In the upper screen (the normal workspace), the insertion point is a flashing vertical line; in the Reveal Codes screen, it shows as a block. The insertion point moves simultaneously in both screens. To close the Reveal Codes screen:

• Choose View ⇒ Reveal Codes ((Alt) + (F3)) again.

The Reveal Codes feature is an ideal way to troubleshoot your document. You can see where an incorrect formatting command has been entered, such as spacing, hard returns, page breaks, and so on. Also, many times when you change the format and a new code is inserted, the old code still remains. It is a good idea to remove old codes. You can do that by dragging them off the screen in Reveal Codes or by selecting them and using the backspace or delete key.

View some of the codes in your letter.

1. Click on <u>V</u>iew

The View menu displays as shown in Figure 2-19.

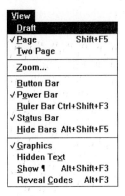

Figure 2-19

2. Click on Reveal <u>C</u>odes

✓ Press (Alt) + (F3)

The window splits into two screens, the lower screen showing both the text and the codes inserted for each feature used. Compare your window to the one shown in Figure 2-20.

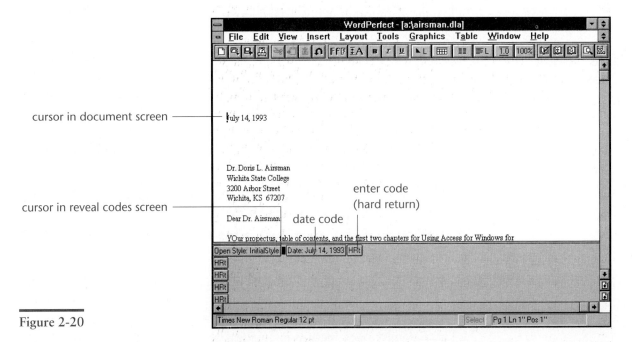

Figure 2-20

Notice the words Open Style:Initial Style. This code contains your default settings. Notice the Date in the code box at the beginning of your document. To the right of the Date is the HRt code. This is where you pressed (Enter) when you typed the letter.

Press the ⊙ until you can see an SRt code at the end of the paragraph's first line. This stands for **soft return**, which indicates that WordPerfect wrapped words to the next line while you were typing the text.

Also, notice the pair of Und codes surrounding the book titles. The first Und code instructs WordPerfect to turn on the underline feature, and the second Und code turns it off. You entered the HSpace code between "November" and "20" to keep them on the same line.

Exit the Reveal Codes screen.

3. Click on <u>V</u>iew ⇒ Reveal <u>C</u>odes

   ✓ Press (Alt) + (F3)

Move the insertion point to the end of the document.

4. Press (Ctrl) + (End)

▌ Using the Speller

Speller checks your documents for misspelled words, double occurrences of a word, and irregular capitalization of text. To spell check a document, from the menu bar:

- Choose <u>T</u>ools ⇒ <u>S</u>peller ((Ctrl) + (F1)).

The options in the pull-down menu under Check are to check: one word; one sentence; one paragraph; one page; the entire document; from the insertion point to the end of the document; selected text; and a specified number of pages. If you want to check a word or a page, your insertion point must be somewhere on that word or page.

WordPerfect compares each word in a document against the words in its two dictionaries: the main dictionary (WP[WP]US.LEX, which contains approximately 125,000 words), and a supplemental dictionary (WP[WP]US.SUP). When Speller finds a word in a document that is not in the main dictionary, such as a proper name, a term that is special to a particular industry, or a typo, Speller flags it as misspelled. You have the option of adding the word to the supplemental dictionary. If you do so, the next time the word appears, it will not be flagged as misspelled.

During a spell check, the Speller is also automatically set to check for double words, numbers within a word, and irregular capitalization. If Speller finds two identical words next to each other, such as "the the," a Duplicate Words Found dialog box appears. You can choose either to delete the second occurrence of the word or to leave the words alone and continue checking.

If Speller finds a word with irregular capitalization, such as "yOUR or YOur," it will flag the word. When irregular capitalization is found, the Irregular Capitalization Found dialog box appears, and you have the options to choose <u>R</u>eplace, to have Speller correct the problem, or to <u>C</u>ontinue, which leaves the irregular capitalization as it is. If a word starts with a capital letter and another capital letter is found somewhere within the word, the word is considered valid and Speller does not flag it.

You can choose to disable the irregular capitalization feature during a spell check by choosing the <u>D</u>isable checking option and then <u>C</u>ontinue from the Irregular Capitalization Found dialog box.

One caveat is that using a spell check program does not take the place of proofreading. Many words can be spelled correctly, but not be used correctly in the document, such as "to," "too," and "two."

You will now type the second paragraph and include a word in boldface. You will use the shortcut key method to boldface the word.

1. Type `We liked your style and approach`

Activate the Bold feature.

2. Press Ctrl + B

3. Type `very much`

Deactivate the Bold feature.

4. Press Ctrl + B

5. Type the remainder of the paragraph as shown below (including the errors):

    `and would be interested in discussing the the possibility of your writing another book forus. At this time we are looking for someone to write a beginning OS/2 book and an advanced Paradox for Windows book.`

    Don't forget to underline the book title.

6. Press Enter twice

7. Type `Pleae let us know if you are interested.`

8. Press Enter twice

9. Type `Sincerely yours,`

10. Press Enter four times

11. Type `your name`

12. Press Enter

13. Type `Editor`

14. Press Enter twice

Save your letter and update the old version of the file with the new one in memory.

1. Click on File ⇒ Save

    ✓ Press Ctrl + S

    CAUTION: It is always advisable to save your document before using a spell check, thesaurus, or grammar correction program in case something happens and you lose your file from memory.

There are several misspelled words in your letter to Dr. Airsman. Use WordPerfect's Speller to help you find them.

1. Click on Tools

The Tools menu is shown in Figure 2-21.

Figure 2-21

2. Click on Speller

   ✓ Press (Ctrl) + (F1)

   The Speller dialog box appears as shown in Figure 2-22. Make sure it states Spell-check: Document. If not, click on the Check pull-down menu and choose Document.

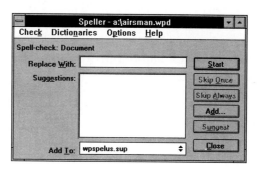

Figure 2-22

3. Click on Start

   Airsman is the first word flagged; since it is a proper name, the Speller cannot find it in either the main or supplemental dictionary. The name *is* spelled correctly, so you have three options. Skip Once will bypass this occurrence of the word, but if Airsman appears in your document again, the Speller will flag it again. Skip Always will bypass "Airsman" every time the Speller locates the word during this spell check. Add will add it to the supplemental dictionary so that the word will never be flagged during any spell check.

   The word Airsman does appear again in the document, so instruct Speller to bypass all occurrences.

4. Click on Skip Always

   "YOur" is now flagged, and the Irregular Capitalization Found dialog box appears. You want to replace "YOur" with "Your."

5. Click on Replace

   The next word flagged is "propectus." The Speller has suggested one possible replacement word, which is "prospectus." Replace "propectus" with "prospectus."

6. Click on Replace

   The word "recieved" is now flagged. The correct spelling is listed and highlighted in the Suggestions box. Replace the incorrect spelling.

7. Click on Replace

   "Microsoft," a proper name, is flagged. You will be using it many times in the future, so add it to the dictionary.

8. Click on Add

   The words "the the" are flagged, and Duplicate Words: "the the" appears above the Replace With: text box.

9. Click on Replace

   The Speller stops at "forus" and displays "focus" as a possible replacement. Place the insertion point after "fo" in the Speller text box.

10. Type r (Spacebar)

11. Press (Del) to delete the "c"

12. Click on Replace

    "Pleae" is then marked for your attention. WordPerfect suggests "plea" as a replacement. You want "please" instead.

13. Press the down arrow key in the Suggestions box until "please" is highlighted and in the Replace With box

14. Click on Replace

    NOTE: Even though "Paradox" and "Windows" are proper names in this letter, they are also ordinary words, and thus are not marked because they are contained in the dictionary.

    The Spell Check Completed option box appears.

15. Click on Yes to close Speller

16. Save the document

Printing a Document

Before you print your letter, be sure that your printer is on, the on-line light is illuminated, and the paper is properly aligned in the printer. To Print the document displayed in the active window:

- Choose File ⇒ Print ((F5)).

The Print dialog box then appears, indicating the selected printer. The Print dialog box allows you to print either the entire document or the current page. If you select the Current Page option, the page on which the insertion point is located will be the page printed.

- Choose Print.

NOTE: If more than one printer is available and the current printer selected is not the one you want, click on the Select button. The Select Printer dialog box then appears. Click on the desired printer and choose Select.

▌ Exiting WordPerfect

There are important reasons to exit WordPerfect properly. First, WordPerfect creates temporary files during an editing session and they must be properly closed. Second, the WordPerfect system files are also open and must be closed properly. Be sure to exit WordPerfect by double-clicking on the control-menu box, by clicking on the control-menu box and choosing Close, or by choosing File ⇒ Exit. If a file has never been saved, or if it has been changed since the last time it was saved, WordPerfect presents a dialog box asking if you wish to save the changes. If so, choose Yes. If not, you can abandon the changes by choosing No. You can cancel the exit procedure by choosing Cancel.

You are now ready to save and print your file and exit WordPerfect.

1. Click on File ⇒ Print

   ✓ Press (F5)

   The Print option box appears as shown in Figure 2-23. Notice in the Options section of the Print dialog box that the Full Document option button is selected indicating that the entire document will print.

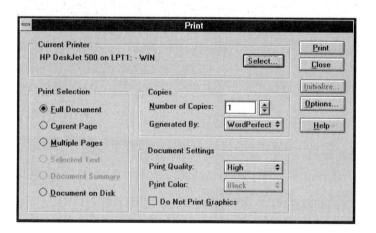

Figure 2-23

2. Click on Print

   Your letter should look similar to a corrected version of Figure 2-11.

3. Click on File ⇒ Exit

   ✓ Press (Alt) + (F4)

   If the Save Changes option box appears:

4. Click on Yes

   You are returned to the Windows program. When you are finished with Windows, be sure to exit by either double-clicking on the Program Manager's control-menu box or choosing File ⇒ Exit.

On Your Own

Review of Commands

Description	Menu Commands	Function Keys
Help	_____	_____
Insert date	_____	_____
Insert Date Code	_____	_____
Underline	_____	_____
Insert hard space	_____	_____
Save a document	_____	_____
Use Reveal Codes	_____	_____
Boldface text	_____	_____
Exit a document	_____	_____
Print a document	_____	_____

Lesson Review

1. Briefly explain the steps to load WordPerfect for Windows 6.0.

2. List the items of information displayed on the left end of the status bar and explain their purpose.

3. List the items of information displayed on the right end of the status bar and explain their purpose.

4. What are the default margin settings?

5. What is the default justification setting?

6. List the two ways to insert a date into a document.

7. Explain the difference between the two ways to insert a date into a document.

8. Explain why you should not press (Enter) at the end of each line of type.

9. What are the commands to begin and end underlines in text?

10. Explain the difference between File ⇒ Save and File ⇒ Save As.

11. What command moves the insertion point to the end of a document?

12. To save a document named LESSON1 after you have added more material, what command would you use?

13. To boldface text as you type, what command would you use?

14. List the types of errors that Speller can find.

15. How do you exit WordPerfect?

▮ Assignments

2-1 Directions

1. Load WordPerfect. Type the following paragraphs. Use (Backspace) to correct errors as you are typing.

An electronic mail package allows the user to send a message via computers within the same room, within the same building, across a campus, or across the ocean. A software package is loaded on some type of computer and every person at a workstation attached to that computer has the capability of sending a message to every other person at a workstation. When a message is received at a workstation, there will be some kind of notification to that person that a message has been received.

When micros are linked together in an organization, an electronic mail package is usually included. When working at home, it is possible to join a public company such as MCI Mail, CompuServe or The Source. You can then send messages which they forward to the intended recipient. These services cost a few dollars a month plus the telephone charges while you are on-line.

---

2. Save the document as Email.wpd (remember, you don't have to type the extension). Where does the document name appear on your screen? What exactly does the screen say?

3. Find the status bar. What is the font size for your document?

4. Place your insertion point on the "r" in the word "received" in the last line of the first paragraph. Look at the status bar. What is your page number? Line number? Position number?

5. Use the keyboard to move the insertion point to the beginning of your document. What command did you give?

6. Use the keyboard to move the insertion point to the end of the first line. What command did you give?

7. Use the keyboard to move the insertion point one word to the left. What command did you give?

8. Use the keyboard to move the insertion point to the beginning of the second paragraph. What command did you give?

9. Use the keyboard to move the insertion point two words to the right. What command did you give?

10. Use the keyboard to move the insertion point to the beginning of the line. What command did you give?

11. Close the document.

2-2 Directions

1. Choose Help from the main menu.

2. Find information about the Speller.

2-3 Directions

1. Select Coach from the Help menu. Select Indent as the topic you wish to be coached on.

2. Follow the steps to indent all lines of a paragraph.

3. List the kinds of indents you can use with WordPerfect. (Hint: you will find them on a submenu.)

2-4 Directions

1. Type the following paragraph. Be sure to include the underlining and boldface.

> Of all the resources available to professionals, time is the most valuable because it is a **fixed quantity**. It <u>cannot</u> be increased; it can only be managed by judicious planning, by prioritizing tasks, and then by working efficiently, effectively, and creatively within the constraints of the calendar. The classic time management question asks: What is the best use of my time right now?

2. When should the (Enter) key be pressed while creating this document? Why?

3. Save the document as Time.wpd. Print the document.

4. Open the Reveal Codes Screen. Find the underline and bold codes. Remove the underlining by grabbing an underline code and dragging it off the screen (be sure to release the mouse button *outside* the Reveal Codes screen). Remove the boldface by deleting one of the bold codes using the backspace or delete key.

5. Spell check the document.

6. Use Save As to save the document with your changes as Time1.wpd.

7. Print the new document. Close the document.

2-5 Directions

1. Type the memo that appears below using the default formatting and the Date Code feature: Press the (Tab) key twice after "To:," "From:," and "Date:" and once after "Subject:." Type the errors as shown (plus any others you inadvertently make).

2. Boldface "outstanding and unusual contributions" as you type the text.

3. Underline "April 3, 1994" as you type, and keep all parts of dates together on each line.

4. Look at the Reveal Codes screen to see if your hard space commands are all in the right places (between the numbers and dates, and between LF 303 and Campus Box 34.)

5. Save the document as Dsawards.wpd.

6. Spell check and save the document again with the corrections made to the text.

7. Print the document.

8. Close the document.

To: Faculty and Staff
From: Alexander Dysert
Vice President of Academic Affairs
Date: (today's date)
Subject: Distinguished Service Award Nominations

The Distinguished Service Award Committee invites all college employes to submit nominations for the distincuished Service Award.

Distinguised Service Awards are given to college clasified staff, contract administrators and faculty who have worked at Cosmopolitan State college for more than 10 years on a full-time basis (hired before September 1, 1994). Service is defined as continous service to CSC characterised by a high standard of quality, longevity, and lasting significance. The emphasis should be on **outstanding and unusual contributions** that are clearly above and beyond the norm.

Important! Please submit materials to the Faculty Senate office, LF 303, or Campus Box 34, by <u>April 3, 1994.</u>

2-6 Directions

1. Type the letter that appears below. Use the default formatting and the Date Code feature.

2. Practice moving the insertion point throughout the letter.

3. Underline "Thank you" in the first paragraph and boldface the phrase "questions regarding your order" in the second paragraph. (Be sure to make the changes as you type.)

4. Type "Mr. James Milton" in such a way that the name cannot be divided between two lines.

5. Name the letter Harder1.wpd and save it.

6. Spell check the letter.

7. Print the letter.

8. Save and exit the document.

February 7, 1994

Mrs. Cathy Harder
127 Meade Way
Westminster, CO 80030

Dear Mrs. Harder:

Thank you for your recent order. The texts you ordered are temporarily out of stock. However, we expect to be able to fill your order within 10 days.

If you have any questions regarding your order, please contact Mr. James Milton in our Order Processing Department.

Sincerely,

Mary L. Warren
Sales Manager

L E S S O N

Basic Editing Features

Objectives

After completing this lesson, you will be able to:

- Open a file
- Change the default justification
- Select text using the mouse and keyboard
- Use the Undelete and Undo features
- Underline and boldface existing text
- Use the Typeover mode
- Display the ruler
- Delete, set, and move tab stops
- Use the Case Conversion feature

Before Beginning

Start both Windows and WordPerfect for Windows. The workspace should be empty, and the title bar should read "Document1-unmodified."

You will be given a chance to practice several new WordPerfect features after a discussion of them. The lesson exercises are divided into a series of numbered exercises even though you may be creating only one document. This gives you places to stop if you have to quit working. If you do stop, be sure to save your file. In fact, it is a good idea to save your file at the end of each exercise.

Opening a Document

When you want to edit or view an existing document, you must first open the file. Opening a file retrieves a copy of the file from the disk and places it into a new document window. To open a file, you choose:

- Choose File ⇒ Open (Ctrl + O).

If you want a blank screen to create a new document:

- Choose File ⇒ New.

▐ Changing the Justification

Justification determines the style of the left and right margins. There are five settings available: Left, Right, Center, Full, and All. The Left option aligns text evenly on the left margin, but leaves the right margin uneven. The Right option aligns text evenly on the right margin, leaving an uneven left margin. The Center option centers the text on the page so that both margins are uneven. The All feature will evenly space letters of a line between the left and right margins. The Full option aligns both the left and right margins evenly. Figure 3-1 shows the result of choosing these options.

This text is left aligned.

This text is right aligned.

This text is center aligned.

This text represents the full justified alignment when creating documents. Notice that all the lines will align at both the left and right margins. You must be sure to press the Enter key at the end of short lines   or   it   may   look   funny .

Figure 3-1

WordPerfect's default setting is Left. To use the Justification feature:

- First you place the insertion point anywhere within the paragraph that is to be changed.
- Choose <u>L</u>ayout ⇒ <u>J</u>ustification.
- Specify the desired alignment.

The shortcut keys are listed in Table 3-1.

Alignment	Shortcut Key
Left	Ctrl + L
Right	Ctrl + R
Center	Ctrl + E
Full	Ctrl + J
All	None available

Table 3-1

Alignment

When the justification for a paragraph is changed, the specified justification takes effect from the Just: code forward in the document. In other words, all text from the Just: code forward is formatted to the specified alignment, until another Just: code is encountered.

▌ **Selecting Text**

Before you can delete, move, or copy text, you must first learn how to select different quantities of text. To **select** means to highlight the text to be changed. You can select text by: (1) using the mouse; (2) using the keyboard (Shift) key plus arrow keys; and (3) using (F8) plus arrow keys.

Using the Mouse to Select Text

To select text by dragging the mouse, position the I-beam immediately to the left of the first character of the text to be selected, press and hold down the left mouse button, and drag the mouse to the end of the text. Once the desired text is selected, release the mouse button.

Or, you can position the insertion point to the left of the first character in the text you want to select. Click the left mouse button once. Then, hold down the (Shift) key and place the insertion point just after the last character of the text to be selected and click the left mouse button.

You can instead position the insertion point to the left of the first character in the text you want to select. Click the left mouse button once. Then, hold down the (Shift) key and place the insertion point just after the last character of the text to be selected, and click on the left mouse button.

You can also select various quantities of text with the mouse as shown in Table 3-2. Read through the commands and select and list the ones you think would be most helpful. For example, selecting text from the insertion point to the end of the document is done by pressing (Shift) + (Ctrl) + (End).

Selection Method	Text Selected
Double-click with I-beam positioned on a word	One word
Triple-click with I-beam positioned anywhere in a sentence	One sentence
Quadruple-click with I-beam positioned anywhere in a paragraph	One paragraph

Table 3-2
Selecting Text via Mouse

Using the Keyboard to Select Text

You can select text by holding down (Shift) or (Shift) + (Ctrl) while pressing an arrow key. Table 3-3 indicates the various key combinations and the text that they select.

CAUTION: When you select text and then begin typing, the selected text is deleted and then replaced with the character(s) you type. Be careful if you have selected text—even one character—when you save the document. You will get a screen asking whether to save the selected text. Just deselect and save again or you may overwrite your file with only the selected text.

Using the (F8) Key

You can also turn on Select mode by pressing (F8) and then using the arrow keys to highlight the chosen text. To deselect text that has been selected,

Selection Method	Text Selected
Shift + →	One character to the right from the insertion point
Shift + ←	One character to the left from the insertion point
Shift + ↑	One line up from the insertion point
Shift + ↓	One line down from the insertion point
Shift + End	From the insertion point to the end of the line (including codes)
Shift + Home	From the insertion point to the beginning of the line (including codes)
Shift + PgUp	From the insertion point to the top of the screen
Shift + PgDn	From the insertion point to the bottom of the screen
Shift + Alt + PgUp	From the insertion point to the first line on the preceding page
Shift + Alt + PgDn	From the insertion point to the first line on the next page
Shift + Ctrl + →	One word to the right from the insertion point
Shift + Ctrl + ←	One word to the left from the insertion point
Shift + Ctrl + ↑	From the insertion point to the beginning of the paragraph
Shift + Ctrl + ↓	From the insertion point to the end of the paragraph
Shift + Ctrl + Home	From the insertion point to the beginning of the document (not including codes)
Shift + Ctrl + End	From the insertion point to the end of the document

Table 3-3

Selecting Text via Keyboard

either press F8 again or click the mouse anywhere in the workspace. F8 is a **toggle switch,** which means you press it once to turn the feature on and press the key again to turn the feature off.

WordPerfect indicates when Select is active with a reverse-type "Select" at the right of the status bar.

After text has been selected, many operations can be performed on the selected text. A list of these operations and their commands are shown in Table 3-4. The majority of the commands are self-explanatory. Some that might not be are: Conditional End of Page, which lets you keep several lines of text together on one page; Protect a Block, which is used to keep a table or graphic on one page; and Append, which allows you to add selected text to the end of material already cut or copied to Windows' Clipboard. You cannot use Append unless you have already stored something in Clipboard. Many of these functions will be demonstrated in the coming chapters.

▌ Deselecting Text

You can deselect text by clicking outside the selected text, or you can move the insertion point to another location without holding down the Shift key.

Functions	Menu Commands	Shortcut Keys
Delete		(Del)
Move	Edit ⇒ Cut	(Ctrl) + (X)
Copy	Edit ⇒ Copy	(Ctrl) + (C)
Insert text	Edit ⇒ Paste	(Ctrl) + (V)
Change the font	Layout ⇒ Font	(F9)
Conditional End of Page	Layout ⇒ Line ⇒ Keep Text Together ⇒ Conditional End of Page	
Center	Layout ⇒ Line ⇒ Center	(Shift) + (F7)
Underline	Layout ⇒ Font ⇒ Underline	(Ctrl) + (U)
Bold	Layout ⇒ Font ⇒ Bold	(Ctrl) + (B)
Convert upper to lower case	Edit ⇒ Convert Case ⇒ Lower	
Convert lower to upper case	Edit ⇒ Convert Case ⇒ Upper	
Convert lower to upper case with first letters capitalized	Edit ⇒ Convert Case ⇒ Initial Capitals	
Print	File ⇒ Print ⇒ Print	(F5)
Save and name	File ⇒ Save As ⇒ file name	(F3), file name
Protect a block	Layout ⇒ Page ⇒ Keep Text Together ⇒ Block Protect	
Append	Edit ⇒ Append	
Search (Find)	Edit ⇒ Find	(F2)
Replace	Edit ⇒ Replace	(Ctrl) + (F2)
Sort	Tools ⇒ Sort	(Alt) + (F9)
Flush right	Layout ⇒ Line ⇒ Flush Right	(Alt) + (F7)
Spell check	Tools ⇒ Speller	(Ctrl) + (F1)

Table 3-4

Available Operations on Selected Text

▌ Deleting Text

You can delete a block of text by first selecting the text to be deleted and pressing the (Del) or (Backspace) key, or by using one of the keystroke combinations shown in Table 3-5.

▌ Undeleting Text

WordPerfect's **Undelete** feature stores your last three deletions in memory so that you can view them and restore them if desired. To restore a deletion:

- Position the insertion point where the deleted text is to be restored.
- Choose Edit ⇒ Undelete ((Ctrl) + (Shift) + (Z)).

Keystrokes	Text Deleted
(Backspace)	Character to the left of the insertion point
(Del)	Character to the right of the insertion point
(Ctrl) + (Backspace)	Nearest word
(Ctrl) + (Del)	From the insertion point to the end of the line

Table 3-5
Deleting Text

- The last deletion is displayed. To restore it, click on Restore.
- You can instead click on Next or Previous; to restore a displayed deletion, click on Restore.

▍ Undoing a Change

The Undo feature reverses the most recent change made to a document. Most actions can be reversed using Undo, including inserting and deleting text, and changing formatting such as margins and tabs. If you use Undo to restore your last deletion, the deleted text is restored at its original location. For example, if you delete a paragraph at the top of the document and then scroll to the end of the document, choosing Undo restores the text to its original location at the top of the document. In contrast, the Undelete command places the deleted text at the insertion point.

If you delete a paragraph and type new text, choosing Undo does not restore the deleted paragraph (since it works only on your last action). Instead, Undo removes the *new* text because that is the most recent change. To restore the deleted text, you would need to use the Undelete command. To use the Undo feature:

- Choose Edit ⇒ Undo ((Ctrl) + (Z)).

Open the rejection letter to Dr. Airsman (airsman.wpd) and practice some of the features discussed.

1. Click on File ⇒ Open

   ✓ Press (F4)

   NOTE: *When you have recently worked on a file, it will be listed at the bottom of the File menu. Clicking on the file name there is a quick way to open it.*

   The Open File dialog box appears as shown in Figure 3-2.

2. Click on airsman.wpd

   The file name is highlighted.

3. Click on OK

   Double-clicking on the file name will also open the file.

With the Airsman letter in your active window and the insertion point positioned at the beginning of the letter, practice selecting text.

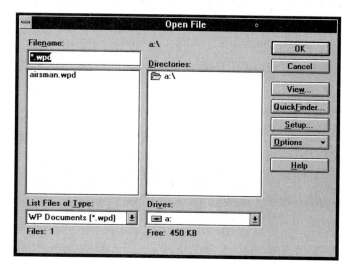

Figure 3-2

1. Position the I beam somewhere in the word Your in the sentence beginning "Your prospectus, table of contents, and . . ."

   Remember, a quick way to position the insertion point is to move the I-beam to the desired place and click the left mouse button once.

2. Double-click the mouse button

   The word Your and the space after it are selected.

3. Place the I-beam anywhere in the first sentence

4. Triple-click the mouse button

   The entire first sentence of the first paragraph is selected.

5. Quadruple-click the mouse button

   The entire first paragraph of the letter is selected. Now deselect the paragraph.

6. Move the I-beam anyplace in the workspace and click the mouse button once

Experiment using (Shift) with various key combinations:

1. Position the insertion point at the beginning of the first paragraph, which reads "Your prospectus, table of contents, and . . ."

2. Press (Shift) + (End)

   The first line of the first paragraph is selected.

3. Deselect the text

4. Press (Shift) + (Ctrl) + (End)

   The text from the insertion point to the end of the document is selected. Now, deselect the text.

5. Press any directional key

Use WordPerfect's Select mode ((F8)) to select text. Position the insertion point at the beginning of the first paragraph.

1. Press (F8)

2. Press (End)

   The first line of the first paragraph is selected. To cancel Select mode:

3. Press (F8)

Before beginning to edit your letter, practice with the Undelete and Undo features.

1. Position the I-beam somewhere in the first paragraph, which reads "Your prospectus, table of contents, and . . ."

2. Click the mouse button four times

   The first paragraph of the letter is selected. Now delete the paragraph.

3. Press (Backspace)

   The paragraph is deleted. Move the insertion point to the bottom of the document.

4. Press (Ctrl) + (End)

   Use the Undo feature to restore the deleted paragraph to its original place.

5. Click on Edit

   The Edit menu is shown in Figure 3-3.

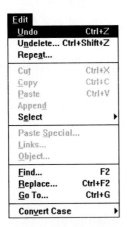

Figure 3-3

6. Click on Undo

   ✓ Press (Ctrl) + (Z)

   The paragraph is restored in its original position. Remember, Undo reverses the last change made to your document.

Now experiment with the Undelete feature.

1. Position the I-beam somewhere in the last paragraph, which reads "Please let us know if you are interested."

2. Click the mouse button three times

3. Press (Del)

   The paragraph is deleted. Next, move the insertion point to the bottom of the document.

4. Press (Ctrl) + (End)

5. Click on <u>E</u>dit ⇒ U<u>n</u>delete

   ✓ Press (Ctrl) + (SHIFT) + (Z)

   The Undelete option box appears, as shown in Figure 3-4.

Figure 3-4

The deleted paragraph is highlighted and shown at the bottom of the document. If you choose the Restore option, the paragraph will be restored at the bottom of the document, which is not where you want it, so cancel Undelete.

6. Click on <u>C</u>ancel

   Remember, the advantage of Undelete is that your last *three* deletions are saved, so you can restore any or all of the deletions. To view the other deletions, click on either <u>N</u>ext or <u>P</u>revious.

7. Move the insertion point back to the paragraph's original position

8. Select Edit ⇒ Undelete

   ✓ Press (Ctrl) + (SHIFT) + (Z)

   The paragraph is shown highlighted and in its correct position.

9. Click on <u>R</u>estore

 You want to leave Dr. Airsman's letter as it is, but you need a similar letter for Mr. Ron Wright. Use Save <u>A</u>s to copy and rename Dr. Airsman's letter.

1. Click on <u>F</u>ile ⇒ Save <u>A</u>s

   ✓ Press (F3)

   The Save As dialog box appears. You want to name the file wright.

2. Type `wright`

3. Click on OK or press (Enter)

Notice that the title bar reads "wright.wpd - unmodified." You are no longer working with Dr. Airsman's letter, but with Mr. Wright's. As you begin to make changes to the letter, notice that unmodified disappears from the title bar (until you save the file again).

 In this exercise you will change the justification to full.

1. Place the insertion point in the first paragraph (move the I-beam there, and click to position the insertion point)

2. Click on <u>L</u>ayout ⇒ <u>J</u>ustification

   The menu shown in Figure 3-5 appears.

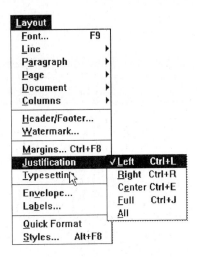

Figure 3-5

3. Click on <u>F</u>ull

   ✓ Press (Ctrl) + (J)

   All paragraphs of your document are now fully justified. Activate the Reveal Codes screen (<u>V</u>iew ⇒ Reveal <u>C</u>odes or (ALT) + (F3)) to see the Just: code box at the beginning of the first paragraph.

   NOTE: To expand the Just: code box, place the red cursor bar to the left of the code box.

4. Exit Reveal Codes

   Select the existing inside address, then replace it with the inside address for Mr. Wright.

5. Select the name and inside address

6. Type: `Mr. Ron Wright`
   `101 Willow Grove`
   `Philadelphia, PA 19118`

   Delete the name in the salutation line.

7. Position the insertion point in front of Dr. in the salutation

8. Press (Ctrl) + (Del)

9. Type `Mr. Wright:`

You will continue working on your document after reading about more WordPerfect features. Save what you have done so far.

Underlining Existing Text

The process for underlining text that has already been typed differs from that for underlining text while you are typing it. After text has been entered:

- Select the text to be underlined.
- Choose Layout ⇒ F<u>o</u>nt ⇒ <u>U</u>nderline ((Ctrl) + (U)).

The text is underlined and remains selected in case you want to make further changes. To deselect the underlined text, either click the mouse button outside the text or press any arrow key.

An Und code is placed before and after the underlined text.

Changing Tab Stops

Tab stops are used to align columns, set up tables, and indent paragraphs. Tab stops are used much the same as on a typewriter: first you set the tab position, then press (Tab) to move the insertion point to the first tab stop. Each time you press (Tab) the cursor moves to the next defined tab stop. WordPerfect inserts a Tab code each time the (Tab) key is pressed.

The two types of tab measurements available are Left Edge, or **absolute**, and Left Margin, or **relative**. Left Margin tabs (the default) are always measured relative to the left margin. For example, if you want to set a tab stop ½" from the left margin, you would specify .5. All Left Margin tabs "float," or move relative to the left margin position. For example, if you have tab stops at every ½", and you decide to move your left margin ¼" to the right, all the tab stops will also move ¼" to the right. In other words, the tabs shift to new positions to remain the same distance from the margin. The code inserted for Left Margin or relative tabs is Tab Set: Rel.

Left Edge (absolute) tab stops are measured from the left edge of the page, regardless of current margin settings. For example, if you wanted a tab stop ½" from the left edge of the text, and the left margin is at 1", you would enter 1.5 for the tab stop. If the left margin of a document is later changed, the tab stops do not float. The code inserted for Left Edge tabs is Tab Set: Abs.

WordPerfect automatically sets tab stops every ½" and the default tab type is relative. There are four tab alignments available and each type can include **dot leaders**—evenly spaced periods preceding the tab stops. Table 3-6 describes each type and shows the icon used in the pull-down menu to identify each one.

An example of each alignment is shown Table 3-7.

The Tab Set Dialog Box

To set and delete tab stops with the Tab Set dialog box from the menu, first position the insertion point where the new tab settings are to take effect. Then:

- Select <u>L</u>ayout ⇒ <u>L</u>ine ⇒ <u>T</u>ab Set.
- Select Clear All.

Tab Type	Icon	Description
Left tab	◣	Aligns the text evenly on the left side of the tab position
Center tab	▲	Centers text over the tab stop
Right tab	◢	Aligns text evenly on the right side of the tab position
Decimal tab	△	Aligns the decimal points of each number under the tab position, thus aligning all the decimal points

Table 3-6
Tab Types

Left	Center	Right	Decimal
Denver	Colorado	1,000	1,000.00
San Francisco	California	200	200.50
Columbia	South Carolina	10	20.75
Salt Lake City	Utah	1	1.00

Table 3-7
Text Alignments

- From the Type drop-down list, select: Left, Center, Right, Decimal, Dot Left, Dot Center, Dot Right, or Dot Decimal.
- In the Position text box, type tab position number.
- Select Relative (left margin) or Absolute (left edge of paper) Position.
- Select Set.
- Repeat as necessary.
- Press (Enter).

To set evenly spaced tabs, as at every 8 spaces, after you Clear All tabs, type the number of the beginning tab position in the Position box, click on Repeat Every, and enter 8.

To return to the default setting, select Default from the Tab Set dialog box.

Using the Ruler Bar

WordPerfect's ruler bar provides a quick way to change various format settings. The ruler bar is marked off in inches, with a total of 8 ½" across the screen.

Each document has its own ruler bar, since different documents can have different format settings. Also, if you have more than one document open, displaying the ruler bar for one document does not automatically display it for others. To display the ruler bar:

- Choose View ⇒ Ruler Bar ((Alt) + (Shift) + (F3)).

To remove the ruler bar, simply repeat the same menu selections. To permanently display the ruler bar, choose File ⇒ Preferences ⇒ Display and click on the radio button preceding "Ruler Bar."

When tabs are set using the ruler bar, Left Margin tab stops are used unless they are otherwise changed using the Tab Set dialog box.

To delete tab stops with the ruler bar as with the commands, first make sure the insertion point is positioned where the new tab settings are to take effect. To delete one tab, drag the tab icon down below the ruler. The icon disappears and the tab setting is deleted.

NOTE: To quickly delete all tab stops, double-click on any tab setting icon. The Tab Set dialog box appears. Click on the Clear All command button and choose OK.

▌ Using the Power Bar

For the most frequently used options, WordPerfect provides a **Power Bar,** shown in Figure 3-6, to expedite the execution of a command. To execute a command contained on the power bar, simply position the mouse pointer on the desired command button (icon) and click once. Commands on all the bars can be accessed only with the mouse—there are no keystrokes available for choosing command buttons. The power bar automatically displays when you open a document.

Figure 3-6

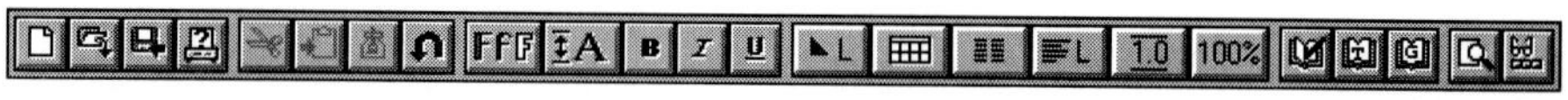

The icon for setting tabs changes, depending on the type of tab last set—right, center, or left. The left tab set is the default icon; it contains a picture of left justified text with an L to the right of the text. If you want to set other types of tabs than the default left tab, you can either click on one of the tab icons on the ruler bar with the *right* mouse button, or you can select the tab icon on the power bar to get a drop-down menu. An advantage to using the power bar is that it will display the ruler bar if the latter is not already displayed. Select each tab's type and then click and hold the mouse pointer on the mark where you want a new tab until a dotted vertical line appears. Release the button and the tab is set.

CAUTION: Be sure you first position the insertion point where the new tabs are to take effect.

Moving a Tab Stop

To move one tab setting, click on the tab marker icon and drag it to the desired position. As you are moving it, the status bar shows your position. Release the mouse button to set the tab.

Copying a Tab Stop

To copy one tab stop, hold down the (Ctrl) key, click on the tab marker and drag it to the new position.

▌ Changing Text to Uppercase

WordPerfect has a feature called Case Conversion that allows you to change text from lowercase to uppercase and vice versa without having to retype the text. To do this:

- First select the text to be converted.
- Choose Edit ⇒ Convert Case, Uppercase, Lowercase, or Initial Capitals.

Mr. Wright also sent some transparency masters. You want to note their receipt.

1. Position the insertion point in front of the letter "a" in the phrase "and first two chapters . . ."

2. Type `transparency masters,`

3. Press (Spacebar) once

The next correction to Mr. Wright's letter is to change the title of the manuscript.

4. Select "for <u>Using Access for Windows for the IBM</u>"

5. Press the (Del) key

6. Type `for First Look At WordPerfect 6.0 for DOS`

Next, underline the title of Mr. Wright's manuscript.

1. Select "First Look at WordPerfect 6.0 for DOS"

2. Click on <u>L</u>ayout-<u>F</u>ont-<u>U</u>nderline

   ✓ Press (Ctrl) + (U)

3. Click the mouse button once to deselect the title

You received Mr. Wright's letter on December 10. You will use the Typeover feature to replace the date.

1. Position the insertion point in front of the "N" in November"

2. Press (Ins)

The prompt on the status bar changes to "Typeover."

3. Type `December 10`

4. Press (Ins) again to deactivate the Typeover feature

5. Put a period after ". . . Publishing Company"

6. Select the rest of the sentence (use (F8) and arrow keys) from ", however" to the end "for us"

7. Press the (Del) key

8. In the second paragraph, position the insertion point at the beginning of the second sentence "At this time . . ."

9. Select the entire sentence

10. Press the (Del) key

11. Type:

   `At this time we will send your manuscript to several of`
   `our reviewers for their opinions.  The reviewers we will`
   `use and the number of days necessary for each of them to`
   `review it are shown in the following table.`

12. Press (Enter) three times

13. Press (↑) once

Your insertion point is positioned on a blank line.

 You will type the table shown in the completed letter in Figure 3-11. The first step is to set three center tabs for the headings.

1. Click on <u>L</u>ayout ⇒ <u>L</u>ine ⇒ <u>T</u>ab Set

The Tab Set dialog box appears, as shown in Figure 3-7.

Figure 3-7

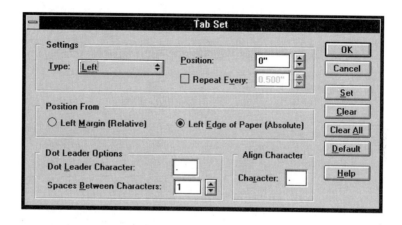

Your first task is to clear all the existing tabs.

2. Click on Clear <u>A</u>ll

Next, select the position.

3. In the Position From box, check that the Left Margin (Relative) position is selected

CAUTION: Be sure to mark the Position From box for Left Margin or Left Edge before you set the tab positions, as they will be set according to what is marked, and they will not change if you later mark the other Position From option.

4. Click on the down arrow button next to Type and hold it down to see a list of tabs

5. Move the pointer down until <u>C</u>enter is highlighted and release the mouse button

Center now appears in the Type text box.

6. Move the I-beam into the <u>P</u>osition box and click the mouse button once

7. Delete any previous settings and Type 1 (for 1")

NOTE: You can also double-click on the number to select it and then type in the new number.

8. Click on the <u>S</u>et command button

Be sure to move the I-beam back to the <u>P</u>osition box each time you set a tab. Be careful not to press (Enter) or you will be returned to your document.

9. Delete the 1 and type **3** (for 3")

10. Click on the <u>S</u>et command button

11. Delete the 3 and type **5** (for 5")

12. Click on the <u>S</u>et command button

13. Click on OK

To see the tab settings, activate the Reveal Codes screen (<u>V</u>iew ⇒ Re-veal Codes or (Alt) + (F3)) and click on the code or press the left arrow—it will expand to show you all the tab positions.

 Display the ruler to see your tab settings marked.

1. Click on <u>V</u>iew ⇒ <u>R</u>uler Bar

   ✓ Press (Alt) + (Shift) + (F3)

The ruler appears below the menu bar. Notice in Figure 3-8 that there are 3 tab markers; they correspond to the 3 center tabs created using the <u>L</u>ayout ⇒ <u>L</u>ine ⇒ <u>T</u>ab Set menu. The reason they are 1" greater than what you entered (1, 3, and 5) is because they are shown relative to the left margin.

Figure 3-8

You are ready to type the headings. The insertion point should be a double space below the text on the left margin.

2. Press (Tab)

3. Type **Reviewer** and press (Tab)

4. Type **Review Days** and press (Tab)

5. Type **Critique Expected** and press (Enter) twice

 Before typing the table you will delete all existing tab settings, then use the ruler to set three new tab stops.

1. Position the mouse pointer on the tab marker icon at 2"

2. Click and drag the tab marker off the ruler line and release

3. Delete the tab markers positioned at 4" and 6"

 You will set 3 new tab settings: a left-aligned tab at 1.56", a right-aligned tab at 4.06", and another left-aligned tab at 5.63".

1. Click and hold the mouse pointer on the ruler line mark at approximately 1.56" (look at the Pos on the status bar to find your place)

A left-aligned tab marker appears with a dotted line as shown in Figure 3-9.

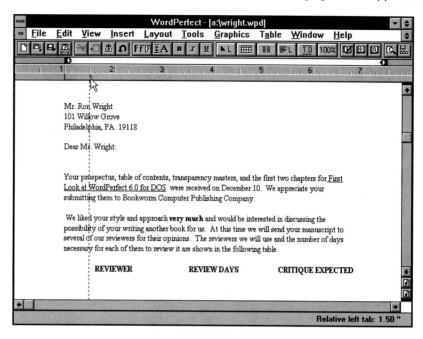

Figure 3-9

2. Move the tab to 1.56 and release

To set a right-aligned tab, with the mouse pointer on the newly-created tab:

3. Click the right button to get a drop-down menu

4. Select Right

5. Set a tab at 4.06

Remember, if you put a tab marker icon in the wrong place, simply place the mouse pointer on the icon and drag it to the desired position. The status bar shows the type of tab alignment and the position.

You will copy another left-aligned tab to position 5.44.

6. Hold down the (Ctrl) key

Be sure to keep (Ctrl) depressed throughout this operation to copy the tab instead of moving it.

7. Click on the tab icon at position 1.56

8. Drag the tab marker to position 5.63

9. Release the mouse button and (Ctrl) key

Once again, if you select Reveal Codes and activate the Tab Set code, you will see tabs set at .56, 4.06, and 4.63, 1" less than the numbers you set as they are positioned from the left margin.

10. Type the columnar table shown below. Press (Tab) before each entry and (Enter) once at the end of each line

```
Curt Weeks          40   January 31
Kathy Jones          9   January 4
Tina Salverson      10   January 5
```

```
Maureen Wilson        40    January 31
Blair Schmitz          8    January 3
Polly Jo Booth        30    January 20
```

11. Press (Enter) twice

You decide that the headings of your columns would look better if they were in all capital letters. Instead of retyping the text, use WordPerfect's Case Conversion feature.

1. Place the I-beam somewhere in the line that reads "Reviewer Review Days Critique Expected" (the column heads)

2. Click the mouse button four times

   The entire line is selected.

3. Click on <u>E</u>dit ⇒ Con<u>v</u>ert Case

   The menu shown in Figure 3-10 appears.

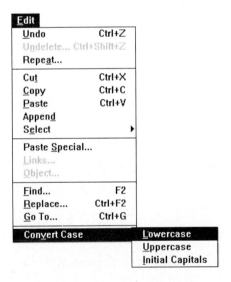

Figure 3-10

4. Click on <u>U</u>ppercase

   You would also like to have the headings of your columns in bold type. The line should still be selected.

5. Click on <u>L</u>ayout ⇒ F<u>o</u>nt ⇒ <u>B</u>old ⇒ OK

   ✓ Press (Ctrl) + (B)

   It is a very good idea to save your document frequently as you create it. Deselect the text and select <u>F</u>ile ⇒ <u>S</u>ave ((Ctrl) + (S))
   You are now ready to continue editing your letter. Position your insertion point on the blank line following the table.

6. Press (Enter) one time

7. Type:

```
If the reviews are positive, we will mail a contract to
you for your approval and signature. For your informa-
tion, our standard royalty schedule for an unpublished
author is as follows:
```

8. Press (Enter) twice

You will use the ruler and the power bar Tab icon to first set Center tabs for the headings, then left- and decimal-aligned tabs for the body of the table. Be sure that your insertion point is positioned at the place in your document where you want the tab stops to take effect.

1. Click on the Tab icon on the power bar and hold it down to display the Set Tabs and Clear All Tabs choices

2. Select Clear All Tabs

3. Click on the Tab icon again and select Center

   Note that the icon changes to a C with text centered on it.

4. Position the mouse pointer on the ruler at approximately 2.31"

5. Click to display a center tab

   A center tab is added because the Tab icon now shows Center.

6. Move the tab to the exact position of 2.31" and release the mouse button

7. Set a center-aligned tab at position 5.56"

8. Press (Tab) before each heading. Type the headings **NUMBER OF BOOKS SOLD** and **ROYALTY PERCENTAGE** in boldface, and press (Enter) twice.

   Be sure to turn Bold off.

9. Clear those tab stops—drag them off the ruler bar or click on the right mouse button from the ruler bar and select Clear All Tabs

10. On your own set a left-aligned tab at 1.81"

11. Set a decimal-aligned tab at 5.63"

12. Type the following table (*not* in boldface), pressing (Tab) before each entry and (Enter) at the end of every line:

```
Up to 3,000      10.0
Up to 6,000      10.5
Up to 10,000     11.0
Up to 15,000     11.5
Up to 20,000     12.0
Up to 25,000     12.5
Over 25,000      13.0
```

Change your tab sets back to the default.

1. Place the mouse pointer in the ruler bar

2. Click the right mouse button

3. Select Tab Set

4. Click on Default

5. Click on OK

The final steps in completing the letter follow.

1. Spell check your document (Tools ⇒ Speller)

   ✓ Ctrl + F1

2. Save the document (File ⇒ Save)

   ✓ Ctrl + S

3. Print the document (File ⇒ Print)

   ✓ F5

Your completed letter is shown in Figure 3-11.

Do not be concerned that your page divides in an unacceptable place. You are not finished with the letter and will fix that in a later lesson.

NOTE: It is extremely important that you make a back-up (additional copy) of your documents onto another disk in case something happens to this disk. It is very easy to make back-ups in WordPerfect. Remove the work disk that's in the drive now, insert another formatted disk, and click on the Save icon. Continue to make back-up copies of your work as you proceed through the lessons.

CAUTION: Be very careful not to insert or remove a disk when the drive light is on. WordPerfect has a save feature that automatically saves files to the disk at regular intervals. If that feature is activated, the light will come on at various times during your lessons as it saves.

4. Exit WordPerfect (File ⇒ Exit)

   ✓ Alt + F4

On Your Own

Review of Commands

Description	Menu Commands	Function Keys
Open existing file	_____	_____
Rename a file	_____	_____
Change the justification	_____	_____
Undelete	_____	_____
Undo	_____	_____
Set tabs	_____	_____
View the ruler	_____	_____

(today's date)

Mr. Ron Wright
101 Willow Grove
Philadelphia, PA 19118

Dear Mr. Wright:

Your prospectus, transparency masters, table of contents, and first two chapters for First Look at WordPerfect 6.0 for DOS were received on December 10. We appreciate your submitting them to Bookworm Computer Publishing Company .

We liked your style and approach **very much** and would be interested in discussing the possibility of your writing another book for us. At this time we will send your manuscript to several of our reviewers for their opinions. The reviewers we will use and the number of days necessar y for each of them to review it are shown in the following table.

REVIEWER	REVIEW DAYS	CRITIQUE EXPECTED
Curt Weeks	40	January 31
Kathy Jones	9	January 4
Tina Salverson	10	January 5
Maureen Wilson	40	January 31
Blair Schmitz	8	January 3
Polly Jo Booth	30	January 20

If the reviews are positive, we will mail a contract to you for your approval and signature. For your information, our standard royalty schedule for an unpublished author is as follows:

NUMBER OF BOOKS SOLD	ROYALTY PERCENTAGE
Up to 3,000	10.0
Up to 6,000	10.5
Up to 10,000	11.0
Up to 15,000	11.5
Up to 20,000	12.0
Up to 25,000	12.5
Over 25,000	13.0

Please let us know if you are interested.

Sincerely yours,

Your Name
Editor

Figure 3-11

Change text to uppercase
or lowercase   _____   _____

Display Typeover or Insert
prompt on the status line   _____   _____

▌ Lesson Review

1. Which justification feature aligns text evenly at both the right and left margins?

2. What menu command gives you right justified text?

3. What keystrokes are needed to select a word?

4. What keystrokes are needed to delete a word at the insertion point?

5. List the steps to underline existing text.

6. Which type of tab stops are measured from the left edge of the paper?

7. Which type of tab stops are measured from the left margin and automatically adjust if the margin is changed?

8. List the steps to display the ruler bar.

9. To replace existing text with new text from the keyboard, which mode must be selected?

10. Which command reverses the last action you took?

11. Which command allows you to restore deleted text to any location in your document?

12. What is the most efficient way to select a word with the mouse?

13. What is the most efficient way to select a sentence with the mouse?

14. How can you select a single paragraph with the mouse?

15. What steps would you take to underline a previously-typed phrase?

16. If you have a tab stop at 2.5", and you want to move it to 3", how could you use the mouse to move the tab stop?

▌ Assigments

3-1 Directions

1. Type the following memo.

Date: (today's date)
To: All Managers
From: Steven Rosenbaum, Vice President of Marketing
Subject: Marketing Survey

A repeat session for the Marketing Opinion Survey has been scheduled for the following time: Thursday, November 11, 1994, 6 p.m. to 9 p.m. The location of the meeting is Conference Room 6, Building 2.

Please announce this repeat session to all key personnel in your departments. This will be the last opportunity for employees to complete this marketing survey.

Employees may want to consider what types of books they feel our company should publish. Request that they come to the session prepared to back up their opinions with facts. Any published data or other documents the employees can furnish will be appreciated.

These surveys are important to the success of our company! Please urge your key employees to attend if they have not attended a previous session.

---

2. Save the document as survey.wpd.

3. Select and delete the third paragraph.

4. Restore the paragraph (hint: use Undelete)

5. Spell check, save, and print the memo.

6. Close the document.

3-2 Directions

1. Open survey.wpd.

2. Save the document as survey1.wpd.

3. Change the justification to full.

4. Change the introductory headings (To:, From:, Date:, Subject:) to uppercase.

5. Bold the introductory Headings.

6. Delete the third paragraph.

7. Type the following sentence in the last paragraph after the first sentence: **Attendance will be taken.**

8. Print, save, and close the document.

3-3 Directions

1. Open survey.wpd.

2. Underline the SUBJECT line.

3. Delete the last paragraph.

4. Place the insertion point before the word "Any" in the last sentence of the third paragraph. Press (Enter) twice to make the last sentence a new paragraph.

5. Add the following text to the end of the last paragraph.

> This data will be reviewed extensively over the next few weeks. It will be the starting point of our research for the next two quarters.

6. Change the justification to full.

7. Save the edited document as survey2.wpd.

8. Spell check, save, print, and close the document.

3-4 Directions

1. Open a new, blank document.

2. Access the Tab Set dialog box from the menu.

3. Clear all existing tabs.

4. Set a new left tab at 2" and another at 5". Close the dialog box.

5. Type the table that appears below.

Smith, A. A.	Houston, Texas	77046
Allen, B. J.	Beaumont, Texas	77707
Zucker, L. L.	Shreveport, Louisiana	59708
Lovely, K. B.	Ruidoso, New Mexico	25769
Klinger, L. M.	Los Angeles, California	98765

6. Display the ruler bar if it is not already displayed. Note the location of the left tabs. Why are the measurements (3" and 6") different from the tab settings you originally set in step 4?

7. Save the document as review.wpd. Print and close the document.

3-5 Directions

1. Open review.wpd and save it as review1.wpd.

2. Make sure the insertion point is at the beginning of the document.

3. Insert three hard returns and move the insertion point to the top of the document again.

4. Center and type the title: **REVIEWERS FOR SOFTWARE PLUS**

5. Insert the column titles above each column: **NAME, GEOGRAPHIC REGION, ZIP CODE**

6. Bold the centered title. Underline the column titles.

7. Make sure the insertion point is in the first line of the table. Using the ruler bar, move the last column (ZIP CODE) tab marker to 6.5" on the ruler bar.

8. Save the document, print it, and close the file.

3-6   Directions

1. Create the following table using the ruler bar and the mouse. Set a Center tab at 3", a Right tab at 5", and a Decimal tab at 7". (Hint: the Decimal tab may not be appropriate for the last column's title. Set a Right tab at 7.2" in place of the Decimal tab for the column title only.)

Computer Software Book Sales

Sales Person	Marketing Area	Sales	Expenses
Jim Spencer	Boston	40,000	$5,700.00
Harold Humphrey	Phoenix	70,000	8,340.00
Lisa Gosek	Sacramento	85,900	9,330.75
Donna Whittaker	New York	763,200	7,567.00
Hillary Smith	Los Angeles	68,500	9,500.30

2. Save the document as sales.wpd. Print the document. Close the file.

3-7   Directions

1. Type the following letter.

2. Determine where the tabs should be placed to give the document a pleasing appearance. Use default justification and margins.

3. Save the letter as gosek.wpd. Spell check, save, print, and close the document.

September 12, 1993

Ms. Martha Gosek
2948 King Street
Westminster, CO 80030

Dear Ms. Gosek:

Here is the information you requested when we spoke the other day . As you can see our sales representatives do a fine job in their respective markets. I am sure they will do as good a job marketing texts this year as they did last year .

Sales Representative	Market	Percentage
B. B. Hunt	New York	98%
R. A. Kane	Montreal	85%
K. V. Jordan	Ottawa	95%
G. O. Thomas	Washington	97%

If you have further questions or need more information about our marketing efforts, please feel free to call me at (303) 555-5515.

Sincerely,

Mary Rogers, Manager
Development and Research

3-8 Directions

1. Retrieve the dsawards.wpd file created in Lesson 2.

2. Save it as award.mem.

3. Change the justification to Full.

4. Boldface the memo headings and make them uppercase.

5. Make a new paragraph after "September 1, 1994."

6. Underline "high standard" in the third paragraph.

7. Using Typeover mode, change the faculty senate office to WC 203.

8. Save, print, and close the file.

Increasing Productivity

Objectives

After completing this lesson, you will be able to:

- Use File Management
- Work with more than one document
- Cut and paste text
- Print a document from disk
- Describe and use the power bar
- Describe and use a button bar
- Select, edit, and create a button bar
- Change the location and appearance of the button bar
- Describe and use QuickMenus

File Management

You will often want to copy a file to another drive or directory, rename a file, or delete a file. To do so:

- Select File ⇒ Open ⇒ File Options.
- Select one of the following: Copy, Move, Rename, or Delete.
- Type the file name in the name text box or click on the file name in the file list box.
- Click on OK.

When copying or moving a file, you must specify the complete path name by including every directory level.

Working with Two Documents Onscreen

WordPerfect allows up to nine open document windows. To open a second window:

- Choose File ⇒ Open (F4).

- Select the file to be opened.
- Choose OK.

You can also select File ⇒ New. An empty window will open for a new document, which becomes the active window and is already maximized. When you have several document windows open, you can go from one to another.

- Select <u>W</u>indow.
- Select the document's name.
- Press (Ctrl) + (Shift) + (F6) (to go to the previous document).
- Press (Ctrl) + (F6) (to go to the next document).

▌ Cutting and Pasting Text

A standard feature in Windows applications is the ability to remove (cut) or move (copy) text from one document and insert (paste) it into another place in the same document, into a different document, or even into a document in an entirely different application. The cut or copied text is stored in Windows' Clipboard and remains there until you cut or copy text again or turn off Windows.

First select the text to be affected.

- Choose <u>E</u>dit ⇒ Cu<u>t</u> ((Ctrl) + (X)) or Edit ⇒ Copy ((Ctrl) + (C)).

To then paste (insert) the cut or copied text in a new location:

- Position the insertion point where the text is to be placed.
- Choose <u>E</u>dit ⇒ <u>P</u>aste ((Ctrl) + (V)).

You can paste text from the Clipboard into other documents as many times as needed without having to select and cut it again.

▌ Printing a Document from Disk

In previous lessons, you printed your document while it was displayed on the screen. WordPerfect also allows you to print a file from disk so that you can work on another document at the same time. You can print either the entire document or only selected pages.

- Choose <u>F</u>ile ⇒ <u>P</u>rint ((F5)).
- Select <u>D</u>ocument on Disk.
- Select Print.
- Type name of the document in the <u>F</u>ilename text box.
- In the <u>P</u>age(s) box; you have three alternatives: accept All to print the whole document; type the numbers of the pages you want to print (such as 1, 3, 4, and 6); or name a range of pages such as 3–7 or 5– [page 5 to the end of the document]).
- Select Print.

▌ The Power Bar

In the last lesson, you used the power bar's Tab icon to quickly set tabs. Several of the other most frequently-used features are available as icons, and, if used when opening, saving, printing, and so on, should save time. For example, to save a document, you might use the menu bar and click on File, wait for the drop-down menu, and choose Save; the shortcut keystrokes are (Shift) + (F3) (which you might not remember); or you can simply click on the Save button (icon) on the power bar. Using the commands from the power bar, (and the other bars available) will often prove to be faster than using other methods. The power bar, with the icons labelled, is shown in Figure 4-1. As you move the mouse pointer over the icons, you will see a description of each icon at the top of the screen.

Figure 4-1

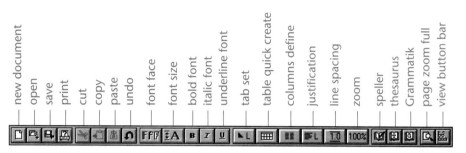

As mentioned, the power bar includes command buttons or icons for the most frequently-used features. The icons reflect the function they perform, such as a printer for Print, a bold "B" for Bold, and an underlined "U" for Underline. Notice that some of the buttons are **grayed**, indicating that they are not available at this time. For example, the Cut, Copy, and Paste buttons are grayed, because no text has been selected to cut or copy.

To execute a command on the power bar, simply position the mouse pointer on the desired button and click once.

NOTE: Commands on the bars can be accessed only via mouse—there are no keystrokes available for choosing command buttons.

Unless previously hidden, the power bar automatically displays when you open a document. To hide it:

• Choose View ⇒ Power bar.

It is very easy to modify the power bar by adding or deleting command icons.

• Select File ⇒ Preferences.
• Double-click on the power bar icon.

To add icons:

• Scroll to the desired item in the Items box, or type the first letter of the item; the list will move to the item beginning with that letter.
• Click on the item; an x will be placed in the check box.

To rearrange icons:

• Drag them to a new location on the power bar.

To remove icons:

• Drag them off the power bar and release the left mouse button.

It is also possible to add spacers between icons for easier readability. Just click on a spacer at the bottom of the Power Bar option box and drag it to the bar. Once you modify the power bar, it will remain that way for all documents. To return to the original arrangement, click on Default.

▌The Button Bar

In addition to the power bar, WordPerfect has various button bars for further commands. Button bars do not automatically display, but once you choose a specific button bar, it will display for all documents until you hide it or choose another button bar.

Creating Your Own Button Bar

You can create your own button bar having command buttons for the features you use most. Once the button bar is created, you can easily change it. The default button bar, which WordPerfect activates when you choose View ⇒ Button bar, is called "WordPerfect." It contains Indent, Bullet, Date Text, Envelopes, Draw, Chart, Figure, Text, Quick Format, and Styles icons. You can customize a copy of this default button bar, or you can build one of your own. The commands available to add to the button bars are divided first into categories, then into features. The categories available are File, Edit, View, Insert, Layout, Tools, Graphics, Table, Window, and Help. These are the same categories listed on the menu bar. The features are the same features contained in each of those pull-down menus.

To create a new button bar, from the main menu:

- Select File ⇒ Preferences.
- Double-click on the Button bar icon.
- Select Create.
- Type a new name at the New Button Bar Name prompt.
- Select OK or press (Enter).
- Mark the radio button Activate a Program Feature.
- In the Categories box, click and hold the down arrow to display all categories.
- Select a category.
- In the Features box, click on desired feature.
- Select Add Button.
- Add features as desired.
- Select OK to close Editor.
- Select Close for Button Bar box.
- Select Close for Preferences box.

The new button bar then displays at the top of your workspace. If more buttons are added than will fit on one row, WordPerfect will scroll the overflow off the screen. When this occurs, up- and down-pointing arrows appear to the right of the button bar. Click on these arrows to scroll the button bar to the right or left.

Button Bars Available

WordPerfect has designed several button bars to be used for performing specialized tasks. For reference, a list of available button bars and their uses is shown in Table 4-1.

Button Bar	Use
Equation Editor	To assist in the Equation Editor
Font	To change font size and style
Generate	For generating indexes and tables of contents
Graphics	To create and edit boxes
Layout	For document layout
Macros	For predefined macros
Outline	To work with outlines
Page	To change page format
Preferences	To customize WordPerfect's settings
Tables	To create and edit tables
WordPerfect	For standard WordPerfect 6.0 commands
WordPerfect 5.2	For WordPerfect 5.2 commands

Table 4-1

Specialized Button Bars

Selecting a Different Button Bar

You may switch among the various button bars. To activate a specific button bar:

- Choose File ⇒ Preferences.
- Double-click on the Button Bar icon.
- Highlight the name of the desired button bar.
- Click on Select.
- Click on Close twice.

The selected button bar displays at the top of your screen below the power bar. As you will see when QuickMenus are discussed later in the lesson, you can position the pointer anywhere in the button bar and click on the right mouse button to display a list of button bars. Clicking on one of them will replace the current button bar.

Editing a Button Bar

You may edit any of the button bars. First, make sure the button bar you want to edit is displayed on the screen. Then, from the menu bar:

- Choose File ⇒ Preferences.
- Double-click on Button Bar icon.
- Highlight the name of the displayed button bar.
- Select Edit.

The Button Bar Editor displays. In the Add a Button To option box:

- Click on the Activate a Feature radio button.
- Select the desired Category, such as View.
- Select the desired Feature, such as Hide Bar.

The Add Button text box is activated.

- Click on the <u>A</u>dd Button.
- Repeat as necessary.
- Click on OK.
- Click on <u>C</u>lose.

Moving and Deleting Buttons

To move a button, from the Editor position the mouse on the button and drag it to the desired location. To delete a command button, position the mouse pointer on the button and drag it off the button bar. When the mouse button is released, the button is deleted.

Moving and Altering the Button Bar

The button bar does not have to be displayed at the top of your screen. It can be positioned at the bottom of the screen or vertically along the left or right side. You can also change the appearance of the buttons by choosing to show only text or only pictures. To change the position and appearance of the button bar, from the menu bar:

- Choose <u>F</u>ile ⇒ Pr<u>e</u>ferences ⇒ <u>B</u>utton Bar ⇒ <u>O</u>ptions

In the following exercises, you will use the power bar and button bar to see the advantage of using only one click to perform various commands that might otherwise involve numerous menus and keystrokes. You will print the first page of your Wright letter from disk (do not open it first). Both the power bar and the default button bar should be displayed at this time.

1. Click on the Print icon

2. Click on <u>D</u>ocument on Disk

3. Click on <u>P</u>rint

The Document on Disk dialog box appears as shown in Figure 4-2.

Figure 4-2

4. In the Filename text box, type `wright.wpd`

5. Press (Tab) to move to the Pages box

6. Type 1 to print the first page

7. Click on Print

> NOTE: *As the page prints, you can continue to work on that file or on another file.*

 You are going to open a new document screen, type the following paragraphs, and save them in a file called collage. You will want to use these paragraphs again when writing to other authors.

 1. Click on the New Document icon

2. Type the following:

```
We are sending Collage Plus under separate cover so that
you can capture and save screen displays as you work
through your manuscript.

To assist you in using this software, we've asked Jane
Monroe, our consultant for this program, to contact you.
Jane is also an experienced project manager and is
available to answer any questions you may have as you
progress. She can be reached at 408/481-1022, Monday
through Friday from 8:30 am to 5:00 pm Pacific time.

Also being sent are some general guidelines to assist you
in capturing and saving your screens in a format best
suited for the production team assigned to your project.
Because of the great variety of program interfaces, it is
not possible to prescribe one specific format that is
correct in every instance. If, after reviewing these
guidelines, you have any questions, please talk with
Jane. In any event, we strongly encourage you to capture
two or three screens and send them to Jane for evaluation
before completing the series needed for your manuscript.
```

 3. Click on the Save icon

4. Save the document as collage, but do not close

 As you can see, the power bar has buttons to open, save, and print a document. Other commands that you will use soon are Cut, Copy, and Paste.
Use the power bar to open the Wright document.

 1. Click on the Open icon

The Open File dialog box appears.

2. Double-click on wright.wpd

Your collage document leaves the screen and the Wright document becomes the active document. To go back to collage:

3. Click on Window

The Window menu is shown in Figure 4-3.

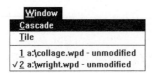

Figure 4-3

4. Click on 1 collage.wpd

   ✓ Press (Ctrl) + (F6)

   Collage becomes the active window.

5. In the collage document, select the text from "We are sending ..." to the end of the third paragraph "... for your manuscript."

6. Click on the Copy icon

   A copy of the text is placed in the Clipboard. You will not see it.

7. Deselect the text (click outside the selected text)

   To go back to your Wright letter:

8. Click on Window in the menu bar

9. Select 2 wright.wpd

   ✓ Press (Ctrl) + (F6)

   The Wright letter becomes the active window.

10. Move the insertion point to the end of "January 20" in the Review table

11. Press (Enter) twice

12. Click on the Paste icon

    The text you selected from the collage document is pasted into the letter.

13. Click on the Save icon

    Use the Window menu to make the collage document active.

14. Click on File ⇒ Close to close collage

    ✓ Press (Ctrl) + (F4)

In this exercise, you will first edit the power bar, then create your own button bar. The Wright document is still on the screen.

1. Click on File ⇒ Preferences

   From the Preferences icon box:

2. Double-click on Power Bar

   The Power Bar Preferences list box shown in Figure 4-4 appears.

Power Bar Preferences

- Add an item by checking box in list.
- Move an item by dragging it to a new position.
- Delete an item by dragging it off the Power Bar.

Items:
- ☒ Attribute Bold
- ☐ Attribute Double Underline
- ☐ Attribute Hidden
- ☒ Attribute Italics
- ☐ Attribute Normal
- ☐ Attribute Outline
- ☐ Attribute Redline
- ☐ Attribute Shadow

OK | Cancel | Default | Options... | Help

Description
Bold Font - Turn on bold font

Spacers
Separate items by dragging a spacer onto the Power Bar.

Figure 4-4

You want to delete the tools Grammatik and View from the button bar, and add View Ruler Bar and Reveal Codes to make it easier to access those commonly-used features.

3. Position the mouse pointer on the Grammatik icon

4. Click and drag the icon off the bar and release

5. Click and drag the View button bar icon off the bar

6. Type **v** and the list will scroll down to the Vs

7. Click on View Ruler Bar and View Reveal Codes to add those two buttons

8. Click on OK

9. Click on <u>C</u>lose

Your new power bar should be similar to the one shown in Figure 4-5.

Figure 4-5

NOTE: Once you modify the power bar, it will stay as modified for all documents until changed again.

10. On your own, undo the changes you've made and return the power bar to its original configuration.

You are going to create a new button bar called "Training" and add the following features to it: Close, Exit, Undelete, Find, Replace, Center Line, View Ruler Bar, View Reveal Codes, and Date Code.

1. Click on <u>F</u>ile ⇒ Pr<u>e</u>ferences and double-click on <u>B</u>utton Bar

The Button Bar Preferences list box displays as shown in Figure 4-6.

2. Click on C<u>r</u>eate

The Create Button Bar dialog box displays as shown in Figure 4-7.

3. Position the insertion point in the New Button Bar Name box and type `Training`

Figure 4-6

Figure 4-7

NOTE: On a network, once one student has created the Training bar it will remain created, and other students cannot later create another Training button bar. Check with your instructor to see if you should give the bar your own name so that each student can have a custom button bar.

4. Click on OK

The Button Bar Editor dialog box displays as shown in Figure 4-8.

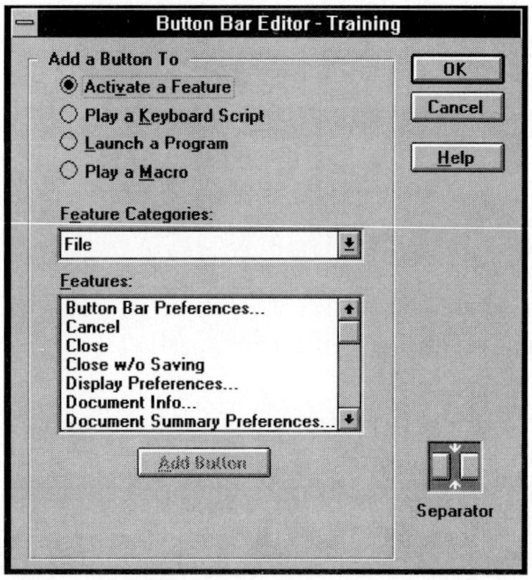

Figure 4-8

In the Add a Button To box, be sure that Activate a Feature is marked.

5. In the Feature Categories box, click the down arrow to display the list

These categories are the same as the ones in the menu bar across the top of the screen.

6. If not selected, select File

The Features box displays (these features are similar to the ones you get from each of the pull-down menus).

7. In the Features box, click on Close

8. In the Features box, click on <u>A</u>dd Button

In the Features box, scroll the down arrow to Exit.

9. Click on Exit

10. Click on <u>A</u>dd Button

11. Select the Edit category

12. Click on Find...

13. Click on <u>A</u>dd Button

14. Click on Replace...

15. Click on <u>A</u>dd Button

16. Click on Undelete...

17. Click on <u>A</u>dd Button

18. In the Layout category, click on Center Line

19. Click on <u>A</u>dd Button

20. In the View category, add Ruler Bar and Reveal Codes, and in the Insert category, add Date Code

Add any other commands you would like to customize your button bar. To delete or move any of the buttons, drag the button off the bar.

21. Click on OK

To save your button bar:

22. Click on Select

CAUTION: *Don't miss this step or the old button bar will display.*

Training has been added to the list of button bars.

23. Click on Close

Your new button bar is now displayed at the top of your Wright document and should look similar to the one shown in Figure 4-9.

Figure 4-9

Your table listing the reviewers and the expected critique dates would read more clearly arranged chronologically. Use the Cut and Paste feature to accomplish this task.

1. Position the I-beam in the line that reads "Blair Schmitz . . ."

2. Quadruple-click to select the line

3. Click on the Cut icon

To paste the line at the beginning of the table:

4. Position the insertion point at the left margin of the line that reads "Curt Weeks …"

5. Click on the Paste icon

6. Select the line that begins "Curt Weeks . . ."

7. Select the Cut icon

8. Position the insertion point at the end of "January 20" and press (Enter)

9. Select the Paste icon

10. Select the line that reads "Maureen Wilson . . ."

11. Press (Ctrl) + (X) (the shortcut keys for Cut)

12. Paste the text after "Curt Weeks" in the table

✓ Press (Ctrl) + (V)

You may have to delete a blank line or two; then compare your table to the one shown in the letter in Figure 4-10.

To save your Wright file:

13. Click on the Save icon

Do not close the file.

In this exercise, you will use the power bar to underline text and move a paragraph. Make sure the Wright document is still open and on your screen. You will also get more practice with the Undo feature, this time using the power bar.

1. Select the text "Collage Plus" in the paragraph below the table

2. Click on the Bold icon

3. Highlight the paragraph below the table beginning "We are sending . . ."

4. Click on the Copy icon

5. Move the insertion point to end of document

✓ (Ctrl) + (End)

6. Click on the Paste icon

Your paragraph is copied to the end of the document.

7. Click on the Undo icon

Your paragraph is removed from the end of the letter.

8. Save and close wright.wpd

(today's date)

Mr. Ron Wright
101 Willow Grove
Philadelphia, PA 19118

Dear Mr. Wright:

Your prospectus, table of contents, transparency masters, and the first two chapters for <u>First Look at WordPerfect 6.0 for DOS</u> were received on December 10. We appreciate your submitting them to Bookworm Computer Publishing Company.

We liked your style and approach **very much** and would be interested in discussing the possibility of your writing another book for us. At this time we will send your manuscript to several of our reviewers for their opinions. The reviewers we will use and the number of days necessary for each of them to review it are shown in the following table.

REVIEWER	REVIEW DAYS	CRITIQUE EXPECTED
Blair Schmitz	8	January 3
Kathy Jones	9	January 4
Tina Salverson	10	January 5
Polly Jo Booth	30	January 20
Curt Weeks	40	January 31
Maureen Wilson	40	January 31

We are sending **Collage Plus** under separate cover so that you can capture and save screen displays as you work through your manuscript.

To assist you in using this software, we've asked Jane Monroe, our consultant for this program, to contact you. Jane is also an experienced project manager and is available to answer any questions you may have as you progress. She can be reached at 408/481-1022, Monday through Friday from 8:30 am to 5:00 pm Pacific time.

Also being sent are some general guidelines to assist you in capturing and saving your screens in a format best suited for the production team assigned to your project. Because of the great variety of program interfaces, it is not possible to prescribe one specific format that is correct in every instance. If, after reviewing these guidelines, you have any questions, please talk with Jane. In any event, we <u>strongly</u> encourage you to capture two or three screens and send them to Jane for evaluation before completing the series needed for your manuscript.

Figure 4-10

continued on next page

If the reviews are positive, we will mail a contract to you for your approval and signature. For your information, our standard royalty schedule for an unpublished author is as follows:

NUMBER OF BOOKS SOLD	ROYALTY PERCENTAGE
Up to 3,000	10.0
Up to 6,000	10.5
Up to 10,000	11.0
Up to 15,000	11.5
Up to 20,000	12.0
Up to 25,000	12.5
Over 25,000	13.0

Please let us know if you are interested.

Sincerely yours,

(your name)
Editor

Figure 4-10
(*continued*)

As mentioned before, WordPerfect's power bar contains many frequently-used commands. Slowly move your mouse pointer over the icons on the power bar. A description of each icon appears in the title bar.

You will type the following paragraph using Bold, Underline, and Speller from the power bar. On your own, you may want to experiment with the other features available on the power bar.

1. Start with a blank screen

2. Type the following paragraph (include the mistakes):

   ```
   I can use the power bar for frequently used commands such
   as spel chek, boldfacing, underlining, saving, and
   printing. The power bar makes my work goe even faster.
   ```

3. Place the insertion point on the word "frequently" and double-click to select the word

4. Click on the Bold icon

5. Triple-click on the second sentence to select it

6. Click on the Italics icon

   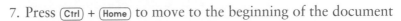

   The sentence becomes italicized.

7. Press (Ctrl) + (Home) to move to the beginning of the document

8. Click on the Speller icon

   Spell check the document.

9. Print the document

In the following exercise, you will use the default button bar (named WordPerfect) for some additional commands not on the power bar. You will type a "To Do" list of the tasks you must accomplish soon and use Word-Perfect's Bullet icon to insert a bullet before each line.

1. Click on the New document icon

    If it is not displayed, select the WordPerfect button bar:

2. Click on File ⇒ Preferences

3. Double-click on the Button Bar icon

4. Click on WordPerfect

5. Click on Select

6. Click on Close

7. Select the Date text icon

    The current date is automatically inserted into your document.

8. Press (Enter) six times, then type the following list:

```
Call Jane to see if new Collage Compleat is in
Check with Brad about due date for Lotus book
Ask Leslie if first draft of WP manuscript is ready
See if First Look reviewers have been contacted
Call airlines about ticket to New York
```

    To insert the bullets:

9. Highlight the listed items

10. Click on the Bullet icon

    The Bullets & Numbers dialog box displays as shown in Figure 4-11. The small circle option is selected.

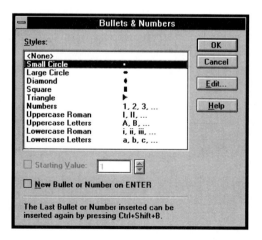

Figure 4-11

11. Click on OK

    Your list now has a bullet preceding each item.

12. Save the list as todo, and print the file

Drag the mouse pointer over the other buttons displayed on the button bar. A description of each button will appear in the title bar.

13. Close todo and the unnamed document

 To experiment with another placement and style of the button bar, move your button bar to the left side of your workspace and change it to show only text on the buttons.

1. Click on File ⇒ Preferences

2. Double-click on Button Bar (be sure "WordPerfect" is highlighted)

3. Choose Options

The Button Bar Options dialog box appears, as shown in Figure 4-12.

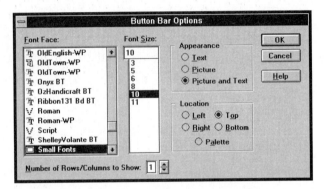

Figure 4-12

4. In the Appearance box, click on Text

5. In the Location box, click on Left

6. Click on OK

Compare your screen to the one shown in Figure 4-13.

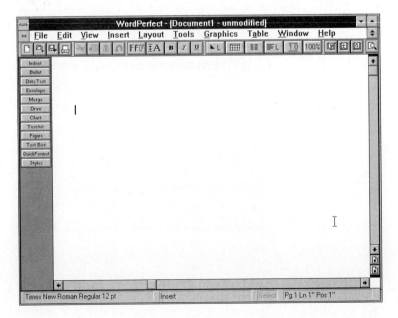

Figure 4-13

7. Click on Close from the Button Bar box

8. Click on Close from the Preferences box

9. On your own, change the appearance and placement of the button bar to your liking

   NOTE: When you open a new file, the button bar will appear as you last saved it until you again change its position or appearance. If you are on a network, your instructor might want you to return the button bar to its original position.

▌ QuickMenus

WordPerfect offers another way of increasing productivity by allowing you to select commands with a minimum of effort. When your mouse pointer is located in the relevant features in your document, you can click on the right mouse button to produce a QuickMenu. Table 4-2 shows some of these menus. To activate them, move the mouse pointer in or on the item and click the right mouse button. For example, to get the Table QuickMenu, move the mouse pointer on the table and click the right mouse button.

Table	Ruler Bar	Selected Text
Paste	Tab Set	Cut
Format	Paragraph format	Copy
Number Type	Margins	Paste
Lines/Fill	Columns	Delete
Insert	Tables	Font
Delete	Hide Ruler Bar	Quick Format
Split Cell	Preferences	Speller
Formula Bar		

Button Bar	Document Window	Bottom and Side Scroll Bars
All other button bars that are available	Paste	Go To
Edit	Quick Format	Bookmarks
Preferences	Font	Preferences
Hide Button Bar	Speller	
	Center	
	Flush right	
	Indent	

Power Bar	Status Bar	Margin
Preferences	Hide Status Bar	Header/Footer
Hide Power Bar	Preferences	Watermark

Table 4-2

QuickMenu Options

You will use some of these options in the following exercises; the others are for future reference. You must click on the right mouse button to activate the QuickMenu, but you can then use either button to select the option.

1. Position the mouse pointer somewhere on the power bar and click the right mouse button

2. Click on Hide Power Bar with the left mouse button

3. Click on View ⇒ Power Bar to redisplay the power bar

Your WordPerfect button bar should still be on the screen. If it is not, click on View ⇒ Button bar.

1. Position the mouse pointer in the button bar and click the right mouse button

2. Click on Hide Button Bar with the left mouse button

3. Click on View ⇒ Button Bar to redisplay the button bar

If the ruler bar is not showing, click on View ⇒ Ruler Bar. You are going to change the margins and the paragraph format, and type a short document.

1. Position the mouse pointer in the top half of the ruler bar

2. Click the right mouse button

3. Click on Margins

4. Set left and right margins at 1.50" on both sides and click on OK

   With the pointer still in the top half of the ruler bar:

5. Click the right mouse button

6. Click on Paragraph Format

   The Paragraph Format option box displays as shown in Figure 4-14. In the First Line Indent option box:

Figure 4-14

7. Type 1"

8. Click on OK

   Your insertion point moves in 1" from the left margin. Position the mouse pointer somewhere near the center of the document window.

9. Click the right mouse button

10. Click on Flush Right

11. Enter today's date

✓ Press (Ctrl) + (D) (or the Date Text icon)

12. Press (Enter) twice

13. Click to get the QuickMenu and Center

14. Type `Batch Printing Program`

15. Press (Enter) twice

16. Type the following paragraphs:

```
Also enclosed is a copy of a batch printing program for
DOS. We've found this program to provide excellent batch
printing capabilities to those authors who need to print
large numbers of screen displays for their projects.
Until batch printing is added to the functionality of our
screen capture program, we offer this utility.

To install the software on your computer, please take a
moment first to read the "README" file that is included
on this disk. The software publisher has provided
specific instructions regarding the installation process
in this file.
```

17. Save the file as batchpnt

Now, to select all the text:

18. Click on <u>E</u>dit ⇒ S<u>e</u>lect ⇒ A<u>l</u>l

19. Click the right mouse button in the selected area

20. Click on Speller

21. Spell check the document

22. Save again and print the document

You now want to copy your batchpnt file to another directory. The following exercise assumes your file is on the A drive. If it is now stored on the C drive, substitute c: for a: in these directions.

1. Click on <u>F</u>ile ⇒ <u>O</u>pen ⇒ File <u>O</u>ptions

The File Options menu displays as shown in Figure 4-15.

2. Click on <u>C</u>opy

3. In the From: text box, type `a:batchpnt.wpd`

You must include the extension. You can also select the name from the directory's list of file names before you select the option.

4. In the To: text box, type `c:batchpnt.wpd`

Check with your instructor before using the C drive.

5. Select <u>C</u>opy

This puts your file in the root directory of your C drive.

Open File

Figure 4-15

Now you'll rename the file.

1. Click on File ⇒ Options
2. Click on Rename
3. In the From: text box, type `a:batchpnt.wpd`
4. In the To: text box, type `a:batch02.wpd`
5. Click on Rename

Now, delete the file from your hard drive.

1. Click on File ⇒ Options
2. Click on Delete
3. In the File to Delete text box, type `c:batchpnt.wpd`
4. Click on Delete
5. Exit WordPerfect

On Your Own

Review of Commands

Descriptions	Menu	Function Keys
Hide/Display power bar	_____	_____
Display/Hide button bar	_____	_____
Display a QuickMenu	_____	_____
Print a file from disk	_____	_____
Go to a previous document	_____	_____
Go to next document	_____	_____
Copy text	_____	_____
Move text	_____	_____
Paste (insert) text	_____	_____

▌ Lesson Review

1. What is the name of the default button bar?

2. What is the advantage of using the power bar and button bar?

3. What is the command to hide the power bar?

4. List three ways to display the button bar.

5. What does the Undo command do in a document?

6. Why does WordPerfect have several different button bars?

7. How do you select a different button bar?

8. How many document windows can you have open at one time?

9. How do you move from one document window to another?

10. Is it possible to print a file not currently displayed in a document window?

11. How can you rearrange the icons on the power bar?

12. Is it possible to select the button bar buttons from the keyboard?

13. List three ways to edit a button bar.

14. What are the general steps in creating a new button bar?

15. Why might you want to modify the power bar?

16. What are the four possible locations for the button bar on your screen?

17. What mouse button must you use to activate QuickMenus?

▌ Assignments

4-1 Directions

1. Open dbms.wpd. Spell check the document and save it as database.wpd.

2. Use the menu commands to copy the first paragraph to a new location below the last paragraph of the document.

3. Use the keyboard commands to move the second paragraph below the third paragraph.

4. Save and close the document.

5. Print database.wpd from your disk without opening the file.

4-2　Directions

1. Open database.wpd. Save it as db1.wpd.

2. Use the power bar to edit the document as shown on the next page.

3. When finished, save, print, and close the document.

4-3　Directions

1. Type the following text. Spell check and save as db2.wpd. Print the document. Do not close the document.

A networking database uses pointers or links within the fields in the records to link the records together. A hierarchical database is more a top-down design like an organization chart. Data is organized within levels where each lower level is a part of the level above.

Relational databases have become popular in the last few years. The structure or organization of the data needs to be visualized before the database can be created. It is very important that the database be designed with a clear understanding of the planned use of the data.

---

2. Open database.wpd. Practice moving between the two open documents (db2.wpd and database.wpd).

3. Make db2.wpd the active document. Copy the second paragraph ("Relational databases . . .") to the Clipboard.

4. Make database.wpd the active document. Position the insertion point just above the last paragraph.

5. Paste the paragraph from the Clipboard into the active document at the insertion point.

6. Save the document as db2.wpd and print the document.

7. Close both documents.

4-4　Directions

1. Open database.wpd. Use the power bar to reverse the order of paragraphs two and three.

2. Delete the last paragraph.

3. Save the document as db4.wpd. Print the document.

4. Close the document.

close up space throughout   full justify entire document

A data base management system is a software package which aids in the creating, maintenance, manipulating and reporting of data. A data base is an orderly collection of related files. In order to understand how a DBMS works, it is necessary to know what fields, records, and files are. A field is one item in a record, such as name, address, social security number. A set of related fields makes up a record. A record contains all the information entered about a client, an employee, a customer, or inventory parts. All the records make up one file. The data base for a company consists of all the files for that company. The more information in the database, the more potential applications of the data base. The more information, however, the greater the cost of setup and maintenance.

of information — under-line

under-line

bold   bold

DBMS are either menu-driven or command driven. Menu-driven systems give users choices and provides a set of patterns to be followed. Menu-driven systems are easy to learn and use, but they can be too inflexible unless menus can be bypassed. Command-driven systems allow user to issue programming commands, rather than selecting from a choice of items on a menu. The command-driven system is more difficult to use because the commands usually have to be learned; however, they are faster because there is no waiting for a menu to appear.

italics

There are two types of data base software packages: file management systems and data base management systems. On file management systems, only one file can be used at a time. Data base management systems can handle several files at one time and produce reports from information contained in several different files. File management systems are better for simple sorting, filing and reporting of single-file data bases. DBMS are best suited for multiple files and complex applications.

bold

There are three types of data bases: relational, hierarchical, and network. A relational data base organizes data into tables of rows and columns called relations. Users then create reports from the data in those tables." — delete

move up one paragraph

"A data base management system is a software package which aids in the creating, maintenance, manipulating and reporting of data. A data base is an orderly collection of related files. In order to understand how a DBMS works, it is necessary to know what fields, records, and files are. A field is one item in a record, such as name, address, social security number. A set of related fields makes up a record. A record contains all the information entered about a client, an employee, a customer, or inventory parts. All the records make up one file. The data base for a company consists of all the files for that company. The more information in the data base, the more potential applications of the database. The more information, however, the greater the cost of setup and maintenance.

delete paragraph

4-5 Directions

1. Modify the power bar with the following changes.
2. Move Speller to the right of Print.
3. Remove Columns and Zoom.
4. Move View Ruler to the right of Undo.
5. Add Edit ⇒ Undelete and File ⇒ Save As.
6. Move File ⇒ Save As to the right of File ⇒ Save.
7. Remember to return the power bar to its original arrangement so that other students may modify it.

4-6 Directions

1. Create a button bar with your first name as its name.
2. Add the following commands: Cancel, Close without Saving, Exit, Insert File, and any other commands of your choice from the menu bar.

4-7 Directions

1. Use the Button Bar Edit feature to add the following buttons to the button bar you created in exercise 4-6: Printer Control and Save All.
2. Move your button bar to the left side of the screen.
3. Display your buttons as text only.
4. Display your button bar in the location of your choice. Choose the appearance option you prefer.

4-8 Directions

1. Display the default button bar (WordPerfect) and make sure the power bar is displayed.
2. Type the letter below in proper format, accessing all the relevant commands from your power bar or button bar. The slashes indicate new paragraphs. Save the document as marold.wpd.

(current date)/(leave six blank lines)/Dr. Louise Marold/3456 Blair Place/Sunnyvale, CA 94067/Dear Dr. Marold:/Thank you very much for submitting your curriculum vitae to us for consideration. However, at this time all of our faculty positions are filled, and we are not hiring any new professors./Your vitae was very impressive, and we will keep it on file in case any openings arise./Sincerely,/Gerald Morrell, Chairman/Information Systems Department

---

3. Use the QuickMenu feature to Select All Text and then italicize it, spell check the document, and print the document.
4. Close the document.

5

More Editing
Features

Objectives

After completing this lesson, you will be able to:

- Delete, Search for, and Replace codes and text
- Recognize a soft page break
- Use Block Protect
- Center a line
- Use Flush Right
- Use Drag and Drop
- Use the Thesaurus
- Understand the use of fonts
- Change font size and appearance
- Use Page View, Draft View, and Two Page View
- Use Zoom

Deleting Codes

Recall that when you instruct WordPerfect to apply special features, such as underlining, centering, and boldfacing, WordPerfect inserts codes in the text to command the printer to print that way. For example, when you underlined the name of Mr. Wright's book, an Und code box was placed before and after the book name. To remove a special feature such as underlining or bolding, you need delete only *one* of the codes—Und or Bold—on either side of the text. One way to locate the code is to display the Reveal Codes screen.

NOTE: If you accidentally delete the wrong code, you can use Undo to reverse your last editing change.

The Find Feature

Scrolling through a long document is tedious when you want to find specific text or delete a code (such as Und). WordPerfect has a feature called Find that will help you locate either text or codes.

When you are searching for text, WordPerfect will find the text even if it is part of another word. For example, if you were to search for the word "the," WordPerfect would also identify "their," "there," and "them." To prevent this, select the "Whole Word" command under the Match pull-down menu. If you want to find words in a specific case, such as Letter or LETTER, select Case and type it in exactly. If you want to find all occurrences, do not select the Case command, and enter the text in lowercase.

You have two choices when searching for codes: Specific Codes under the Type pull-down menu, or Codes under the Match pull-down menu. The Codes option lets you find any code, regardless of value, such as any font size code. Specific Codes lets you find a specific value, such as a font size of 18 points.

To activate the Find feature:

- Choose Edit ⇒ Find (F2).

The Find Text dialog box appears, with the insertion point in the Find text box. You can enter either text or codes. To search for text, simply type the text you want to find. To search for a specific code, such as left justify, choose Type to display the Specific Codes dialog box. An additional dialog box will display for you to select the specific code, such as left. Then scroll to highlight Justify and choose OK. To select non-specific codes, such as Bold, select Match ⇒ Codes, select the desired code, and select Insert.

To begin the search, choose Find. When the first occurrence of the search string is found, the insertion point appears at the end of the search string. To locate the next occurrence of the search string:

- Choose Edit ⇒ Find Next (Shift + F2).

To find the previous occurrence:

- Choose Edit ⇒ Find Prev (Alt + F2).

To include searching in headers and footers, and so on, select Options and check Include Headers, Footers, and so on. If you begin the search in the middle of your document, select Options, and check Begin Find at Top of Document.

Replacing Text

The Replace feature allows you to locate and replace text or codes in a single operation. You can do this in forward or backward, for a single occurrence, or for the whole document. If you wish to implement this option for the entire document, make sure the insertion point is either at the very beginning or the very end. Be sure to proofread your document after using the Replace feature. It is easy to make mistakes when using Replace.

To activate the Replace feature, you first:

- Choose Edit ⇒ Replace (Ctrl + F2).

The Find and Replace Text dialog box appears. In the Find text box, enter the text and/or codes that are to be searched for; in the Replace With text box, type the replacement text and/or codes. In the Type box, select Text, or Specific Codes. For non-specific codes, select Match ⇒ Codes. As in Find, use the Match ⇒ Case command only if you want to replace a specific case. If you want to replace only a specific font style or size, select Match ⇒ Font and mark the attributes desired.

To replace one occurrence at a time, which allows you to confirm or reject the replacement, choose <u>R</u>eplace. When the text string is found, either choose <u>R</u>eplace (to replace the occurrence) or <u>F</u>ind (to leave the text or code as it is and skip to the next occurrence). To replace all occurrences of the text string without having to confirm each one, choose Replace <u>A</u>ll. To replace codes, select Replace ⇒ C<u>o</u>des. You have the option of going forward or backward in the document by selecting <u>D</u>irection ⇒ <u>F</u>orward or <u>B</u>ackward. To close the Find and Replace text dialog box, choose Close.

To delete text or codes throughout a document, type the item to be deleted in the Find box, press (Tab) to move to the Replace box, and select Replace All. In other words, you are replacing something with nothing.

Soft Page Breaks

Recall that soft page breaks are those inserted by the system automatically, and hard page breaks can be inserted by the writer at any time. WordPerfect inserts a soft page break when the text reaches the default length of 9.65". Page breaks show in your workspace as a double horizontal line—black above gray. In the Reveal Codes screen, soft page breaks are indicated by an SPg code. This type of page break can be altered by changing the top or bottom margins, or by using options such as the Block Protect feature (covered in the next section). In the Page mode, a bottom margin of 1" will show before the page break and the insertion point will drop down 1" from the top of the page.

Protecting a Block of Text

The Block Protect feature prevents a block of text, such as a table or paragraph, from being divided across pages. To use this feature, first select the block of text to be protected.

- Choose <u>L</u>ayout ⇒ <u>P</u>age ⇒ <u>K</u>eep Text Together.
- In the <u>B</u>lock Protect box, mark Keep selected text together on one page.

Block Pro codes are placed at the beginning and end of the selected text. You can add or delete lines anywhere between the codes, and WordPerfect will still keep the block of text on one page.

Centering a Line of Text

The Center feature in WordPerfect positions the insertion point midway between the left and right margins. As you type the text, WordPerfect automatically centers it and inserts a Hd Center on Marg code before it.

To center a line as you type, first position the insertion point on the left margin.

- Choose <u>L</u>ayout ⇒ <u>L</u>ine ⇒ <u>C</u>enter ((Shift) + (F7)).
- Type the text.
- Press (Enter).

There is another method to achieve the same result.

- Select Justification ⇒ Center from the power bar.
- Type the text.
- Select Justification ⇒ Left.

If the text has already been typed, first place the insertion point in front of the text to be centered.

- Choose Layout ⇒ Line ⇒ Center (Shift + F7).

If more than one line of text needs to be centered, select the text and execute the Center command. However, be aware that if a Tab code precedes the center code, the line of text will not be centered.

Using Flush Right

The Flush Right feature is used to align a single line of text, such as the date or a letterhead, to the right margin

- Choose Layout ⇒ Line ⇒ Flush Right (Alt + F7) or select Justification ⇒ Right from the power bar.
- Type the text.
- Select Justification ⇒ Left.

If more than one line of text needs to be aligned on the right margin, select those lines of text first, then choose Layout ⇒ Line ⇒ Flush Right.

In the following exercises, you will practice some of the features just described. Open your wright.wpd letter and display the WordPerfect button bar.

In the fifth paragraph of Mr. Wright's letter, the word "strongly" is underlined. You want to remove the underlining and so will find and delete the underline code.

1. Move the insertion point to "strongly"

2. Click on View ⇒ Reveal Codes

   ✓ Press Alt + F3

3. In the Reveal Codes screen, position the I-beam to the right of either Und code box and click to display the red cursor bar

4. Press Backspace

   The underline is removed.

5. Exit the Reveal Codes screen

Now you want to delete the bold commands on the phrases "very much" in the second paragraph and on "Collage Plus" in the fourth paragraph. Instead of searching for the codes yourself in the Reveal Codes screen, you will use the Search feature to locate the bold code.

1. Press Ctrl + Home

2. Display the Reveal Codes screen

3. Click on Edit ⇒ Find

   ✓ Press (F2)

   The Find Text dialog box displays as shown in Figure 5-1.

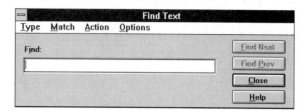

Figure 5-1

4. Click on Match

   The Match menu displays as shown in Figure 5-2.

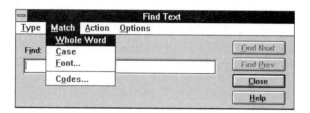

Figure 5-2

5. Click on Codes

   The Codes dialog box appears, as shown in Figure 5-3.

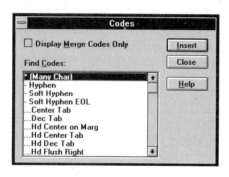

Figure 5-3

6. Using the down scroll arrow, locate the Bold On code

7. Highlight the Bold On code

8. Click on Insert

   Now close the Code dialog box.

9. Click on Close

10. Click on Options in the Find Text box

    The Options drop-down list is shown in Figure 5-4.

11. Click on Begin Find at Top of Document

12. Click on Find Next

Find Text
<u>T</u>ype   <u>M</u>atch   <u>A</u>ction   <u>O</u>ptions

<u>B</u>egin Find at Top of Document
<u>W</u>rap at End of Document
Limit Find Within Selection

✓ <u>I</u>nclude Headers, Footers, etc. in Find

F<u>i</u>nd:

[Bold On]

Help

Figure 5-4

13. Click on <u>C</u>lose

Notice that in the Reveal Codes screen, the insertion point is positioned to the left of "very much," and the Bold code is to the left of the insertion point. Now, delete the code.

14. Press (Backspace) (you may have to press it twice)

To search for another bold code:

15. Click on <u>E</u>dit ⇒ <u>F</u>ind ⇒ <u>F</u>ind Next

The insertion point stops on the bold code before "Number of Books Sold." You don't want to delete that one.

16. Click on <u>F</u>ind Next

The Bold code in the phrase "Collage Plus" has been located. The insertion point is to the left of "Collage Plus," and the Bold code is to the left of the insertion point. Delete the code.

17. Press (Backspace) (you may have to press it twice)

18. Exit Reveal Codes

You want to see by what day Polly Jo Booth's review is supposed to be in, and a fast way is to find her name. (It doesn't matter where your insertion point is.)

1. Click on <u>E</u>dit ⇒ <u>F</u>ind

✓ Press (F2)

2. Click on <u>T</u>ype

3. Click on Te<u>x</u>t

4. Click on <u>M</u>atch

5. Click on <u>W</u>hole Word

6. Click on <u>A</u>ction

7. Click on <u>S</u>elect Match

8. Click on <u>O</u>ptions

9. If not already marked, click on <u>B</u>egin Find at Top of Document

10. In the text box, type `Polly Jo Booth`

The previous selection will be deleted as you begin typing.

11. Click on <u>F</u>ind Next

"Polly Jo Booth" is found and you can see the review due date.

12. Click on <u>C</u>lose

13. Deselect the text

Obviously, this doesn't make a lot of sense for such a short letter. However, if you were looking in a 30-page document, the computer can search much faster than you can.

 Using the <u>R</u>eplace feature, you will search for the word "manuscript" and replace it with "text book."

1. Position the insertion point at the beginning of the document

    ✓ Press `Ctrl` + `Home`

2. Click on <u>E</u>dit ⇒ <u>R</u>eplace

    ✓ Press `Ctrl` + `F2`

    The Find and Replace Text dialog box appears, as shown in Figure 5-5, with the insertion point positioned in the <u>F</u>ind text box.

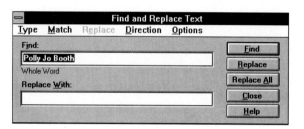

Figure 5-5

3. Type `manuscript` (in lower case)

    The previous selection will be deleted as you begin typing.

4. Press `TAB`

    In the Replace <u>W</u>ith text box:

5. Type `text book`

    The Whole Word option is automatically selected.

6. Click on <u>D</u>irection

7. Click on <u>F</u>orward (if not already marked)

8. Click on <u>F</u>ind

    The first occurrence of "manuscript" is found in the second paragraph.

9. Click on <u>R</u>eplace

    The next occurrence of "manuscript" is selected.

10. Click on <u>R</u>eplace

    Continue to search for "manuscript" and replace it with "text book" until a "manuscript" Not Found option box displays.

11. Click on OK

12. Click on <u>C</u>lose to close the text box

A faster way to replace all occurrences is to click on Replace All, which replaces without stopping for confirmation. You will do that in the next exercise.

 You want to replace the words "text book" with "composition," and will use the Replace <u>A</u>ll feature to do this.

1. Press (Ctrl) + (Home)

2. Click on <u>E</u>dit ⇒ Replace

   ✓ Press (Ctrl) + (F2)

   In the Find and Replace text box:

3. Type `text book`

4. Press (TAB)

   The insertion point is now in the Replace <u>W</u>ith text box.

5. Type `composition`

   Replace all occurrences without confirmation.

6. Click on Replace <u>A</u>ll

   Every occurrence of "text book" is automatically replaced with "composition."

7. Click on <u>C</u>lose

 Using the Flush Right feature, move the date to align at the right margin. Position the insertion point to the left of the date.

1. Press (Ctrl) + (Home)

2. Click on <u>L</u>ayout ⇒ Line ⇒ <u>F</u>lush Right

   ✓ Press (Alt) + (F7)

   The date is now positioned on the right margin.

3. Press (Ctrl) + (End)

 Scroll until you see the horizontal line (soft page break), indicating that the text below the line will be printed on another page. You are considering deleting the paragraph beginning "Also being sent …," which would make the soft page break split your royalty table in two. Use the Block Protect feature to prevent that from happening.

1. Select the entire table

2. Click on <u>L</u>ayout ⇒ <u>P</u>age ⇒ <u>K</u>eep Text Together

   The Keep Text option box displays as shown in Figure 5-6. Under the Block Protect option:

3. Mark Keep selected text together on same page

4. Click on OK

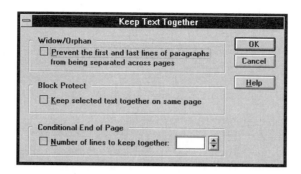

Figure 5-6

5. Deselect text

Now, no matter where the table falls when the document is printed, the entire table will appear on one page.

In the following exercise you will insert a centered line above the royalty table.

1. Position the insertion point on the left margin (just to the left of the "n" in "number") of the first line of the royalty table, which reads "NUMBER OF BOOKS SOLD …"

2. Press (Enter) twice

This will create two blank lines.

3. Press (↑) twice

The insertion point is positioned on the first blank line. Now center a line.

4. Click on <u>L</u>ayout ⇒ <u>L</u>ine ⇒ <u>C</u>enter

✓ Press (Shift) + (F7)

The insertion points jumps to the middle of the screen.

5. Click on the Bold icon

6. Type BCPC ROYALTY SCHEDULE

7. Save your document

Using Drag and Drop

You've learned how to move text to a different location using the menu, shortcut keys, and the power bar. WordPerfect has another feature called Drag and Drop that allows you to move text simply by selecting it and dragging it to a new location.

To use Drag and Drop, simply select the desired text. Place the mouse pointer within the selection and press the left mouse button. Notice that the mouse pointer changes shape—it now has a rectangle at the bottom of it. While holding the left mouse button down, drag the pointer to a new location. Release the left mouse button. The selected text is removed from the old location and placed in the new location.

In this exercise you will move a paragraph in wright.wpd.

1. Open wright.wpd if it is not already open

2. Select the first paragraph ("Your Prospectus …")

3. Place your mouse pointer within the highlighted paragraph

4. Press and hold the left mouse button

5. Move the mouse pointer below the second paragraph

> Make sure the insertion point is lined up at the left margin directly below the second paragraph.

6. Release the left mouse button

> Remember to press Undo if the text does not appear in the correct location.

7. Deselect the text

8. Position your insertion point at the left margin, to the left of "Your"

9. Press (Enter) once to create a blank line between the paragraphs

> Moving the mouse pointer correctly may take a little practice. Fortunately, the Undo feature allows you to correct your mistakes quickly.

 10. On your own, move the same paragraph back to its original location (click on the Undo icon)

> *NOTE: Another way of keeping the document in its original state is to close without saving changes.*

Using the Thesaurus

WordPerfect includes a program called Thesaurus, which is similar to a book thesaurus. It displays **synonyms** (words that have the same or similar meanings) and **antonyms** (words with opposite meanings) for words in your document. The Thesaurus is helpful if you're not happy with the word or words you've already used. The Thesaurus also shows the parts of speech (noun, verb, or adjective) of the synonyms.

To use the Thesaurus, you first position the insertion point in the pertinent word in your text.

• Choose T̲ools ⇒ T̲hesaurus ((Alt) + (F1)) or click on the Thesaurus icon

The Thesaurus dialog box appears, listing alternative words. If you do not see a word you'd prefer, you can have the Thesaurus suggest additional ones by either (1) double-clicking on a listed word that is preceded by a bullet; or (2) typing a word in the W̲ord text box and choosing L̲ook Up. The bullet indicates that there is a group of synonyms and antonyms available for that word. The additional words are listed in the scroll box to the right. Once the desired replacement word is located, click on the word, and choose Replace.

Selecting a Font

A **font** is a complete set of characters in a specific typeface (such as Times Roman, Courier, Ariel, and Helvetica), with a specific style or appearance (such as bold, italic, shadow, outline, and superscript), and a specific size, such as 10 point (pt) or 10 characters per inch (cpi). Depending on the capability of your printer, you can select a variety of fonts to fine-tune your document's appearance. For example, you might want to use a different size or typeface for your company name and address.

If a font is **proportionally spaced,** the size is indicated in points, and different letters will have different widths. For example, a capital "M" will require more space than a lowercase "i." There are 72 points per vertical inch; therefore, if you select a point size of 72, the characters will be 1" high. A 12-point font is commonly used for regular text; this is about equivalent to 10-pitch type or 10 horizontal characters per inch. If you choose a **monospaced** font, each letter will require the same amount of horizontal space. The size is indicated in characters per horizontal inch (cpi). Proportionally spaced fonts are measured in points (pt) and monospaced fonts are measured in characters per inch (cpi).

Typefaces can also be **serif** or **sans serif.** Serif characters have small lines at the ends of the letters themselves; sans serif type lacks these small lines.

Fonts come from three sources: **resident,** which are pre-installed on your printer; **add-on,** which are added from a cartridge on your printer; and **soft fonts,** which are stored on your hard disk and sent to the printer as needed.

Fonts may be either **bit mapped** or **outline.** Bit mapped fonts create characters by arranging bits (pixels) in certain patterns. All available sizes and styles have to be stored on the disk, such as 8 pt, 10 pt, and 12 pt regular, 12 pt bold, 12 pt italic, and so on. Bit mapped fonts print faster than do outline fonts.

Outline fonts use mathematical descriptions to generate each character as an outline consisting of a series of points. An H could be described as a series of 12 lines connecting the 12 dots at each inside and outside corner of the capital letter. To get a larger H, the computer moves the dots farther apart. These are known as *scaleable* fonts. From one definition, you can create an infinite range of font sizes and styles. Obviously, these fonts require less hard disk space, but it takes a little longer to print them.

Some font sizes and styles are shown in Table 5-1.

This is Stone Sans typeface, 36 pt, italic, sans serif

This is Sabon, 12 pt, Bold, serif

This is Sabon, 14 point, regular style, serif

`This is Courier, 12 cpi, regular style, serif`

This is Stone Sans, 12 pt, regular, sans serif

This is Stone Sans, 14 pt, regular, sans serif

`This is Courier, 10 cpi, serif`

Table 5-1

Changing a Document's Initial Font

When WordPerfect was installed on your computer, an **initial (default) font** was selected by the installer. If one was not selected, WordPerfect automatically selects a font that will work with your printer. When new documents are created, WordPerfect chooses that font for your document.

It is important to understand the difference between changing a document's initial font and making a regular font change within a document. To change the font for the entire document, including the page numbers, header, footer, footnotes, endnotes, captions for graphics boxes, and so on:

- Choose Layout ⇒ Document ⇒ Initial Font.
- Highlight the desired font from the Fonts list box.

If you have a PostScript printer, a LaserJet III, or any other printer with proportional fonts, you will also need to specify the point size. Finally, click on OK. When a document's initial font is changed, it doesn't matter where the insertion point is located; all of the document's text is altered.

To change the text from the insertion point forward in the document until another font change is encountered:

- Choose Layout ⇒ Font.
- Select desired font.
- Click on OK.

The new font will remain in effect (in that document only) until you select a new font. If you open a new document, the font will revert to the initial font.

Changing the Font's Size and Appearance

You can change the size or appearance of a font either as you type the text or after it has been typed. In the latter case, you must first select the text. Changes to the size and appearance of a font are based on the font currently selected. Changing the size dictates the height and width of characters. The options are Fine, Small, Large, Very Large, and Extra Large; the sizes are a percentage of the currently selected font. For example, if the current font is 12 pt Times Roman, and Large is selected, the text will increase to 120 percent.

Table 5-2 illustrates size changes on a 10 pt font as rendered by a PostScript printer.

Attribute	Percentage	Example
Fine	60%	Fine
Small	80%	SMALL
Large	120%	Large
Very Large	150%	Very Large
Extra Large	200%	Extra Large

Table 5-2

To change the size of a font while typing the text:

- Choose Layout ⇒ Font ((F9)).
- Click on Face, Style, Size, and Appearance.
- Type the text.

To turn off the feature, repeat the same steps.

 *NOTE: You can also use the power bar icons, but you must use one icon (left icon in margin) to change the style of the font and another (right icon in margin) to change the size.*

If the text is already typed, select the desired text, choose Layout ⇒ Font, and then click on the check box of the desired attributes. There is no need to deactivate the feature because it applies only to the selected text.

The Appearance options control the style of the text. Table 5-3 shows the available style options and shortcut keys, if any, again illustrated by a 10-point font rendered by a PostScript printer (the appearance of Outline, Shadow, and Redline will vary depending on your printer). The Redline/Strikeout feature is very useful when preparing documents that require heavy editing. Redline is used to mark text that is to be added to the document, and Strikeout marks text that is to be deleted from the document. You need read only the marked revisions each time instead of the entire document.

Menu Commands	Appearance	Shortcut Keys
Bold	**Bold**	(Ctrl) + (B)
Underline	Underline	(Ctrl) + (U)
Double Underline	Double Underline	
Italic	*Italic*	(Ctrl) + (I)
Outline	Outline	
Shadow	Shadow	
Small Cap	SMALL CAP	
Redline	Redline	
Strikeout	Strikeout	

Table 5-3

To apply any of these appearances as you enter text, choose Layout ⇒ Font, the desired Appearance, and type the text. To turn off the Appearance, execute the same commands you did to turn it on.

If the text is already typed, select the text and choose the desired command from those in Table 5-3.

Using Page and Two Page Mode

This version of WordPerfect allows you to see your document onscreen as it will be printed out. Known as WYSIWYG (what you see is what you get), you can now see headers and footers, top and bottom margins, page numbers, correct font sizes, styles, and attributes in the Page mode (the default mode). The Two Page mode allows you to see two pages side by side onscreen. The text is "Greeked"—made so small you cannot read it. However, you can edit in this mode. You can use Page Up and Page Down to see other pages.

- Select <u>V</u>iew ⇒ <u>P</u>age.

For Two Page mode:

- Select <u>V</u>iew ⇒ <u>T</u>wo Page.

Using Draft Mode

It is also possible to type your documents in Draft mode, which does not show correct margins, headers, footers, page numbers, or graphics. Because the screen doesn't show the details of the printed page, it takes somewhat less time to redraw the screen. To change to Draft mode:

- Choose <u>V</u>iew ⇒ <u>D</u>raft.

Using Zoom

Zoom shows a magnification of a particular area or displays an entire page at one time, and you *can* edit the text. Zoom cannot be used in Two Page mode.

To activate the Zoom feature:

- Choose <u>V</u>iew ⇒ <u>Z</u>oom ⇒ <u>F</u>ull Page ⇒ OK or select the Page Zoom Full icon.

To see a magnification of your text:

- Select <u>V</u>iew ⇒ Zoom-x%(percent of enlargement) ⇒ OK.

Zoom is for viewing purposes only; it does not change the size of your text permanently.

Viewing Options

Table 5-4 shows the various options for viewing the current page.

Zoom Option	Shows
50%	half the actual size of the print
75%	three-fourths of the actual size of the print
100%	the actual size of the print
150%	one and one-half of the actual size
200%	the text at twice its normal size

Table 5-4

You also have a choice of the Other option, which allows from 25 percent to 400 percent. The default is 100 percent.

In the following exercises, you will practice some of the features described. You want to change some of the words in your letter and will use the Thesaurus feature to do so.

In the fourth paragraph of your letter, beginning "To assist you . . ." you want another word for "progress."

1. Position the insertion point in the word "progress"

2. Click on Tools ⇒ Thesaurus

   ✓ Press (Alt) + (F1) or Thesaurus icon

   The Thesaurus dialog box appears, as shown in Figure 5-7.

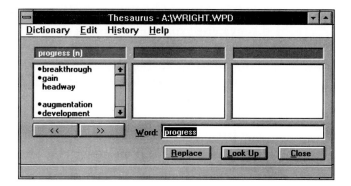

Figure 5-7

"Progress" is a verb, so scroll down to the verbs. You decide you would rather have the word "proceed."

4. Click on "proceed"

5. Click on Replace

   In the fifth paragraph, beginning "Also being sent ..." you want to replace "prescribe" and "specific."

6. Position the insertion point in the word "prescribe"

7. Click on Tools ⇒ Thesaurus

   ✓ Press (Alt) + (F1) or Thesaurus icon

   Scroll down until you see the word "establish" and click on it. You like the word, but you would also like to see if there are any better words. Notice that "establish" is preceded by a bullet, indicating that there is a group of synonyms and antonyms available for that word. Look at those additional words.

8. Double-click on "establish"

   Your Thesaurus dialog box will now appear as shown in Figure 5-8.

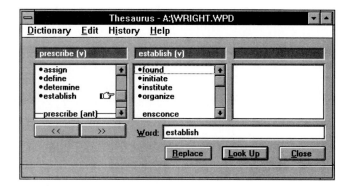

Figure 5-8

You have decided on the word "establish," so you need to replace "prescribe" with "establish."

9. Click on "establish"

10. Click on <u>R</u>eplace

11. On your own, find a suitable synonym for the word "specific"

 In this exercise, you will choose a different initial document font for your letter to Mr. Wright. Remember that the fonts available to you will depend on your printer's capabilities. It doesn't matter where the insertion point is in the document; the code will be placed at the beginning of the document.

1. Click on <u>L</u>ayout ⇒ <u>D</u>ocument ⇒ Initial <u>F</u>ont

The Document Initial Font dialog box appears. Your dialog box will be similar to the one shown in Figure 5-9, but will vary depending on your printer.

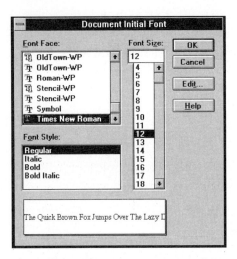

Figure 5-9

Check the way the different fonts will look in the sample box before choosing one.

2. Choose a font

3. Click on OK

Notice that the name and point size of the new font are now displayed at the left end of the status bar. Remember, any new font code will override the initial font.

Now, apply the Italic appearance and Large size to the text "Collage Plus" in the fourth paragraph of the letter.

4. Select "Collage Plus"

5. Click on <u>L</u>ayout ⇒ <u>F</u>ont ⇒ <u>I</u>talic

In the Relative Size drop-down menu:

6. Click on <u>L</u>arge

7. Click on OK

8. Deselect the text

See what your screen looks like in Draft mode.

1. Click on <u>V</u>iew ⇒ <u>D</u>raft

Notice that your margins are not correctly shown.

2. Click on <u>V</u>iew ⇒ <u>P</u>age to return to normal mode

In this exercise, you will use Zoom to magnify part of the letter and Full Page to see the full page.

1. Position the insertion point at the beginning of the letter

2. Click on <u>V</u>iew ⇒ <u>Z</u>oom

The Zoom option box is shown in Figure 5-10.

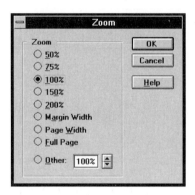

Figure 5-10

3. Click on <u>F</u>ull Page

4. Click on OK

You can see what a full page looks like, but cannot read the text, as shown in Figure 5-11.

5. Click on <u>V</u>iew ⇒ <u>Z</u>oom ⇒ 200% ⇒ OK

6. Press (PgDn) twice

You will see your text enlarged.

7. Click on <u>V</u>iew ⇒ <u>Z</u>oom ⇒ 50% ⇒ OK

8. Press (PgUp)

The size of the text is so small that it is now barely possible to read.

To return to normal:

9. Click on <u>V</u>iew ⇒ <u>Z</u>oom ⇒ 100% ⇒ OK

10. Click on <u>V</u>iew ⇒ <u>T</u>wo Page to see two pages side by side

11. Return to the default <u>P</u>age

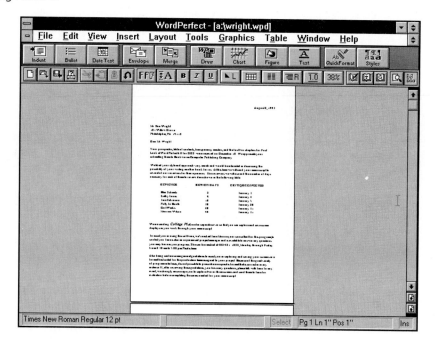

Figure 5-11

12. Select <u>F</u>ile ⇒ <u>C</u>lose

    ✓ Press (Ctrl) + (F4)

13. Save the changes and print your document

14. Exit WordPerfect

On Your Own

Review of Commands

Description	Menu Commands	Function Keys
Find	_____	_____
Find Next	_____	_____
Find Previous	_____	_____
Replace	_____	_____
Flush Right	_____	_____
Block Protect	_____	_____
Center Line	_____	_____
Thesaurus	_____	_____
Initial Font	_____	_____
Font	_____	_____
Page Mode	_____	_____
Two Page Mode	_____	_____
Draft Mode	_____	_____
Zoom	_____	_____

▌ **Lesson Review**

1. How can you remove underlining and other features from text?

2. What option do you select in order to search for short words, such as "he" or "his," without selecting all words that contain "he" or "his"?

3. Describe how the Replace feature works.

4. What is the purpose of the Block Protect feature?

5. What is the purpose of the Thesaurus?

6. What is a font?

7. Name one of the fonts on your system.

8. When you change the initial font, what happens?

9. How can you change the font for just a portion of text in your document?

10. What does the Flush Right command do?

11. What is meant by "drag and drop"?

12. Describe a quick way to remove all underlining from a document.

13. How do you execute a Find command that searches all text, including headers and footers?

14. How do you align more than one line of text at the right margin?

15. What is a soft page break?

16. What is a synonym? What is an antonym?

▌ **Assignments**

5-1 Directions

1. Type the letter on the following page.

2. Use Flush Right to type the heading.

3. Use Center Line to type the lists in the body of the letter.

4. Save the Document as courses.wpd. Spell check, print, and close the document.

5-2 Directions

1. Open courses.wpd. Save it as courses1.wpd.

2. Use the Find feature to locate "Paul Williams." What course did he just complete?

Janet Moore   Cosmopolitan State College
Information Science Department   September 19, 1993

Mr. Robert Thomas, Director of Marketing
Harrington Computer Corporation
3127 West Allison Boulevard
Denver, CO 80222

Dear Mr. Thomas:

The following employees of your department have completed courses at CSC for the Fall semester. The courses were part of our regular Information Science degree program and are each worth <u>three credits</u> of college level work. Transcripts will be sent to you about twelve weeks after the end of the semester.

use a different font

CMS 101 <u>Introduction to Computers</u>

Ron Salem
Barbara Loftus
Keith Deaner
Paul Williams
Jane Howerton

CMS 490 <u>Introduction to Digital Electronics</u>

Jason DeVilla
Grant McCormick

CMS 390 <u>Microprocessors</u>

Anthony DiRipparat
Mary Sakata
Ulda Rasmussen

small

Course descriptions are available in our College Catalog, which I will be happy to send you. We will be offering a wide variety of courses for Spring semester. Please enroll early to ensure a position in our popular courses.

Sincerely,

Janet Moore

3. Use the Find feature to locate the word "variety." Use the Thesaurus to find a synonym. Replace "variety" with the synonym of your choice.

4. Use the Replace feature to locate all the underlined text and remove it.

5. Use the Replace feature to remove bold from all text.

6. You want the course listings to be in numeric order. Use the Drag and Drop feature to reverse the position of the CMS 490 list and the CMS 390 list.

7. Save, print, and close the document.

5-3 Directions

1. Open database.wpd. Save it as db5.wpd.

2. Center and bold the title: "Introduction to Databases" above the text (allow two lines below the title).

3. Change the initial font to a sans serif font of your choice.

4. Use the Drag and Drop feature to reverse paragraphs two and three.

5. Place the current date flush with the right margin, three lines above the title.

6. Save, print, and close the document.

5-4 Directions

1. Open marold.wpd. Save it as marold1.wpd.

2. Use the QuickMenu feature to make the date flush with the right margin.

3. Remove the italics.

4. Use the QuickMenu feature to select the text and change it to a sans serif font of your choice.

5. Save, print, and close the document.

5-5 Directions

1. Open db1.wpd. Save it as db6.wpd.

2. Center and bold the title "Introduction to Databases" above the text (allow two lines below the title).

3. Change the initial font to a sans serif font of your choice.

4. Use the Replace feature to remove all bold and underlining from text.

5. Delete the last paragraph.

6. View the document in Draft mode. What is different about the screen when you are in draft mode?

7. Save, print, and close the document.

5-6   Directions

1. Open courses.wpd. Save it as courses2.wpd.

2. Block Protect each course listing and associated text (be sure to block each list separately).

3. Insert the following text after the first paragraph.

Many corporations require a form to be filled out by the registrar and/or the instructor indicating that their employees have passed a course and marking the grade the student has received. The student must return this form to his/her employer to receive compensation for tuition and fees. We will be glad to provide any information needed on such a form. A student need only send the form to our department and we will forward it to the appropriate person.

The students listed below have passed their course with a C or better. This means that they have received at least a 72 percent average on completed coursework and examinations. Cosmopolitan State College has *rigorous standards* for their courses. Students should be congratulated for completing their courses in addition to working a full-time job at Harrington Computer Corporation.

---

4. You want the course listings to be in numeric order. Use the Drag and Drop feature to reverse the position of the CMS 490 list and the CMS 390 list.

5. Save, spell check, print and close the document.

5-7   Directions

1. Open courses2.wpd.

2. Change Page View to Two Page. How does the document appear?

3. Return to Page View.

4. Select Draft View. How does the document appear differently from when in Page View?

5. Close the document.

Formatting Enhancements

Objectives

After completing this lesson, you will be able to:

- Change top, bottom, left, and right margins
- Change line spacing
- Enter a hard page break
- Center a page vertically
- Select different sizes of paper
- Cascade and Tile WordPerfect documents
- Create and edit headers and footers
- Suppress and discontinue a header or a footer
- Move within a long document

Changing the Margins

The default left, right, top, and bottom margins are all 1". If the top and bottom margins are changed, WordPerfect places a Top/Bot Mar: code box at the top of the current page, regardless of where you are in the document when inserting the command. Thus, the new margins are in effect from the top of the current page forward.

If the left and right margins are changed, WordPerfect inserts a Lft/Rgt Mar: code at the beginning of the paragraph in which the insertion point is positioned. The new left and right margins are in effect from the beginning of the paragraph forward in the document.

To change the current margin settings:

- Choose Layout ⇒ Margins (Ctrl + F8).

The Margins dialog box appears, allowing you to change the top, bottom, left, and right margins. Click on the up arrow to increase the margin, or the down arrow to decrease the setting. To save the settings, choose OK.

The left and right margins can also be changed with the ruler. First, display the ruler by choosing <u>V</u>iew ⇒ <u>R</u>uler Bar. Then position the mouse pointer on the margin marker, which appears above the numbers on the ruler bar, and drag it to the desired position.

Changing Line Spacing

As mentioned, the default line spacing—the number of blank lines between lines of text—is single spacing. Line spacing can be in increments of .1, from .01 to virtually any number. In printing, the term for line spacing is *leading*, and WordPerfect's ability to change leading incrementally is very useful when typing headlines in documents. A line spacing code will display at the beginning of the paragraph in which the change is made and will stay in effect until a new code is entered. To change the spacing of an already-typed document, move the insertion point to the beginning of the document and enter the new line spacing code. To change the line spacing:

- Select <u>L</u>ayout ⇒ <u>L</u>ine ⇒ <u>S</u>pacing.
- Click on the up arrow to increase setting.
- Click on the down arrow to decrease setting.
- Click on OK.

Creating a Hard Page Break

Soft page breaks were covered in the last lesson. A hard page break is inserted at the insertion point; any text following the insertion point will be printed on a new page. A hard page break shows onscreen the same as does a soft page break—pages are divided by black and gray lines. In the Reveal Codes screen, it is indicated by one of two codes: a HPg code box if (Ctrl) + (Enter) is used, or a Force: New code if the command is executed from the menu (both codes have the same effect).

To insert a hard page break, you first move the insertion point to the left of the character to be the first character of the new page, then:

- Choose <u>L</u>ayout ⇒ <u>P</u>age ⇒ <u>F</u>orce Page ⇒ New <u>P</u>age ⇒ OK ((Ctrl) + (Enter)).

To delete a hard page break code, in the Reveal Codes screen place the insertion point to the right of the HPg code and press (Backspace). You can also click on the code box and drag it off the screen.

Centering a Page Vertically

The Center Page feature centers the text vertically on a page between the top and bottom margins. This is very useful when creating a title page. It looks much nicer to have your name, the title, and date at the center of the page than at the very top or bottom. A nice feature is that regardless of where the insertion point is in the page, WordPerfect inserts the code (Cntr Cur Pg:On) at the top of the page in which the insertion point is positioned. To activate the Center Page feature:

- Choose <u>L</u>ayout ⇒ <u>P</u>age ⇒ <u>C</u>enter.
- Select Current Page.
- Select OK.

Selecting Paper Sizes

When a printer is selected, either during installation or before printing, a list of predefined paper sizes and types is included in the printer definition. This list will vary depending on the printer selected. Most printers include paper sizes for: standard 8 ½-by-11" paper; 11-by-8 ½" (for printing lengthwise on a standard sheet of paper); and business envelopes, 9 ½ by 4". Even though the paper sizes are the same for different printers, the settings for each type can vary. For example, you might need to manually feed an envelope into one printer, whereas another will have a tray for automatically feeding envelopes.

To view the predefined paper sizes and types included in your printer definition:

- Choose Layout ⇒ Page ⇒ Paper Size.

The Paper Size dialog box appears, listing definitions and displaying the selected orientation.

Adding an Envelope Definition

If an envelope definition does not appear in your Paper Size dialog box, you will need to add it to your list. A paper size definition need be added only once; it then becomes a permanent definition in the list.

To add an envelope definition:

- Select Layout ⇒ Page ⇒ Paper Size.
- Select Create.
- In the Paper Name text box, type Envelope.
- In the Paper Type drop-down list box, choose Envelope.
- In the Paper Size drop-down list box, select Envelope #10 4 ⅛ x 9 ½ in. The left drop-down box should show 4.12". The right drop-down box should show 9.50".

In the Orientation box, you have a choice of Rotated Font and Wide Form. "Orientation" refers to the direction a printer prints a page. (If you have a dot-matrix printer, this option may not be available.) Many printers allow you to choose between portrait and landscape orientation. **Portrait** prints vertically on the page, and **landscape** prints sideways—even if the page is inserted vertically into the printer.

If you have a laser printer, you will choose the Rotated Font check box. In the Paper Location drop-down box, choose Envelope Manual Feed if you do not have an envelope feed on your printer, or Auto Sheet Feeder if you do.

To save the definition, click on OK. You are returned to the Paper Size dialog box and Envelope is added in the Paper Definition. Click on Close to exit the dialog box.

Creating an Envelope

You can create an envelope using the mailing address from your current document and a stored return address. WordPerfect will select the mailing address from your current document and show it in the Envelope feature. You can add that address for future use in the Envelope dialog box and you can type and add return addresses for future use.

NOTE: While the post office prefers addresses to be in all capital letters with no punctuation, it is not advisable to write the fields into your database that way because of the different uses for the data. A better choice might be to create the envelope file from the database and then use Case Conversion to make the address all capitals.

To activate the Envelope feature:

- Select <u>L</u>ayout ⇒ En<u>v</u>elope (the mailing address of the current letter will display).
- Select New Address to use an available address or type a return address.
- In the Envelope Definitions drop-down list, select Envelope if it is not already selected.

If you want a return address printed, be sure the Print Return Address box is marked.

- Select <u>P</u>rint Envelope.
- Choose <u>S</u>elect.

To produce an envelope without an accompanying letter, select <u>L</u>ayout ⇒ En<u>v</u>elope and type in a new address or select an available address from the New Address box.

▍ Cascade

It is possible to have several documents open at one time and to move among those documents. If they are scattered on the screen, you can organize them by using the Tile or the Cascade options as done in Windows.

The <u>C</u>ascade option arranges open windows so that they overlap with title bars showing. To cascade all open document windows:

- Choose <u>W</u>indow ⇒ <u>C</u>ascade.

▍ Tile

The <u>T</u>ile option reduces all the open documents to small windows that can all be viewed on the desktop at once. To activate the Tile feature:

- Choose <u>W</u>indow ⇒ <u>T</u>ile.

Your letter to Dr. Airsman would look nicer with the text centered vertically on the page. In this exercise, you will use the Center Page feature to accomplish this task.

1. Open the Airsman letter

2. Click on <u>L</u>ayout ⇒ <u>P</u>age ⇒ <u>C</u>enter

   The Center option box displays as shown in Figure 6-1.

3. Click on the Current Page button

4. Click on OK

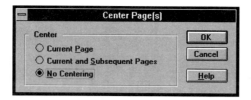

Figure 6-1

Use the Zoom feature to view your letter.

5. Click on <u>V</u>iew ⇒ <u>Z</u>oom

6. Click on <u>F</u>ull Page ⇒ OK

Your letter should be centered vertically on the page. To return to the normal page mode:

7. Click on <u>V</u>iew ⇒ <u>Z</u>oom ⇒ 100% ⇒ OK

In the next exercise, you will create an envelope for your letter. You will first look at the predefined paper size and type definitions for your printer, and if you do not have an envelope definition, follow the instructions to add one. Do not be concerned if the numbers of your envelope definition do not exactly match ours. The options and definitions vary among printers. Also, if you do not have envelopes available to you, just simulate on regular paper.

1. Click on <u>L</u>ayout ⇒ <u>P</u>age ⇒ Paper <u>S</u>ize

The Paper Size dialog box appears as shown in Figure 6-2. Remember, the definitions will depend on the type of printer selected and may vary from the one shown in the figure.

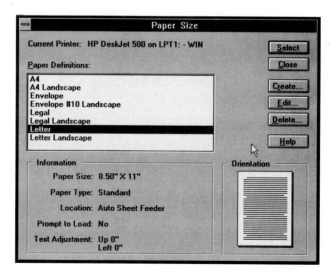

Figure 6-2

Scroll to see if you have a 4.12" x 9.5" (or similar) Envelope option.

2. Click on Close

If your Paper Size dialog box did not list an envelope, follow the instructions in the next exercise. If the dialog box does list an envelope, skip the next exercise and go to the one following.

1. Click on <u>L</u>ayout ⇒ <u>P</u>age ⇒ Paper <u>S</u>ize

2. Click on C<u>r</u>eate

The Create Paper Size dialog box appears as shown in Figure 6-3. In the <u>P</u>aper Name text box:

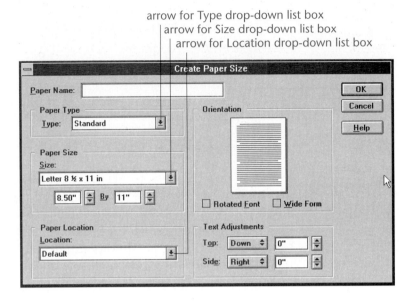

Figure 6-3

3. Type `Envelope`

Click on the Paper <u>T</u>ype drop-down list box, which is shown in Figure 6-4.

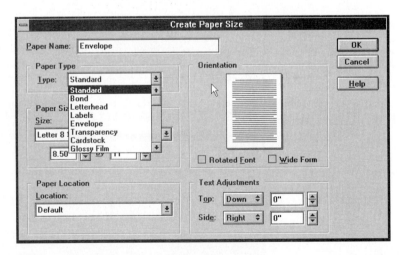

Figure 6-4

4. Select En<u>v</u>elope

5. Click on the Paper <u>S</u>ize drop-down list box, which is shown in Figure 6-5

6. Select <u>E</u>nvelope #10 4 1/8 x 9 1/5 in, or a similar one

7. If not shown, click the arrow of the left size box to 9.50"

8. If not shown, click the arrow of the right size box to 4.12"

The up arrow increases size, the down arrow decreases size.

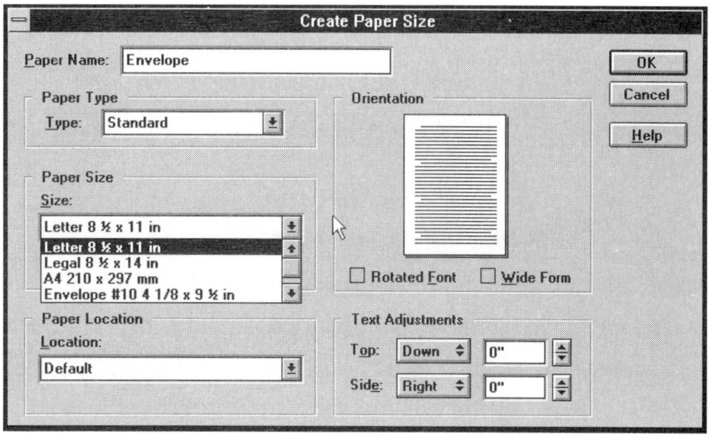

Figure 6-5

9. In the Orientation option box, click on Wide Form

10. In the Paper Location drop-down list box, shown in Figure 6-6, click on Manual Feed

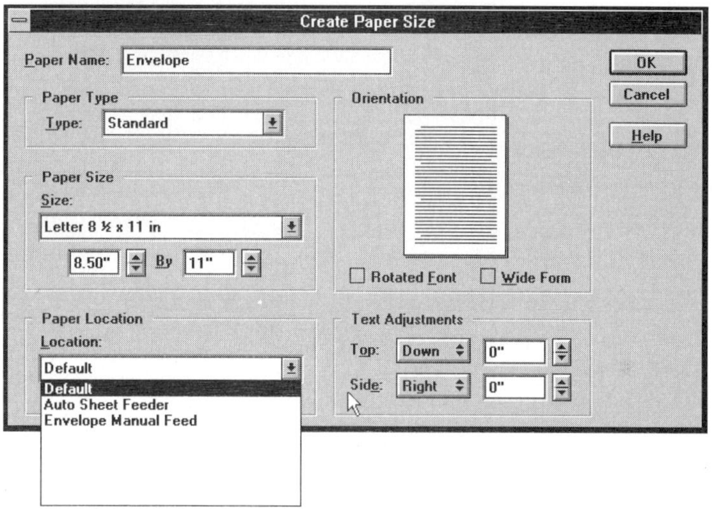

Figure 6-6

Your screen should look similar to that in Figure 6-7. Now save the definition.

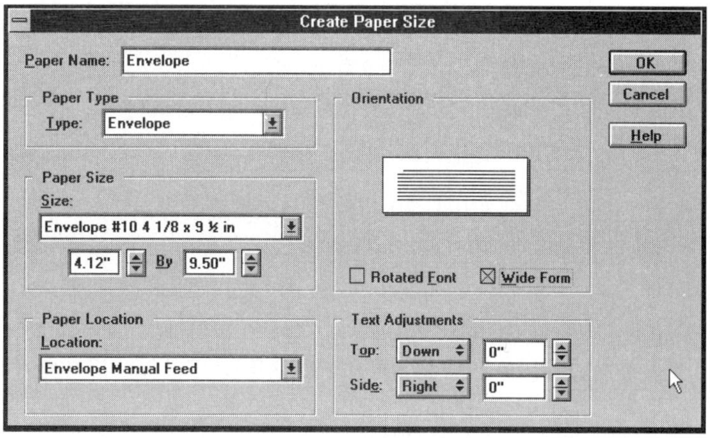

Figure 6-7

11. Click on OK

You are returned to the Paper Size dialog box.

12. Click on Select

You are ready to create your envelope for Dr. Airsman. Be sure the document is open onscreen.

1. Click on Layout ⇒ Envelope

The Envelope dialog box displays, as in Figure 6-8, and the mailing address for Dr. Airsman shows in both the Mailing Address text box and on the displayed envelope.

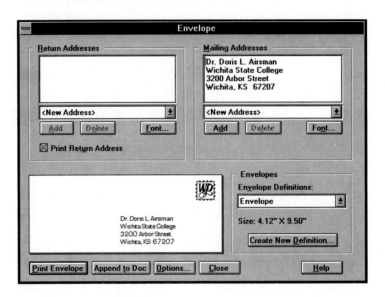

Figure 6-8

Position the insertion point in the Return Address text box.

2. Type your name and address

Be sure to type the two-letter state abbreviation in capitals and leave two spaces before the zip code.

3. Click on the Print Return Address box (if not selected)

Save the return address for future use.

4. Click on Add

To save the mailing address:

5. Click on Add

6. Click on Print Envelope

7. Click on Close

You also want to create an envelope for Mr. Wright, so open wright.wpd. (The Airsman document remains open but is now in the background.) Follow the preceding steps to make an envelope for Mr. Wright. To use your same return address, click on the New Address down arrow and select it.

In this exercise, you will open a third document window—the Collage document—change the left and right margins, center it on the page, and double-space it.

1. Click on <u>F</u>ile ⇒ <u>O</u>pen

   ✓ Press (F4) or Click on the Open icon

2. Click on collage.wpd

3. Click on <u>O</u>pen

   Collage is now the active window.

4. Center and bold the title "Collage Plus"

5. Click on <u>L</u>ayout ⇒ <u>L</u>ine ⇒ <u>S</u>pacing

   The Line Spacing dialog box opens as shown in Figure 6-9.

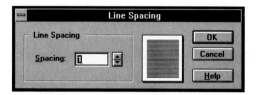

Figure 6-9

6. Click on the up arrow to 2

   Notice that the page display shows double spacing.

7. Click on OK

   To center it vertically:

8. Click on <u>L</u>ayout ⇒ <u>P</u>age ⇒ <u>C</u>enter ⇒ Current Page ⇒ OK

9. Press (Ctrl) + (Home)

   This is an important step, because your changes take place from the cursor forward.

10. Click on <u>L</u>ayout ⇒ <u>M</u>argins

    ✓ Press (Ctrl) + (F8)

    The Margins option box displays as shown in Figure 6.10.

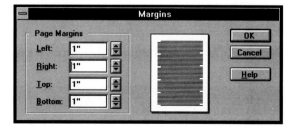

Figure 6-10

11. Click the up arrow in the left margin box to change it to 1.50"

12. Click the up arrow in the right margin box to change it to 1.50"

13. Click on OK

Use the Zoom Full Page feature to see your document.

14. Save the document, but do not close it

Now switch to Dr. Airsman's letter:

15. Click on Window-1 airsman.wpd

✓ Press Ctrl + F6

Continuing to press Ctrl + F6 cycles you through the open windows.

 You will cascade the three document windows you have open so that they overlap with their title bars showing.

1. Click on Window ⇒ Cascade

Compare your desktop to the one in Figure 6-11. Notice that each window has its own minimize and maximize buttons.

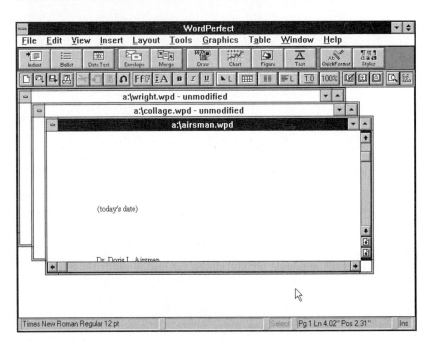

Figure 6-11

 Remember, to make a document window active, simply click anywhere inside the window. The window will move forward and the title bar will be a different color to indicate that it is the active window. Tile the windows.

1. Click on Window ⇒ Tile

Compare your desktop to Figure 6-12.

2. Activate and close the Collage document

3. Activate and close the Airsman document

4. Restore the Wright document

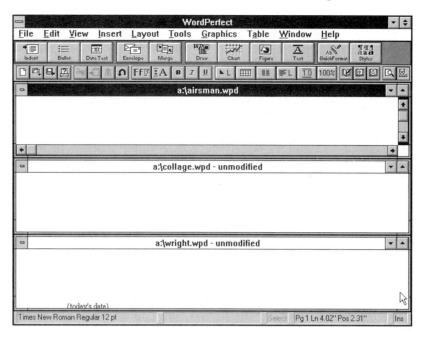

Figure 6-12

▎ Creating Headers and Footers

You may sometimes want to print a date, name, title, page number, or phrase at the top or bottom of every page of a document. A **header** is text printed at the top of every page; a **footer** appears at the bottom of every page. You type a header or footer only once in a special screen. WordPerfect takes care of printing the header or footer on every page of the document, starting with the page on which you activate the Header/Footer feature. You can see headers and footers in Page mode, but not Draft mode.

You can create two headers (labeled A and B) and/or two footers (also labeled A and B) in a document. Two headers might be used when you want one header on odd-numbered pages and a different one on even-numbered pages. When you are creating header or footer text, almost any WordPerfect feature can be used, including font changes, alignment settings, date codes, page numbers, and graphics.

WordPerfect prints headers just below the top margin and adds a blank line between the header and the first line of text. Footers are printed just above the bottom margin, and one blank line is inserted between the last line of text and the footer.

To create a header or footer, position the insertion point on the page where you want the header or footer to first appear (normally at the beginning of the document).

- Choose Layout ⇒ Header/Footer.

The Header/Footer dialog box appears. If you are creating only one header, leave Header A selected. For a second header, select Header B. For one footer, select Footer A; for an additional footer, select Footer B. Select Create. A feature bar appears across the top of the document. Type the header's text.

To include a page number, click on the Number command button on the feature bar and select Page number. The current page number is inserted in the header at the insertion point. To insert a date code, choose Insert ⇒ Date ⇒ Date Code (Ctrl + Shift + D) from the menu bar.

To specify the pages on which you want the header/footer, select Placement and click on the Every Page radio button if it is not already selected (other options are Odd Pages and Even Pages). Click on OK. When you are finished typing the text of the header or footer, choose Close. A code box with Header A: Every Page [Open Style] [Pg Num Display] is inserted in your document.

CAUTION: Be sure to close the header/footer screen and return to your document. If you continue to type in the header/footer screen instead, you may lose what you type. The only way to tell if you are in the header/footer screen or in the document body is by looking at the title bar. You could conceivably type pages of text in the header/footer screen. All you have to do to return to the document body is move the insertion point.

Editing Headers and Footers

An existing header or footer can be edited at any time. If you have more than one header or footer, make sure the insertion point is positioned to the right of the header or footer code you want to edit. If you have only one header or footer, the insertion point can be anywhere in the document. To edit a header or footer:

- Choose Layout ⇒ Header/Footer.
- Select the header or footer you wish to edit.
- Select Edit.
- Make the desired changes.
- Select Close.

Suppressing a Header or Footer

The Suppress feature allows you to turn off any combination of formats for the current page only; you might suppress page numbering, a header, or a footer. To activate the Suppress feature, first position the insertion point on the page where the suppression is to occur.

- Choose Layout ⇒ Page ⇒ Suppress.
- Mark the item(s) to be suppressed or mark All.
- Select OK.

WordPerfect inserts a Suppress code when this feature is used.

Discontinuing a Header or Footer

To turn off a header or footer for the rest of the document, first position the insertion point on the page where you want to discontinue the header or footer, then:

- Choose Layout ⇒ Header/Footer ⇒ Discontinue.

An End Header A or Footer code is placed in the document. Should you decide not to discontinue a header or footer, delete the End code. Once the header or footer has been discontinued, you cannot turn it on again for subsequent pages; you must create it again.

In this exercise, you will create a header for your letter to Mr. Wright.

1. Position the insertion point at the beginning of the document

    ✓ Press (Ctrl) + (Home)

2. Click on Layout ⇒ Header/Footer

    The Header/Footer dialog box appears, as shown in Figure 6-13, with the Header A radio button selected.

Figure 6-13

3. Click on Create

    The WordPerfect Header A window appears as shown in Figure 6-14.

header/footer feature bar

header window area (above data)

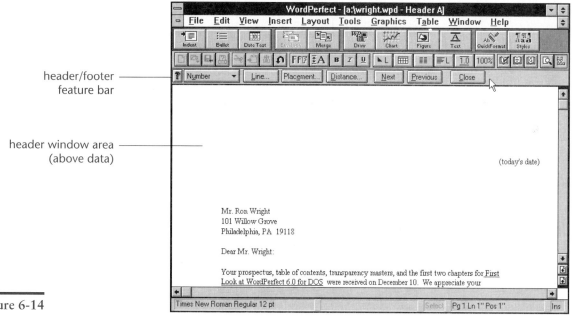

Figure 6-14

4. Type **Mr. Ron Wright**

5. Press (Enter)

    Because you are in Page mode, you will see your header as it will look when printed. Enter the Date code:

6. Click on Insert ⇒ Date ⇒ Date Code

    ✓ Press (Ctrl) + (Shift) + (D)

7. Press (Enter)

Instruct WordPerfect to automatically insert a page number in the header.

8. Click on Number on the control bar

9. Click on Page Number

A "1" is inserted in your letter.

10. Click on Close

 In this exercise, you are going to edit your header to insert the word "Page" before the page number and bold the header type.

1. Click on Layout ⇒ Header/Footer

The Header A radio button is selected.

2. Click on Edit

The Header A window appears.

3. Move the insertion point in front of the page number "1"

4. Type **Page** and press (Spacebar)

5. Select the name, page number, and date

 6. Click on the Bold icon

Now exit the Header window.

7. Click on Close

 You are going to suppress header A on the first page of your letter. Be sure the insertion point is positioned somewhere on the first page.

1. Click on Layout ⇒ Page ⇒ Suppress

The Suppress option box is shown in Figure 6-15.

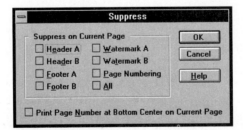

Figure 6-15

2. Click on Header A

3. Click on OK

If you activate the Reveal Codes screen, you will see a Header A Suppress code box inserted at the top of that page.

4. Click on View ⇒ Two Page to see that your header shows on the second page, but not the first

5. Return to Page View

In this exercise, you are going to turn off Header A.

1. Press (Ctrl) + (End)

   To create a new page:

2. Click on <u>L</u>ayout ⇒ <u>P</u>age ⇒ <u>F</u>orce Page ⇒ New <u>P</u>age ⇒ OK

   ✓ Press (Ctrl) + (Enter)

   This is one command that is obviously *much* more efficient from the keyboard.

3. Click on <u>L</u>ayout ⇒ <u>H</u>eader/Footer

   The Header <u>A</u> option button is selected.

4. Click on <u>D</u>iscontinue

   The header disappears from the third page and will not appear on any subsequent pages.

5. Save and print wright.wpd

▍ Moving from Page to Page

In a multi-page document, you often want to move from page to page. Table 6-1 lists some keystroke combinations to assist you in quickly moving through a long document.

Keystroke	Moves to
(Alt) + (PgUp)	Top of the previous page
(Alt) + (PgDn)	Top of the next page
(Alt) + (Home)	Top of the current page
(Alt) + (End)	Bottom of the current page
(Ctrl) + (Home)	Top of document
(Ctrl) + (End)	End of document

Table 6-1

The Go To feature allows you to specify a page or move to the previous (last) position of the insertion point, among other choices. To use the Go To feature to get to a specific page:

- Choose <u>E</u>dit ⇒ <u>G</u>o To ((Ctrl) + (G)).
- Select Page <u>N</u>umber and type the number.

To move to the insertion point's previous position:

- Choose <u>P</u>osition ⇒ Last Position ⇒ OK.

To move to a specific page, type the desired page number in the Page <u>N</u>umber text box (you can also use the arrows to select the number) and choose OK.

In this exercise, you will practice moving the insertion point from page to page in your Wright letter.

1. Position the insertion point at the top of the document

   ✓ Press (Ctrl) + (Home)

   Now move to the top of page 2.

2. Press (Alt) + (PgDn)

   Move back to the top of page 1.

3. Press (Alt) + (PgUp)

4. Press (↓) six times

   Now move to the bottom of page 1.

5. Press (Alt) + (End)

   Move to a specific page.

6. Click on Edit ⇒ Go To

   ✓ Press (Ctrl) + (G)

   The Go To dialog box is shown in Figure 6-16. The insertion point is positioned in the Go To Page Number text box.

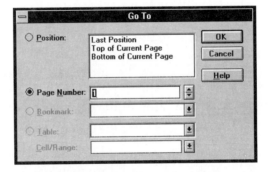

Figure 6-16

7. Type 2

8. Click on OK

9. Close wright.wpd

10. Exit WordPerfect

On Your Own

Review of Commands	Description	Menu Commands	Function Keys
	Center page	_____	_____
	Hard page break	_____	_____
	Paper size	_____	_____

Envelope   _____   _____

Margins   _____   _____

Line Spacing   _____   _____

Cascade windows   _____   _____

Tile windows   _____   _____

Headers/Footers   _____   _____

Move to top of previous page   _____   _____

Move to top of next page   _____   _____

Move to bottom of current page   _____   _____

Move to top of current page   _____   _____

Move to bottom of document   _____   _____

Move to top of document   _____   _____

▍ Lesson Review

1. What are the keystrokes used to force a page break?

2. List the two possible print orientations and describe them.

3. How would you change the side margins using the ruler bar?

4. How many open documents does WordPerfect allow you to have?

5. Describe the appearance of cascaded documents on the desktop.

6. Describe the appearance of tiled documents on the desktop.

7. What are headers and footers?

8. What command turns a header off for the remainder of the document?

9. What header command turns a header off for one specific page?

10. What keystrokes could be used to move quickly from page 2 to 25?

11. You wish to create a one-page document that has approximately the same top and bottom margin. What command could you use to quickly accomplish this task?

12. You wish to move through a long document page by page. What command would you use?

13. What are the two ways to create and save an envelope?

14. Name two ways to change your side margins.

15. Name the command to move to the end of your document.

16. Name the command to move to the bottom of the current page.

▌ Assignments

6-1 Directions

1. Create the document on the next page. Save it as software.wpd.

2. Create the following header for the letter.

Jane Kelso, Director Research and Development	Software Plus (555) 555-1234

3. Place a hard page break above the last paragraph of the body of the letter.

4. Save, spell check, and print the letter.

6-2 Directions

1. Open software.wpd. Save it as soft1.wpd.

2. Double-space and block protect the list of questions following paragraph four.

3. Use the ruler to change the side margins to 1.25" (don't forget to change the margins in your header).

4. Change the top margin to 2".

5. Remove the Hard Page Code and replace it at an appropriate place in the document, if necessary.

6. Create an envelope for the letter (append it to your document). Use the following return address:

Software Plus
Research and Development Division
228 Market Street
Denver, CO 80212

7. Save, print, and close the document.

(today's date)

Mr. John Evanston
9335 East Wilson Way
Carlisle, PA 17013

Dear Mr. Evanston:

Thank you for talking with me the other day about your organization and your experience with office automation. As I told you, our company, Software Plus, is involved with creating software that meets the needs of all types of users. We create and market word processing, spreadsheet, database, and integrated packages for every need. In addition, we tailor packages to individual companies, if necessary.

Currently, we are developing a new software package that can meet clerical and administrative needs of small to medium-size companies. This package needs to be easy to learn and to use. It needs to be able to handle all aspects of office work from accounting to human resources. We think we are well on our way to developing such a package and are recruiting reviewers to try the package and give us their opinions.

In looking over our list of reviewers, we have noticed that there are no reviewers from your part of the nation. While office procedures, wants, and needs are basically the same throughout our country, it is amazing how different perspectives can emerge from different regions. Therefore, we would like to invite you to review our software before it is released and give us your opinion. You will receive compensation for your time in addition to the satisfaction of knowing you helped us develop a satisfying product.

If you decide to help us with this project, I would like you to think about the following:

-Does the software run smoothly?
-Is the interface pleasant and easy to understand?
-How long did it take you to become reasonably proficient with the program?
-Do you think others will find the program easy to use?
-Does the software contain all the applications needed to run a small to medium-size office?
-What improvements might you like to see made to the software?

If this project looks like something you would like to participate in, please call me by October 10, and I will arrange to have the software sent to you. I hope you choose to help us. Your input can help us to create a superior product.

Sincerely,

Jane Kelso, Director
Research and Development

6-3 Directions

1. Open soft1.wpd and review1.wpd. Tile the windows.

2. Make soft1.wpd the active document. Add the following text to the end of the third paragraph.

> Here is a list of our current reviewers. You may recognize some of the names from your organizational activities.

3. Make review1.wpd the active document. Copy the table and title to just below the third paragraph in soft1.wpd.

4. Suppress the header on the first page of the document.

5. Save the document as soft2.wpd.

6. Spell check, save, and print soft2.wpd. Close all documents.

6-4 Directions

1. Open database.wpd. Save it as data1.wpd.

2. Indent the first line of each paragraph five spaces.

3. Use the QuickMenu to select the last paragraph and delete it.

4. Use the power bar to double-space the document, removing the extra HRt code between the paragraphs.

5. Add three blank lines above the text. (You need to make sure your insertion point is before the Line Space code.) Center and underline the title: **Introduction to Databases.**

6. Type the following text right-aligned in a header.

> Database Technology
> (today's date)

7. Edit the header. Bold the text and reduce the font size.

8. Move the insertion point to the end of the document. Open and copy the text from db2.wpd to the end of data1.wpd. Edit appropriately.

9. Save, print, and close the document.

6-5 Directions

1. Open data1.wpd. Save it as data2.wpd.

2. Add the following text to the end of the document (double-spaced).

Obviously, it is possible to extract reports only about data that has been entered into the database, a fact which makes it extremely important that the database be set up originally with all the necessary information.

Following are examples of reports that can be produced from a database:
- A list of clients, customers, or employees in alphabetical order.
- A list of employees' salaries in ascending or descending order.
- A list of customers who purchased more than $5,000 of goods in January.
- A list of faculty members making less than $20,000 who have been teaching more than five years.

3. Suppress the header on the first page.

4. Save, spell check, print, and close the document.

6-6   Directions

1. Open marold.wpd. Save it as marold6.wpd.

2. Remove any extra lines (hard returns) above the date.

3. Remove the italics.

4. Center the letter vertically on the page.

5. Use the ruler bar to change the side margins to 2".

6. Create an envelope for the document. Use your address for a return address.

7. Save, print, and close the document.

6-7   Directions

1. Use the post office preferred method of addressing an envelope to go to:

MIDWESTERN COLLEGE
924 STATE STREET
TERRE HAUTE IN 47803

Use your name and address as the return address.

2. Print and close the document.

7 Creating and Editing Macros

Objectives

After completing this lesson, you will be able to:

- Define a macro
- Record a macro
- Play a macro
- Assign a macro to the Macro pull-down menu
- Assign shortcut keys to a macro
- Assign a macro to the button bar

Defining a Macro

The Macro feature allows you to save or **record** frequently used keystrokes, such as text characters and menu selections, in a file. You can use or **play** a macro saved in a file at any time, and WordPerfect will automatically execute the saved keystrokes for you.

Macros are useful timesavers if you regularly use the same text or series of keystrokes. Examples include the name of your company, the closing of a letter, and forms such as interoffice memoranda. For example, if you always end a letter with "Sincerely yours," leave four blank lines, then type your name and title, you can create a macro to do that, then play the macro in future letters with only a keystroke or two.

Creating a Macro

To create a macro from the menu bar:

- Choose Tools ⇒ Macro ⇒ Record (Ctrl + F10).
- Select Location ⇒ File on Disk.
- Type in a file name in the Name text box.
- Select Record.
- Perform all the actions you wish to record.
- Select Tools ⇒ Macro ⇒ Record (Ctrl + F10).

If you select Location, you can also store your macro in a template (a form). The default stores the macro in the wpwin60\macros subdirectory.

▮ Playing a Macro

When you play a macro, WordPerfect executes all the saved keystrokes, starting at the current position of the insertion point. To play a macro, from the menu bar:

- Select <u>T</u>ools ⇒ <u>M</u>acro ⇒ <u>P</u>lay (⟨Alt⟩ + ⟨F10⟩).

The Play Macro dialog box appears. You can either click the icon beside the Name text box to get a list of all your macros and double-click on the desired macro or type the name of the macro in the Name text box, then click on <u>P</u>lay. If the macro is stored on a floppy disk, designate the letter of the drive.

In this exercise, you will create a macro for your signature block use every time you write a letter. Begin with a blank screen.

1. Click on <u>T</u>ools ⇒ <u>M</u>acro

The pull-down menu shown in Figure 7-1 appears.

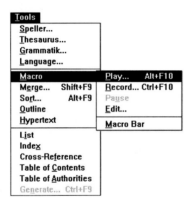

Figure 7-1

2. Click on <u>R</u>ecord

✓ Press ⟨Ctrl⟩ + ⟨F10⟩

The Record Macro dialog box appears, as shown in Figure 7-2, with the insertion point blinking in the Name text box.

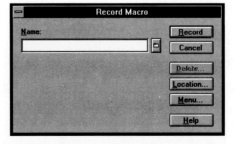

Figure 7-2

You want to save this to your floppy disk drive. If you don't, it may not work correctly on a network or a shared hard drive.

3. Click on Location

The Location option box displays as shown in Figure 7-3.

Figure 7-3

4. Click on File on Disk

5. Click on OK

With the insertion point in the Name text box:

6. Type `a:sign` (or `b:sign`)

7. Click on Record

The middle of the status bar prompts "Macro Record." Now type your signature block.

8. Type `Sincerely yours,`

9. Press (Enter) four times

10. Type your name

11. Press (Enter)

12. Type `Acquisitions Editor`

Stop the recording of this macro.

13. Click on Tools ⇒ Macro ⇒ Record

✓ Press (Ctrl) + (F10)

14. Close the file without saving it

The macro is saved on your floppy disk—check to see.

 After you wrote the letter to Dr. Airsman, you were promoted to Acquisitions Editor. The letter has not yet been mailed, so play your newly-created macro to update the closing.

1. Open airsman.wpd

2. Select the signature block of the letter

To delete the signature block:

3. Press (Del)

Now play your sign macro to insert the new signature block.

4. Click on Tools ⇒ Macro ⇒ Play

✓ Press (Alt) + (F10)

The Play Macro dialog box appears, as shown in Figure 7-4. In the Name text box:

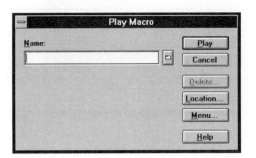

Figure 7-4

5. Type `a:sign`

   Be sure to have the macro's floppy disk in the correct drive.

6. Click on Play

   The new signature block is automatically inserted.

7. Close the letter to Dr. Airsman and choose Yes to save your changes

Assigning a Macro to the Macro Menu

For easier access, you can assign a macro to the Macro menu. Up to nine of your most frequently used macros can be placed in this menu. (The last macros used will display in the menu, also until the limit is reached.) To play a macro from the Macro menu, simply choose it the same way you would any other menu option. To assign a macro to the menu:

- Create and name the macro.
- Select Tools ⇒ Macro ⇒ Play.
- Select Menu.
- Select Insert.
- Select desired macro name-OK. (Type in the macro name, click the drop-down list button, or press (F4) to get list of available macros.)
- Choose Select.
- In the Assign Macro to Menu box, click on OK.
- Select Cancel in the Play Macro box.

Deleting a Macro from the Menu

When you no longer need a macro, it's a good idea to delete it from the menu. To do so:

- Select Tools ⇒ Macro ⇒ Play ⇒ Menu.
- Select the macro to delete.
- Select Delete.
- Select OK.
- Select Cancel.

Assigning a Macro to Shortcut Keys

You can assign macros to a (Ctrl) + (Shift) + letter combination. The letters *b*, *d*, *l*, *o*, *p*, and s have already been used by WordPerfect for macros; however, the others should be available for use.

To assign the keystroke to the macro:

- Select Location ⇒ File on Disk.
- With the insertion point in the Name text box, press (Ctrl) + (Shift) plus the letter.

If WordPerfect has already assigned that combination, it will not warn you of that but will use the WordPerfect macro when played, ignoring your macro.

- Click on Record.
- Create your macro.

Assigning a Macro to the Button Bar

Another way to play a macro is to assign it to the button bar. To play the macro, simply click on the corresponding button. To assign a macro to the button bar, you must first select and display the appropriate button bar. From the menu bar:

- Choose File ⇒ Preferences ⇒ Button Bar.
- Select desired button bar.
- Select Edit.

The Button Bar Editor dialog box displays. In the Add a Button To option box:

- Select the Play a Macro radio button.
- Select Add Macro.

In the Select Macro Name text box:

- Type the name of the macro you wish to assign to the button bar (or click on the icon and select the macro from the Select File list).
- Choose Select.
- Choose OK in the Button Bar Editor dialog box.
- Select Close in the Button Bar Preferences menu.
- Select Close in Preferences menu.
- Choose OK.

As you will be using your signature block macro frequently, you want to assign it to the Macro menu. Create the macro again and assign it to the menu.

1. Click on Tools ⇒ Macro ⇒ Record
2. In the Name text box, type `signatur`
3. Click on Record
4. Create your signature block again
5. Click on Tools ⇒ Macro ⇒ Record

To assign it to the Macro menu:

6. Click on Tools ⇒ Macro ⇒ Play

7. Click on Menu

The Assign Macro to Menu option box displays as shown in Figure 7-5. Don't be concerned if your dialog box does not match the figure exactly.

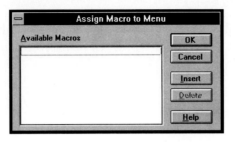

Figure 7-5

8. Click on Insert

9. Click on the file drop-down box or press (F4)

A list of available macros displays.

10. Select signatur.wcm ⇒ OK

11. Click on Select

12. Click on OK in the Assign Macro to Menu box

13. In the Play Macro option box, click on Cancel

See if your macro is on the menu.

14. Click on Tools ⇒ Macro

It should appear as 1 or 2signatur.wcm.

 You are now back in the workspace, and will open the letter to Mr. Wright, then play your macro from the Macro menu.

1. Open Mr. Wright's letter—wright.wpd

2. Select and delete the letter's signature block

3. Click on Tools ⇒ Macro ⇒ 1 Sign

The signature block is automatically inserted into your document.

Leave Mr. Wright's letter open in your workspace. You will use it in a later section.

 In this exercise, you will use a shortcut key to create a new macro. You should open a new document.

1. Click on Tools ⇒ Macro ⇒ Record

2. Click on Location ⇒ File on Disk

3. Press OK

With your insertion point in the Name text box:

4. Press (Ctrl) + (Shift) + (W)

5. Click on Record

   ✓ Press (Ctrl) + (F10)

6. Type `Bookworm Computer Publishing Company`

7. Click on Tools ⇒ Macro ⇒ Record

   ✓ Press (Ctrl) + (F10)

8. Close the untitled document without saving the changes

Give your new macro a try. Mr. Wright's letter is still in your workspace. First, you need to delete the text "Bookworm Computer Publishing Company" in the first paragraph, which begins "Your Prospectus . . ."

1. Select and delete "Bookworm Computer Publishing Company"

Now play your macro.

2. Press (Ctrl) + (Shift) + W

If you select Tools ⇒ Macro ⇒ Play, you will see that ctrlsftw.wcm is listed first as your last-used macro. However, it has not been permanently assigned to your menu.

3. Close Mr. Wright's letter and choose Yes to save the changes

Because you write so many memos, you will create a memo macro, typing in an asterisk to easily find the place for your insertion point. You will then assign it to a button on the WordPerfect button bar.

1. Click on Tools ⇒ Macro ⇒ Record

2. Click on Location ⇒ File on Disk ⇒ OK

In the Name text box:

3. Type `memo`

4. Click on Record

To leave a 2" top margin:

5. Press (Enter) six times

In a font of your choice (if you have Windows TrueType fonts, Arial 16 pt is good), centered and in boldface:

6. Play your macro for "Bookworm Computer Publishing Company"

7. Press (Enter) twice

In the same font, centered:

8. Type `Interoffice Memorandum`

9. Press (Enter) twice

   Change back to your regular font (Times New Roman, 12 pt), and in boldface:

10. Type **DATE:**

    Be sure to turn bold off.

11. Press (Tab)

    NOTE: You may have to tab a different number of times to line up the items, depending on the font you are using.

12. Click on Insert ⇒ Date ⇒ Date Code

    ✓ Press (Ctrl) + (Shift) + (D)

13. Press (Enter) twice

14. Type **TO:** (in bold)

15. Press (Tab) twice

16. Type * (an asterisk)

17. Press (Enter) twice

18. Type **FROM:**

19. Press (Tab)

20. Type * (an asterisk)

21. Press (Enter) twice

22. Type **SUBJECT:**

23. Press (Tab)

24. Type * (an asterisk)

25. Press (Enter) twice

26. Type * (an asterisk)

    To stop recording:

27. Click on Tools ⇒ Macro ⇒ Record

    ✓ Press (Ctrl) + (F10)

    Your screen should appear similar to Figure 7-6.

28. Close the document without saving

 You will now assign the Memo macro to the WordPerfect button bar.

1. Select and display the WordPerfect button bar

2. Click on File ⇒ Preferences ⇒ Button Bar ⇒ WordPerfect ⇒ Edit

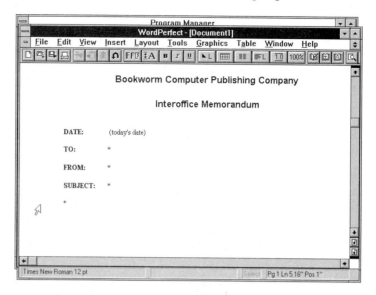

Figure 7-6

The Button Bar Editor ⇒ WordPerfect dialog box appears as shown in Figure 7-7.

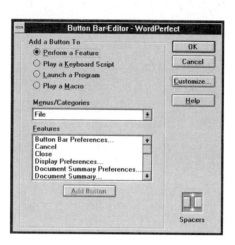

Figure 7-7

In the Add a Button To dialog box:

3. Click on the Play a <u>M</u>acro radio button

4. Click on <u>A</u>dd Macro

The Select Macro dialog box displays as in Figure 7-8.

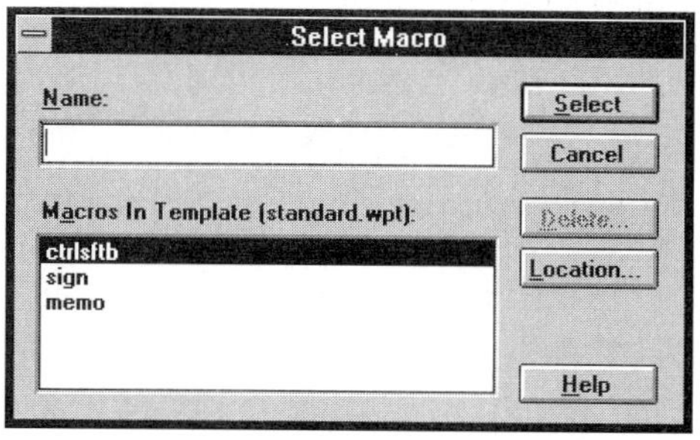

Figure 7-8

5. Select Memo

6. Click on OK

7. Click on <u>S</u>elect

If you are prompted to "Save macro with full path," click on <u>Y</u>es. You are returned to the Button Bar Editor dialog box. Remember, you can also double-click on the macro file name in lieu of step 5.

8. Click on OK

9. Click on <u>C</u>lose in the Button Bar Preferences dialog box

10. Click on <u>C</u>lose in the Preferences dialog box

You are returned to your workspace, and the button bar now has a command button called WP Macro. You may have to scroll to see it, depending on how many buttons are already on the bar.

You need to write a memo to the BCPC staff telling them about your upcoming vacation. To do so, play the macro from the button bar.

1. Click on WP Macro in the button bar

The macro displays.

2. Select the asterisk after TO:

3. Type BCPC Personnel

4. Select the asterisk after FROM:

5. Type your name

6. Select the asterisk after SUBJECT:

7. Type Summer Vacation

8. Select the last asterisk

9. Type:

I will be out of the office on vacation from August 1 until August 15. Meg White will handle my responsibilities while I'm gone. Her extension is 3401. She will be able to reach me in case of an emergency.

10. Save the document as vacation

11. Print the document from the power bar

Your memo should be similar to that in Figure 7-9.

12. Close the document and exit WordPerfect

Bookworm Computer Publishing Company

Interoffice Memorandum

DATE: (today's date)

TO: BCPC Personnel

FROM: your name

SUBJECT: Summer Vacation

I will be out of the office on vacation from August 1 until August 15. Meg White will handle my responsibilities while I'm gone. Her extension is 3401. She will be able to reach me in case of an emergency.

Figure 7-9

On Your Own

Review of Commands

Description	Menu Commands	Function Keys
Create a macro	_____	_____
Play a macro	_____	_____
Add a macro to a button bar	_____	_____

Lesson Review

1. What does a macro do?

2. How many macros can be assigned to the Macro menu?

3. Where else may frequently used macros be located?

4. Why would you assign macros to the button bar or menu?

5. What key combination assigns a macro to the keyboard?

6. What are the general steps to assign a macro to the button bar?

7. What is the default location for macro file storage?

8. What actually happens when you play a macro?

9. When might a macro be convenient?

▌ **Assignments**

7-1 Directions

1. Create a macro for your personal letterhead as follows.

YOUR NAME
Your Street Address
Your City, State, and Zip

---

2. Bold the text and use a font of your choice.

3. Name the macro Lhd.

4. Play the macro for your instructor or another student to observe.

7-2 Directions

1. Play the macro Lhd.

2. Type a letter to a friend discussing what you have learned about WordPerfect.

3. Save and print the letter.

7-3 Directions

1. Assign Lhd to the Macro menu.

2. Display the Macro menu, with Lhd listed, to your instructor.

7-4 Directions

1. Create a macro for a company memorandum or for personal use. Format and insert the text as follows: YOUR COMPANY'S NAME/ MEMORANDUM/ TO:/FROM:/DATE:/ SUBJECT:. Be creative in your use of fonts, bold type, and so on.

2. Name the macro Memo1.

3. Play the macro for your instructor or another student.

7-5 Directions

1. Play the macro Memo1.

2. Type a memorandum reminding your employees of the company picnic as follows.

Don't forget that the company picnic is this Friday at 2 p.m. Sign-up sheets are posted in the break room. Please sign up to bring a side dish or dessert.

Remember to dress casually so that you can participate in all the games and activities.

---

3. Save the memorandum.

4. Print the document.

7-6 Directions

1. Assign Memo1 to the WordPerfect Button Bar.

2. Display the button bar to your instructor and demonstrate how to play the macro using the button bar.

7-7 Directions

1. Create a macro for a document that has 2" side margins and double line spacing. Place a date code on the first line.

2. Assign the macro to the keyboard: (Ctrl) + (Shift) + (N) (for note).

3. Play the note macro you just created.

4. Type a note to your classmates reminding them that WordPerfect 6.0 allows you to assign shortcut keys to macros as follows:

---

date/
Don't forget that you can use shortcut keys to name your most commonly-used macros. This saves time when creating documents.

Creating Tables

Objectives

After completing this lesson, you will be able to:

- Create a table
- Move within a table
- Insert and delete rows and columns
- Select cells, rows, and columns
- Join cells together
- Change the appearance of a table
- Move and copy rows and columns
- Insert a formula and perform calculations
- Copy a formula
- Format numbers in a table

▊ Creating a Table

WordPerfect's Table feature offers users the ability to create "tabular" columns without entering tabs or tab settings. It also lets the user create complex forms and multicolumn documents, while incorporating a variety of font attributes and sizes.

The basic structure of a table consists of horizontal **rows** and vertical **columns**. Columns are labeled alphabetically from left to right, and rows are numbered sequentially from the top down, as shown in Figure 8-1. You can have up to 32 columns and 32,765 rows in one table.

The rectangle at which a row and column intersect is called a **cell**. Each cell has an **address**, consisting of its column letter and row number, which indicates the cell's position in the table. The address of the cell in which the insertion point is positioned is indicated in the status bar. For example, if the insertion point is positioned in the first cell of the table, the status bar will read "Cell A1."

Columns

	A	B	C
1			
2			
3			
4			
5			
6			
7			
8			

Figure 8-1

 There are two ways to create a table in WordPerfect. You can use either the Table command button on the power bar (the button that looks like a grid) or choose the Table option from the menu bar.

To create a table using the power bar, first position the mouse pointer on the Table button, then click and hold the left mouse button to display the table sizing grid. Drag the mouse until the desired number of columns and rows is displayed, and release the mouse button.

NOTE: *When you create a table using the power bar, the maximum size is 32 columns by 45 rows.*

To create a table using the menu bar:

- Choose Table ⇒ Create.
- Type in the desired number of columns and rows.
- Choose OK.

Moving Within a Table

The (Tab) key moves the insertion point one cell forward and (Shift) + (Tab) moves it one cell back. You can also position the I-beam at any location within the table and click the mouse button to place the insertion point. Listed in Table 8-1 are additional keystrokes that can be used to move the insertion point within a table.

Inserting Rows and Columns

Rows and columns can be inserted at any time, anywhere in a table. To insert a row or column:

- Choose Table ⇒ Insert.
- Choose Rows or Columns.
- Type the number of rows or columns to be inserted (or click on the up/down arrow to select a number).
- In the Placement box, click on Before or After (to have the new row or column inserted either before or after the insertion point).
- Choose OK.

The new rows or columns are inserted either immediately before the row or column where the insertion point is positioned or after it, depending on your

Keystroke	Result
↑	Moves up one line at a time in the current column
↓	Moves down one line at a time in the current column
←	Moves one character to the left
→	Moves one character to the right
Alt + ↑	Moves to the beginning of the cell above
Alt + ↓	Moves to the beginning of the cell below
Alt + ←	Moves to the beginning of the cell to the left
Alt + →	Moves to the beginning of the cell to the right
Home , Home	Moves to the first cell in a row
End , End	Moves to the last cell in a row

Table 8-1

choice. The new rows and columns will have the same formatting features (attributes, justification, column width, and lines) as the row in which the insertion point is positioned.

One row can also be inserted by:

- Pressing Alt + Ins (inserts a row at the insertion point position).
- Pressing Alt + Shift + Ins (inserts a row below the row in which the insertion point is located).

▌ Selecting Cells

Before you can edit or format a cell, you must first select the cell(s), row(s), or column(s) to be affected. And before you can select a cell, row, or column, the mouse pointer must be displayed as an arrow. Moving the mouse pointer to either the left or top of a cell turns it into an arrow. Table 8-2 shows how to select different areas of a table.

Area to Be Selected	Steps
Cell	Display either the left or up arrow and click once
Row	Display the left arrow on any cell in the row and double-click
Column	Display the up arrow on any cell in the column and double-click
Entire table	Display either the left or up arrow anywhere in the table and triple-click
Several cells, rows, or columns	Display either the left or up arrow in a corner of a cell and drag the mouse to the opposite corner of the block to be selected

Table 8-2

NOTE: You can drag the mouse to select text in a single cell. However, if you drag the mouse across the cell's boundary into an adjacent cell, the block of cells—instead of only the text—becomes selected. Use (F8) *to select only text when crossing into another cell.*

▌ Deleting Rows or Columns

To delete a row or column, first position the insertion point anywhere in the row or column to be deleted.

- Choose Table.
- Choose Delete.
- Type the number of rows or columns to be deleted (or use the up or down arrow).
- Choose OK ((Alt) + (Del)).

To delete more than one row or column, position the insertion point in either the topmost row or the leftmost column to be deleted. You may also select the rows or columns to be deleted. When you do so, you are not prompted for the number of rows or columns to be deleted because WordPerfect assumes you want to delete those that have been selected. To delete cell contents only, mark the Cell Contents radio button.

Using the Table button on the power bar, you will create a table that is 3 columns wide and 12 rows long and enter the data shown in Figure 8-2.

Using WordPerfect for Windows	15,000	20,000
Word for Windows	12,500	15,500
Guide to Ami Pro	7,500	9,000
WordPerfect 5.2 for OS/2	6,000	4,500
First Look at Lotus 1-2-3	16,000	17,000
Running Excel 4.0	12,000	13,500
Quattro Pro Made Easy	4,000	6,000
Beginning dBase IV	9,000	10,500
Mastering Fox Pro	8,500	12,000
Learning Paradox	4,500	3,000
Unix and C++	5,200	6,000
Programming with COBOL	3,200	1,000

Figure 8-2

1. Position the mouse pointer on the Table icon

2. Depress the left mouse button

   The table sizing grid displays.

3. Drag the mouse until the sizing grid displays "3x12"

4. Release the mouse button

The table is created. Note that WordPerfect evenly divided the space between the left and right margins into three columns. The insertion point is positioned in the first cell, and the center of the status bar reads, "TABLE A Cell A1."

Now you are ready to enter text into cell A1 of your table. (Use the status bar or the top left of the title bar to determine the address of the current cell.)

5. Type `Using WordPerfect for Windows`

   Do not press (Enter). If you already have, press (Backspace) to delete the HRt code. Notice that WordPerfect expanded the cell vertically to accommodate the text. Now move to the next cell, B1.

6. Press (Tab)

   If you accidentally press (Tab) more than once, press (Shift) + (Tab) to back up one cell.

7. Type `15,000`

   To move to the next cell, C1:

8. Press (Tab)

9. Type `20,000`

   To move to cell A2:

10. Press (Tab)

   Complete the table as shown in Figure 8-2. Remember, do not press (Enter) after the text in a cell has been typed; use the (Tab) key and arrow keys to move around.

You need a descriptive title for your table showing that it represents 1994 book sales. In this exercise you will use both of the methods previously described to insert rows. As you proceed through the following exercises, refer to the finished table in Figure 8-2.

1. Position the insertion point in the first row

2. Click on T<u>a</u>ble

   The Table pull-down menu appears, as shown in Figure 8-3.

Figure 8-3

3. Click on Insert

The Insert Columns/Rows dialog box appears as shown in Figure 8-4.

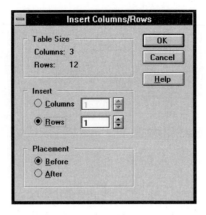

Figure 8-4

4. Click on the Rows radio button (if not already marked)

You want to insert two rows, so enter that number in the Rows text box (you can also use the arrow box to select the desired number).

5. Type 2

Make sure the Before button is selected in the Placement box to have the blank row appear *before* the insertion point.

6. Click on OK

Using keystrokes, you are going to insert a blank row after the word processing books, the spreadsheet books, and the programming books to later subtotal those divisions.

7. Position the insertion point in the row that reads "First Look at Lotus 1-2-3"

8. Press (Alt) + (Ins)

9. On your own, insert a new row above the row that reads "Beginning dBase IV" and another one above the row that reads "Unix and C++"

Now insert a row at the end of the table.

10. Position the insertion point in the last row

11. Press (Alt) + (Shift) + (Ins)

12. On your own, add three more rows at the end of the table

13. Click on Save in the power bar

14. Name the file bksales

In this exercise, you will practice selecting areas of a table. Be sure your table is displayed on your desktop. It does not matter where the insertion point is located.

1. Position the mouse pointer in the first cell of the table (A1)

2. Position the I-beam against the left edge of cell A1 to display the left arrow

Compare your screen to the one in Figure 8-5.

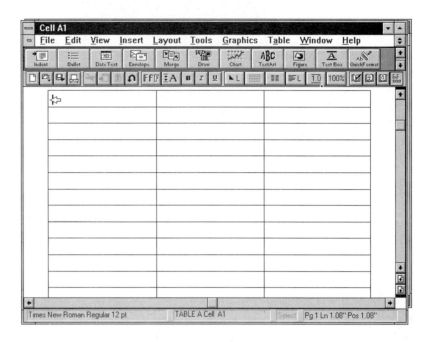

Figure 8-5

3. Click the mouse button

Cell A1 is selected. To deselect the cell:

4. Click the mouse anywhere once

Now select the entire first row.

5. Display the left arrow

6. Double-click the mouse button

The entire first row of your table is selected. Don't forget to deselect the row. Now, select the first column of your table:

7. Display the up arrow, then double-click the mouse button

Select the first two rows of your table and deselect them.

8. Display the left arrow in cell A1

9. Drag the mouse to the lower corner of cell C2

You have four blank rows at the bottom of the table and you need only two, so you'll delete two rows using two different methods.

1. Select the last row of the table

2. Click on Table ⇒ Delete

The Delete Columns/Rows dialog box appears, as shown in Figure 8-6, and Rows should be marked.

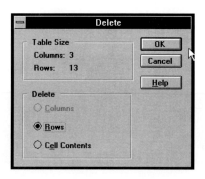

Figure 8-6

3. Click on OK

The selected row is deleted. Remember, if you accidentally delete more than you intend to, use Edit and either Undo or Undelete to recover the deleted portion of your table.

Using keystrokes, you will delete one of the three remaining blank rows at the end of the table.

4. Position the insertion point in the last row of the table

5. Press (Alt) + (Del)

Your table now has two blank rows at the end.

Joining Cells

The Join feature allows you to remove the boundaries (lines) between cells, combining the contents of the cells. Cells may be joined either before or after text is entered. You might, for example, want to join several cells to include a heading at the top of your table or to create preprinted forms. To join cells, first select the cells to be joined.

• Choose Table ⇒ Join ⇒ Cell

The selected cells are joined into a single cell. You can also join tables by using the Table ⇒ Join ⇒ Table command.

NOTE: If you accidentally join cells that should not be joined, use the Split feature to return them to their original states.

Formatting Text in a Table

You can format text in a single cell, a column, a row, or an entire table. You can change the vertical alignment, the justification, the appearance, and the position and size of the text. A small preview window in the screen shows how the text will appear, given your selections.

To change the format for a column, first position the insertion point in the column to be affected. If more than one column is to be formatted, select *one* cell in each column; do not select all the cells in the columns.

• Choose Table ⇒ Format ⇒ Column

The Format Column dialog box appears, allowing you to add boldfacing, italic, underlining, and so on; choose the text size and position (normal, superscript, or subscript); choose the justification; adjust the column width and column margins; and determine the number of digits shown to the right of the decimal point.

To change the format for a cell, position the insertion point in the cell to be affected. If more than one cell is to be formatted, select those cells.

- Choose T<u>a</u>ble ⇒ F<u>o</u>rmat ⇒ C<u>e</u>ll

The Format Cell dialog box appears, giving you the same appearance, alignment, justification position, and size options as for a column. It also allows you to lock cells (to protect the contents from being written over), and ignore cells when calculating.

To format a row or rows, first select the rows, then:

- Choose T<u>a</u>ble ⇒ F<u>o</u>rmat ⇒ R<u>o</u>w

The Format Row dialog box displays, giving you options for either single or multiple lines per row, automatic or fixed row height, and row top and bottom margins.

To change the format for an entire table:

- Choose T<u>a</u>ble ⇒ F<u>o</u>rmat ⇒ T<u>a</u>ble

The Format Table dialog box gives you virtually the same options as the Format Column screen above, with the two additional choices of Table Position and Disable Cell Locks.

Changing the Width of a Column

The easiest way to change the width of a column is to use the ruler. Simply position the mouse pointer on the column markers (the downward-pointing arrows above the numbers in the ruler) and drag the column marker to the desired position. The right side of the status bar will display the position as it changes.

If you need a column to be a specific width, you can position the insertion point in the column to be changed and choose T<u>a</u>ble ⇒ F<u>o</u>rmat ⇒ Col<u>u</u>mn. The Format Column dialog box appears. Then specify the desired dimension in the Column Width text box and choose OK.

Changing Lines and Shading Cells

When a table is first created, WordPerfect automatically puts a single line around the perimeter of the table and single lines inside it. You then have options of choosing different types of lines for individual cells, blocks of cells, the lines inside the table, and the lines around the outside of the table (the border). If you want to change more than one cell, be sure to select them before changing the line style.

Actually, you can change only the left, right, top, bottom, inside, or outside line styles for a cell or a block of cells. You have almost infinite choices, such as double, triple, thick, extra thick, color, and so on. If working with color, you can change line color and foreground and background color.

Cells can also be shaded to add appeal to a table. You can use shading in titles or to emphasize a particular cell or column. The default percentage of shading depends upon the fill style you choose. However, the percentage of shading for a table can be changed. A preview window in the screen displays what your selected styles will look like. To change line styles or shading, first select the appropriate area.

- Choose T<u>a</u>ble ⇒ <u>L</u>ines/Fill ⇒ Current C<u>e</u>ll (or Selection or Table)

The Current Cell option gives you the individual line style choices and the color and fill style choices. Only the cells selected would be affected.

The Table option gives you inside table line styles and color choices, border line choices, and fill options. The entire table would be affected by the changes.

Moving or Copying Rows or Columns

To move or copy rows or columns in a table, select the row(s) or column(s) and choose Edit ⇒ Cut or Copy. To retrieve the cut or copied portion of the table, position the insertion point where the row or column is to be inserted and choose Edit ⇒ Paste.

NOTE: When a row or column is moved, the line style for that row or column is also moved or copied. The same is true of multiple rows and columns.

Determining the Row Height

As text is typed into a cell, WordPerfect automatically adjusts or expands the row height to accommodate the text. That is, if one cell in a row has six lines, the height of the entire row expands to fit six lines. Similarly, if text is deleted from that cell, the row height decreases. If the size or attribute of the text changes, the row height either decreases or increases to fit the new text size.

You can also manually set the height of a row, which is useful when creating preprinted forms because it's important to maintain the design of the form, regardless of the amount of text entered.

To set the row height manually:

• Choose Table ⇒ Format ⇒ Row

The Format Row dialog box appears. If you choose Single Line, only one line of text will be shown in that row. If you choose Multi Line or Auto, the row adjusts to the specified dimension. However, all the text within a given cell in that row must fit within the row height. Any text that does not fit within the fixed row height will not be visible.

NOTE: When row height is specified or the Single Line option is chosen, text that is not visible is still stored in the cell in case the row height is later increased to accommodate the additional text.

In this exercise, you are going to join cells A1, B1, and C1 so that you can insert a title across the top of your table, and you will format the cell to make the title more attractive.

1. Select cells A1, B1, and C1

2. Click on Table ⇒ Join ⇒ Cell

   Notice that the cell address for the joined cells is A1.

3. Position the insertion point in cell A1

4. Click on Table ⇒ Format ⇒ Cell

   The Format dialog box appears as shown in Figure 8-7.

5. Click on Bold

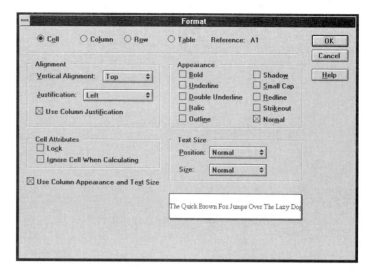

Figure 8-7

6. Click on the Text Size: Si_ze arrow and, in the drop-down box, drag the pointer to _Very Large

7. Click on the _Justification arrow and, in the drop-down box, drag the pointer to _Center

Note that the preview window shows what your text will look like.

8. Click on OK

You do not have to turn off Center, Bold, and Justification, because only that cell was formatted.

9. In cell A1, type `BCPC 1994 Book Sales`

 In the next exercise, you will format cells A2, B2, and C2 so that the subtitles will be bold and centered in the cells.

1. Select cells A2, B2, and C2

2. Click on T_able ⇒ F_ormat

The Format Row dialog box displays as shown in Figure 8-8.

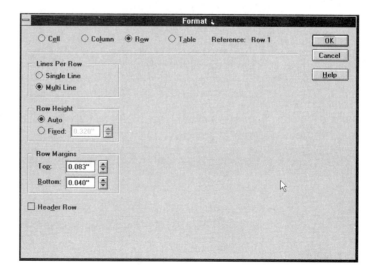

Figure 8-8

3. Click on Cell

4. Click on Bold

5. Click on Justification ⇒ Center

6. Click on OK

7. Position the insertion point in cell A2

8. Type **Book Title**

9. Position the insertion point in B2

10. Type **Jan - Jun**

11. In cell C2, type **Jul - Dec**

 In the following exercise, you will set columns B and C to be right-aligned so that the numbers will line up properly. You will also specify no digits to the right of the decimal point, as you will need this later in the lesson.

1. Select cells B3 and C3

   Remember, when you are changing the format of more than one column, you need select only one cell in each column.

2. Click on Table ⇒ Format ⇒ Column

   The Format Column dialog box appears as shown in Figure 8-9.

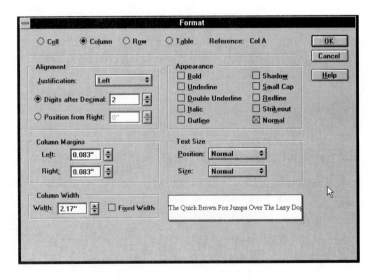

Figure 8-9

3. Click on Justification ⇒ Right

   You want to specify no digits to the right of the decimal point, so move to the Digits after Decimal option box.

4. Type **0** or click on the down arrow to select 0

5. Click on OK and deselect the columns

   The numbers in columns B and C are now aligned to the right side of each cell. You have made several changes to your table. To save it:

 6. Click on the Save icon

You are going to change the width of column B (using the ruler) and column C (using the menu). This will enable you to add another column later in the lesson. Display the ruler bar.

1. Position the mouse pointer on the second column marker, as shown in Figure 8-10.

   Your insertion point *must* be positioned in the column to get the column marker to display.

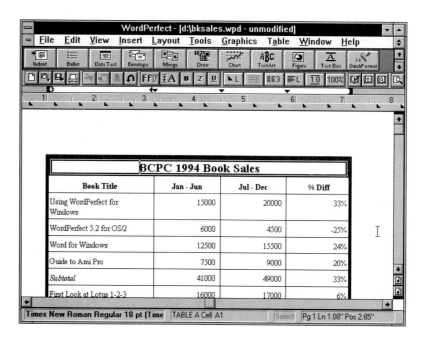

Figure 8-10

2. Drag the column marker to the left until the status bar reads "Position 4.5"" and release the marker

   Now change the width of column C.

3. Position the insertion point in column C

4. Click on T̲able ⇒ F̲ormat ⇒ Co̲lumn

5. In the Column Width Box, type `1.33"`

6. Click on OK

Add a column to the right side of your table so that later in the lesson you can calculate the percentage of increase between the two six-month periods.

1. Position the insertion point in column C

2. Click on T̲able ⇒ I̲nsert

   You want to increase the number of columns by 1.

3. Click on the C̲olumns radio button

4. Type `1` or select 1 from the arrow box

   In the Placement option box:

5. Click on A̲fter

6. Click on OK

7. On your own, join cells A1 and D1

8. In cell D2, type **%** `Diff`

It is centered and bold as are the previous cells.

 In this exercise you will first change the border around your table, then enhance the title of your table.

1. Position the insertion point in cell A1

2. Click on Ta̲ble ⇒ L̲ines/Fill ⇒ T̲able

The Table Lines/Fill dialog box displays as shown in Figure 8-11.

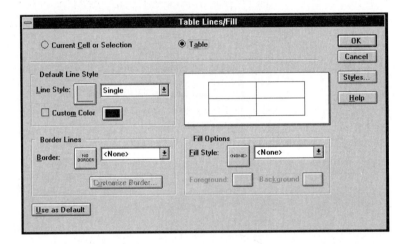

Figure 8-11

3. In the Border Lines box, click on the "No Border" button to see a display of the choice of borders as shown in Figure 8-12

Figure 8-12

4. In the top row, click on the fourth one from the left

You can also click on the arrow beside the text box to see a list of styles and scroll to select the Thick option.

5. Click on OK

   A thick black border surrounds your table.

6. Select cell A1 (title cell)

7. Click on Table ⇒ Lines/Fill ⇒ Current Cell

   The Table Lines/Fill dialog box displays as shown in Figure 8-13.

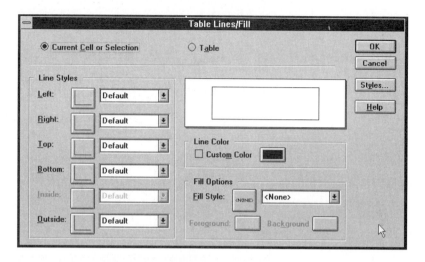

Figure 8-13

8. In the Line Styles ⇒ Outside text box, click on the arrow to display a list of choices as shown in Figure 8-14

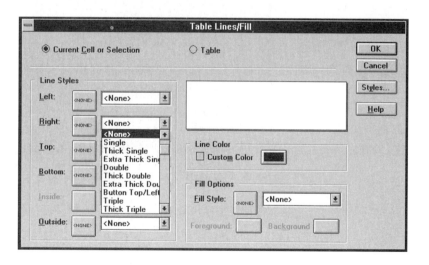

Figure 8-14

9. Scroll (if necessary) to select Thick Double

   In the Fill Options box:

10. Click on the Fill Style "NONE" button

    The fill pattern styles display as shown in Figure 8-15.

11. Select the first option after None

    The default for shading is 10 percent.

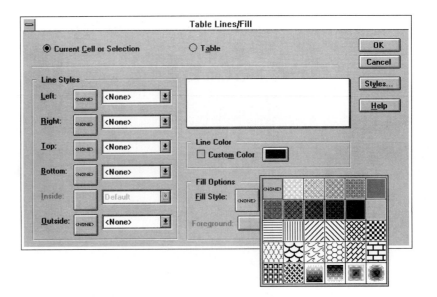

Figure 8-15

12. Click on the text box arrow to the right of the 10 percent fill box

13. Click on the up arrow

The percent of shading possible is shown in Figure 8-16.

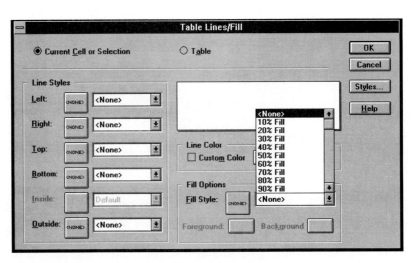

Figure 8-16

14. Select 20% Fill

15. Click on OK

 In this exercise, you will move the row that reads "Word Perfect 5.2 for OS/2" to follow "Using WordPerfect for Windows."

1. Select the row that reads "WordPerfect 5.2 for OS/2"

 2. Click on the Cut icon or choose Edit ⇒ Cut

   ✓ Press Ctrl + X

The Table Cut/Copy dialog box appears as shown in Figure 8-17.

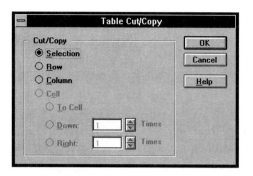

Figure 8-17

3. Click on <u>R</u>ow

4. Click on OK

5. Position the insertion point in the row below the row that reads "Using WordPerfect for Windows"

6. Click on the Paste icon or choose <u>E</u>dit ⇒ <u>P</u>aste

   ✓ Press (Ctrl) + (V)

   The "Word for Windows" row moves down one row.

7. Make the text in cells A7, A11, A15, A18, and A19 bold and italic

   Don't forget to use the status bar to determine the address of the cell in which the insertion point is positioned, and use the title bar to show the address of the cell when only the mouse pointer is in it.

8. In cells A7, A11, A15, and A18, type `Subtotal`

9. In cell A19, type `TOTAL`

10. Save the changes and close the file

▌ Performing Calculations in Tables

WordPerfect can perform mathematical calculations within a table. Formulas can add, subtract, multiply, divide, subtotal, and total a column of numbers. You also can designate the way the numbers display in a cell, a column, or a table, similar to the way you format text in a table.

Creating a Formula

To enter a formula, first position the insertion point in the cell in which the formula is to be entered. Numbers in a table can contain decimal points, commas to separate thousands, and initial dollar signs ($). A negative number can be marked either by a leading minus sign or one enclosed in parentheses. Any combination of the arithmetic operators shown in Table 8-3 can be used in a formula. You must use the operators on your number pad, not those above the letter keys.

These operators will work with numbers, cell addresses, or both. If a formula contains two or more operators, they are calculated from left to right. However, enclosing any part of a formula in parentheses will cause that portion of the formula to be calculated first. If parentheses are **nested** (one or more pairs of parentheses are enclosed within another pair), the innermost

Operator	Operation
+	Addition
−	Subtraction
*	Multiplication
/	Division

Table 8-3

expression is calculated first. Table 8-4 has some sample formulas that show how this works.

Formula	Result
A1 + B1	Adds the numbers in cells A1 and B1
D2*100/B2	The amount in D2 is multiplied by 100; the result is divided by the contents of cell B2
5/(G1 + 50)	Adds the amount in cell G1 to 50; then divides the result by 5

Table 8-4

Copying a Formula

A formula can easily be copied from one cell to another or to adjoining rows or columns. WordPerfect will automatically adjust the copied formula to reflect the correct cell address. For example, if the original formula is A1 + A2 and the formula is copied to column B, the formula will be adjusted to read B1 + B2.

To copy a formula, first position the insertion point in the cell that contains the formula to be copied.

- Choose Table ⇒ Copy Formula.

To copy the formula to a specific cell, choose To Cell and enter the cell address. To copy the formula in the same row to the right, choose Right and enter the number of cells to which it is to be copied. Likewise, to copy the formula down in the same column, choose Down and enter the number of cells to which the formula is to be copied. Finally, click on OK.

Formatting Numbers in a Table

To specify the way you want numbers to be displayed in a cell, column, or table, place the insertion point in the correct location, then:

- Choose Table ⇒ Number Type or click the right mouse button.
- Choose Cell, Column, or Table.
- In the Available Types box, choose one of the types in Table 8-5.

Type	Function
Accounting	Displays number with up to 15 decimal places, aligns the currency symbol at the edge of the column, adds a comma to separate thousands.
Commas	Displays numbers with up to 15 decimal places, uses commas for thousands separators, and displays negative numbers in parentheses.
Currency	Displays numbers with up to 15 decimal places, adds the currency symbol, thousands separators, and a decimal align character.
Date/Time	Converts numbers into the current date and time format.
Fixed	Displays numbers with up to 15 decimal places, but does not display the thousands separator.
General	Displays numbers without a thousands separator and with no zeros to the right of the decimal point.
Integer	Rounds numbers to eliminate decimals.
Percent	Displays numbers as percent values (multiplied by 100) with the percent symbol (%) and the number of decimal places you set. A value of .45 is shown as 45%.
Scientific	Displays up to 15 decimal places in scientific (exponential) notation. For example, with 2 as the number of decimal places, the number 3,450,000 is converted to 3.45e + 06.
Text	Treats the contents of a cell as text, which cannot be used for calculations.

Table 8-5

In this exercise, you are going to use the Sum and Copy Formula commands from the Table formula bar.

1. Open bksales.wpd

2. Position the insertion point in cell B7 (the blank row to the right of "Subtotal")

   Activate the formula bar and use the Sum feature to subtotal the sales of word processing books for January through July.

3. Click on Table ⇒ Formula Bar

   The formula bar appears as shown in Figure 8-18.

Figure 8-18

4. Click on Sum

Notice that the subtotal amount is entered in the cell, the status bar shows the formula for cell B7, and the formula text box displays the formula, also.

You will now copy the formula one cell to the right. Be sure the insertion point is positioned in cell B7.

5. Click on Copy Formula

The Copy Formula dialog box displays as shown in Figure 8-19.

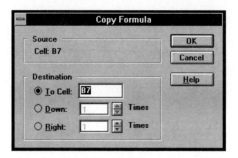

Figure 8-19

6. Click on the <u>R</u>ight radio button

The text box automatically displays a 1, which shows that the formula will be copied one time to the right.

7. Click on OK

Now you will enter a formula to subtotal the other categories of books. Move your insertion point to cell B11, then move the mouse pointer to the text bar immediately after the check mark (✔) and click to activate the insertion point. You will no longer see the insertion point in the cell.

8. Type sum(B8:B10)

9. Press (Enter)

10. On your own, sum the database and programming books for the period from January to June and copy the formulas to subtotal the column for July to December

Now enter a formula to get the total for the subtotals.

11. Position the insertion point in cell B19

12. Move the mouse pointer to the formula text box and click

13. Type B7 + B11 + B15 + B18

14. Press (Enter)

15. Copy the total formula to cell C18

Soon you will enter a formula to calculate the difference between the two six-month time periods as a percentage of increase over the first six-month period's sales. First, however, you want to format the column to display the formula's output as a percentage.

1. Position the insertion point in cell D3

2. Select the column

3. Select Ta̲ble ⇒ Nu̲mber Type

✓ Press (Alt) + (F12)

The Number Type dialog box displays as shown in Figure 8-20.

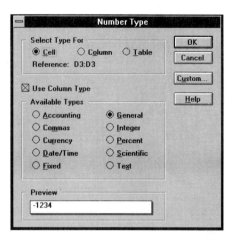

Figure 8-20

4. In the Available Types option box, select P̲ercent

5. Click on Cu̲stom

The Customize Number Type dialog box appears as shown in Figure 8-21.

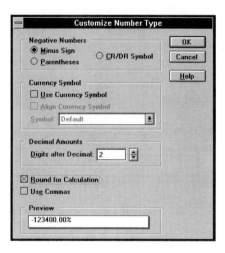

Figure 8-21

6. In the D̲igits after Decimal text box, type 0 or click the down arrow until the box reads 0

7. Click on OK

8. Click on OK again

Column D is now formatted to display percentages. Next enter a formula to calculate the percentage difference between columns B and C.

9. Position the insertion point in cell D3

10. Move the mouse pointer to the Formula text box and click

11. Type (C3-B3)/B3

12. Press (Enter)

13. Copy the formula down 16 times

Compare your table to the one shown in Figure 8-22.

BCPC 1994 Book Sales			
Book Title	**Jan - Jun**	**Jul - Dec**	**% Diff**
Using WordPerfect for Windows	15000	20000	33%
WordPerfect 5.2 for OS/2	6000	4500	-25%
Word for Windows	12500	15500	24%
Guide to Ami Pro	7500	9000	20%
Subtotal	41000	49000	20%
First Look at Lotus 1-2-3	16000	17000	6%
Running Excel 4.0	12000	13500	13%
Quattro Pro Made Easy	4000	6000	50%
Subtotal	32000	36500	14%
Beginning dBase IV	9000	10500	17%
Mastering Fox Pro	8500	12000	41%
Learning Paradox	4500	3000	-33%
Subtotal	22000	25500	16%
Unix and C++	5200	6000	15%
Programming with COBOL	3200	1000	-69%
Subtotal	8400	7000	-17%
Total	103400	118000	14%

Figure 8-22

14. Close the formula bar, then save and print your table

15. Close bksales.wpd

In this exercise, you are going to create the calendar shown in Figure 8-23.

1. Click on the Table icon and create a table seven cells wide by seven high

2. Select the top row (A1 through G1)

3. Click on Table ⇒ Join ⇒ Cell

Now specify that the top row can accommodate only one line of text and give it a fixed height of 1".

4. Select the top row (now cell A1)

September						
Sun	Mon	Tues	Wed	Thu	Fri	Sat
				1	2 check on book sales for Aug	3
4	5 2:00 meeting w/First Look authors	6	7	8 10:00 meeting to set date for Institute	9	10
11	12	13 12:00 lunch w/ publisher	14	15	16 9:30 - 4:00 interviews for new assistant	17
18	19	20 call about WP Beta	21	22	23	24
25	26	27	28 check on new book for WP for DOS	29	30	

Figure 8-23

5. Click on T**a**ble ⇒ F**o**rmat ⇒ R**ow**

6. Click on Single Line

7. Click on Fi**x**ed

   To specify a fixed line height, enter the measurement in the Fi**x**ed text box.

8. Type **.5**

9. Click on OK

   The next step is to boldface, center, and enlarge the title cell for the name of the month.

10. Select the top row (cell A1)

11. Click on T**a**ble ⇒ F**o**rmat ⇒ C**e**ll

12. Click on **B**old

13. Click on Si**z**e ⇒ **E**xtra Large

14. Click on **J**ustification ⇒ **C**enter

15. Click on OK

The next step is to specify that the second row will accommodate only one row of text.

16. Select the second row (A2 through G2)

17. Click on T̲able ⇒ F̲ormat ⇒ R̲ow

18. Click on Single Line ⇒ OK

Auto Row Height should already be marked. The next step is to center the cells for the days of the week, and make the type large and bold.

19. Make sure the second row (A2 through G2) is still selected

20. Click on T̲able ⇒ F̲ormat ⇒ C̲ell

21. Click on B̲old

22. Click on L̲arge

23. Click on J̲ustification ⇒ C̲enter

24. Click on OK

Now you want to make the row height for the body of your calendar 1".

25. Select rows 3 through 7

26. Click on T̲able ⇒ F̲ormat ⇒ R̲ow

27. Click on Fi̲xed

To specify the row height, enter the number in the F̲ixed text box:

28. Type 1 (for 1")

Be sure to leave the Lines Per Row setting at M̲ulti Line.

29. Click on OK

The next step is to change to a small type size for the body of the calendar.

30. Make sure rows 3 through 7 are still selected

31. Click on T̲able ⇒ F̲ormat ⇒ C̲ell

32. Click on Si̲ze ⇒ S̲mall

33. Click on OK

34. In row 2, type the days of the week, referring to Figure 8-23 if necessary

35. Save the calendar as calform

You will keep this as a template or model for use with other months.

36. Type september in the first cell and enter the rest of the text for the calendar

Now save the calendar under a new file name, thus leaving your original form intact.

37. Click on F̲ile ⇒ Save A̲s

✓ Press (F3)

38. Name the file septcal

39. Print septcal

40. Close the file

On Your Own

Review of Commands

Description	Menu Commands	Function Keys
Create a table	_____	_____
Insert a row	_____	_____
Delete a row	_____	_____
Join cells	_____	_____
Format cells	_____	_____
Number type	_____	_____
Shade cells	_____	_____
Change width of column	_____	_____
Change lines	_____	_____
Move/copy rows or columns	_____	_____
Change row height	_____	_____

Lesson Review

1. List the keystroke(s) to move the insertion point:

   Up one line in the current column _____

   Down one line in the current column _____

   One character to the left _____

   One character to the right _____

   To the beginning of the cell above _____

   To the beginning of the cell below _____

   To the beginning of the cell to the left _____

   To the beginning of the cell to the right _____

   To the first cell in a row _____

   To the last cell in a row _____

2. What is the intersection of a row and column called?

3. What is one example of a cell address?

4. What formatting features would already be included in an inserted row?

5. What must be done to cells, rows, and columns before they can be edited or formatted?

6. Explain the steps to delete three rows at a time.

7. What happens when you join three cells, such as B1, C1, and D1?

8. What are some of the appearance characteristics that can be used in a table?

9. What are some of the size characteristics available?

10. What justification options are provided for tables?

11. How can a column be formatted to display currency symbols?

12. What are some of the types of lines available?

13. List four of the arithmetic operators available in the Table feature.

14. What formula would add cells A1, A2, and A3, and divide by cell D2?

▌ Assignments

8-1 Directions

1. Create a table consisting of: your scheduled daily activities, hour by hour, for one day. List the hours vertically in the first column. Leave the second column blank so that you can fill in your activities. Make each cell in the columns at least 1" in height.

   In the first row, type **HOUR** and **ACTIVITY** in the first and second columns, respectively. Then type each hour from **8 A.M.** to **4 P.M.** in the first column.

2. Save the file as schedule.cms.

3. Print and close the table.

8-2 Directions

1. Create a calendar for the current month.

2. Insert the days and times your WordPerfect class meets and include other classes or appointments if you wish.

3. Save the calendar as month.wpd.

4. Print and close the file.

8-3 Directions

1. Design a table showing your monthly expenses for three months.

   First row: **EXPENSES/JAN/FEB/MAR/TOTAL**
   First column beneath the title row: **RENT/CAR PAYMENT/UTILITIES/ GROCERIES/CLOTHING/ENTERTAINMENT/TOTAL**
   Second through fourth columns: fill in monthly expenses
   Fifth column: enter formula(s) to total expenses

2. Save the table as expenses.wpd

3. Calculate totals horizontally and vertically.

4. Save the table again, then print and close it.

8-4 Directions

1. Design a table that lists all college coursework you have taken in your major and the number of credit hours you have earned for each course.

   First row: COURSE NAME/CREDITS
   Last row: TOTAL CREDITS/CREDITS REMAINING

2. In the last row, insert a formula that calculates the number of credit hours you have remaining in your major.

3. Save the table as credit.wpd.

8-5 Directions

1. Design a form for a survey you are conducting on pet owners. Include the following information: First, Middle, and Last Name; Address with City, State, and Zip; Age; Type of Pet; and any other pertinent information.

2. Make the form attractive and easy to use.

3. Include at least one change of type appearance and font.

4. Put a thick line around the border of the form and shade the title row.

5. Save the form as formpet.wpd.

6. Print and close the document.

8-6 Directions

1. Design a log sheet that allows you to record the number of hours spent practicing and completing assignments on the computer. Insert enough rows for at least ten entries.

   First row: DATE/HOURS
   Last row: TOTAL HOURS

2. Include a cell to display a running total of the hours completed.

3. Save the log sheet as log.wpd.

4. Record three or four days of computer time.

5. Save, print, and close the document.

9

Setting Up
Text Columns

Objectives

After completing this lesson, you will be able to:

- Discuss the difference between parallel columns and newspaper columns
- Create parallel columns
- Change column widths
- Move and copy columns
- Convert parallel columns to a table
- Create newspaper columns
- Retrieve a file into an open document

▊ Preliminaries

Because you will need fairly long documents to use the features in the rest of the lessons, we have supplied files on a data disk for your instructor. Check with the instructor to get copies of the disk or the documents. We suggest that you open the file you need from the data disk, insert your work disk, and save the document to your work disk each time you work with a new document. That way, you will always be able to go back to the original document.

▊ Types of Text Columns

Two different styles of text columns are available in WordPerfect: newspaper and parallel. **Newspaper columns** are designed for text that flows continuously from one column to the next. When the first column is filled with text, the insertion point automatically moves to the top of the next column, and so on, through all the columns. If you want to end a column before the bottom of the page, press (Ctrl) + (Enter) to insert a hard page break. The Balanced Newspaper option lines up potentially uneven columns, that is, instead of having one full column and one-fourth of the next one, this option will make them even.

Parallel columns are designed for documents in which the information in the first column relates to information in the second (and subsequent) columns, and they are uneven numbers of lines. Examples of this type of document include employment resumés, scripts for plays, and lists with uneven lines. If the lines are all the same length, using tab stops is more efficient. A Parallel with Block Protect option keeps all rows of the columns together across page breaks.

Creating Parallel Columns

To create parallel columns, first type any title and subtitle you want before the columns start, then:

- Choose Layout ⇒ Columns ⇒ Define.
- Select Number of Columns desired.
- Select Parallel or Parallel with Block Protect.
- Select OK.

WordPerfect equally divides the space between the left and right document margins into the specified number of columns, inserting between columns the measurement specified in the Spacing Between Columns text box. The default space setting is ½" (.500) and can be changed in any increment. If you specified 4 columns, for example, WordPerfect would calculate the space between the left and right margins, insert the designated space between the columns, then evenly divide the remaining space into 4 columns.

To choose columns of different widths with varying spaces between them, use the Column Widths ⇒ Width option box to designate the desired widths for each column. The Fixed option lets you designate columns and spaces to remain as set, regardless of changes in other columns. Another available option for this feature is Line Spacing Between Rows. The default is 1 and it increases in increments of .5.

WordPerfect will automatically turn on the Column feature when you exit the Define Columns dialog box.

Typing the Text

After defining the columns, type the first column's text (which might be a column heading), then select Layout ⇒ Columns ⇒ Column Break or Ctrl + Enter to position the insertion point in the next column. Pressing Ctrl + Enter after typing the last column moves the insertion point to the beginning of the first column.

Turning Columns Off

Turning columns off is necessary only if you are combining columns with regular text or are using different types or widths of columns in one document. To turn columns off, choose Layout ⇒ Columns ⇒ Off.

Parallel Column Codes

At the point in the document at which the columns are defined, a Col Def code is inserted with the description of the columns hidden in the code box. To see the full description, move the insertion point to the right of the code box and press the ⟨←⟩. An HCol code is inserted at the end of each column where ⟨Ctrl⟩ + ⟨Enter⟩ is pressed. Another Col Def code is inserted when the Layout ⇒ Column ⇒ Off feature is selected.

▌ Moving the Insertion Point in Columns

Table 9-1 shows how to move the insertion point when in columns.

To move	Press
One column to the right	⟨Alt⟩ + ⟨→⟩
One column to the left	⟨Alt⟩ + ⟨←⟩
To previous entry in same column	⟨Alt⟩ + ⟨↑⟩
To next entry in same column	⟨Alt⟩ + ⟨↓⟩

Table 9-1

Column Insertion Point Movement

The insertion point can also be positioned by moving the I-beam and clicking the mouse button once. All editing keys work as usual within the column in which the insertion point is positioned.

▌ Changing the Space Between Columns

To change the amount of space between columns, position the insertion point anywhere in the column to be changed.

- Choose Layout ⇒ Columns ⇒ Define or click on the Columns icon in the power bar and select Define.
- Type the desired width in the Spacing Between Columns text box.
- Choose OK.

The text will automatically adjust to the new width and a preview window will show the general results of your selections.

CAUTION: Be sure your insertion point is positioned in the first line of the column.

▌ Changing Column Widths

To change the width of a column, first position the insertion point in the column to be changed.

- Choose Layout ⇒ Columns ⇒ Define.
- Select the desired width for each column.
- Click on OK.

Another method is to position the mouse pointer on the spacing bar (the solid gray area between columns) shown on the ruler bar and drag it to a new position. As you drag the bar, the status bar shows the position in inches.

▌ Moving or Copying Columns

You can select any amount of text either by dragging the mouse diagonally from one corner of the block to the opposite corner, or by placing the insertion point before the first character, pressing ⟨F8⟩, and using the arrow keys to select text. You must have the Reveal Codes screen displayed and stop selecting text before a Col Def Off code.

- Choose the Cut or Copy icon or Edit ⇒ Cut or Copy.
- Position the insertion point where the text is to be inserted.
- Choose the Paste icon or Edit ⇒ Paste.

Converting Parallel Columns to a Table

Should you decide that you would like to have your parallel columns converted into a table, the task is quite easy. Simply select the text to be converted to a table, then:

- Select Table ⇒ Create.
- Choose the Parallel Column option.
- Choose OK.

You are now ready to begin the exercise for creating parallel columns. When defining the columns, you will specify three parallel block-protected columns and accept the default space of ½". The document you will create is shown in Figure 9-1.

New Book Projects

1994-1995

Name of Book	Description	Publish Date/Binding
First Look at Access	By Kathy Kline and Brian Findlay. Number of pages in manuscript should be approximately 300; final copy from 100-150 pages; first draft due February 15, 1994.	October, 1994 Soft cover
Using CorelDraw	By Mike Williams and Sharon Lewis. Number of pages in manuscript approximately 600; final copy not more than 450. First draft due by April 30, 1994.	December, 1994 Spiral
Working with Focus	By Gayle Allen, Linda Evans, and Vu Nguyan. Number of pages in manuscript should be approximately 450; final copy not more than 375. First draft due by August 1, 1994.	February, 1995 Comb

Figure 9-1

---

1. Choose center justification and very large and bold font. Use Layout ⇒ Justification and Layout ⇒ Font

2. Type New Book Projects

3. Press (Enter) twice

4. Type 1994-1995

Don't forget to turn off the formatting features now and in the following exercises. A fast way is to press (End), which takes the cursor beyond formatting codes such as Bold, Extra Large, and so on. Turn on Reveal Codes to see how that happens.

5. Press (Enter) three times

6. Choose left justification

You are now ready to define the columns.

7. Click on Layout ⇒ Columns

The Columns drop-down menu appears as shown in Figure 9-2.

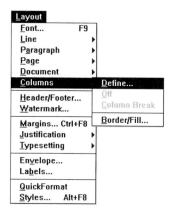

Figure 9-2

8. Click on Define

The Define Columns dialog box appears, as shown in Figure 9-3, with the insertion point blinking in the Number of Columns text box. You want to set three columns.

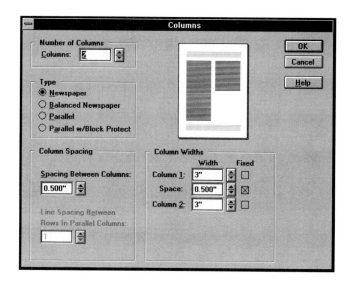

Figure 9-3

9. Type **3** or click on the arrow box to select 3

Move to the Type section of the dialog box.

10. Click on Parallel w/Block Protect

For the remainder of the settings you will accept WordPerfect's defaults. WordPerfect will evenly divide the space into three columns and place a 1/2" (.500") space between the columns.

11. Click on OK

Display the ruler bar to see the margins for the three columns as shown in Figure 9-4.

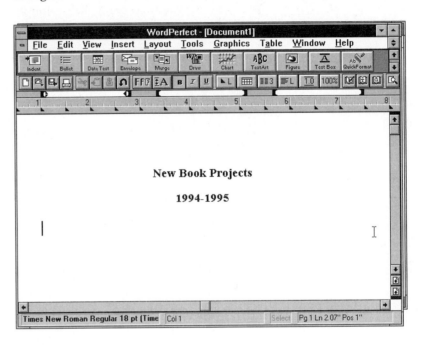

Figure 9-4

12. On your own, activate the Reveal Codes screen and view the codes that have been inserted in your document

Compare your screen to the one shown in Figure 9-5. Press ⊖ to return the insertion point to the correct position for column definition.

You are now ready to begin typing the first column.

13. In bold, type `Name of Book`

To position the insertion point at the top of the second column:

14. Click on <u>L</u>ayout ⇒ <u>C</u>olumns ⇒ <u>C</u>olumn Break

✓ Press Ctrl + Enter

Notice that the status bar reads "Col 2." Now type text for the second column:

15. In bold, type `Description`

16. Press Ctrl + Enter

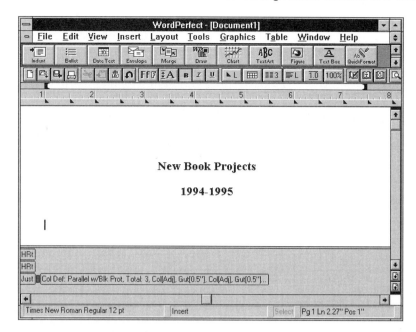

Figure 9-5

Notice that the status bar reads "Col 3." Now type the text for the third column:

17. In bold, type `Publish Date/Binding`

18. Press (Ctrl) + (Enter)

The insertion point is positioned in the first column. Type the text of the second block in the first column:

19. Type `First Look at Access` (don't forget to turn off bold)

20. Press (Ctrl) + (Enter)

21. Type:

    `By Kathy Kline and Brian Findlay; number of pages in manu-`
    `script should be about 300, final copy about 100-150; first`
    `draft due February 15, 1994.`

    Do *not* press (Enter) as you type the text; WordPerfect will automatically keep the text within the column width. (Don't be concerned if your text does not break exactly as shown in Figure 9-1.)

22. Press (Ctrl) + (Enter)

23. Type `October, 1994`

    To position the cursor on the next line:

24. Press (Enter)

25. Type `Soft cover`

26. Press (Ctrl) + (Enter)

27. On your own, type the remainder of the text as shown in Figure 9-1, being sure to press (Ctrl) + (Enter) after each column of text is typed

Your last step is to turn the columns off:

28. Click on <u>L</u>ayout ⇒ <u>C</u>olumns ⇒ O<u>ff</u>

29. Save the document and name it projects

 In this exercise, you will change the space between columns to ¼" and make the middle column larger by dragging the spacing bars on the ruler bar. If you make a mistake at any stage, click on Undo.

1. First, save your document as project2 to keep the original intact

2. Place the insertion point in the column headings line

3. Click on <u>L</u>ayout ⇒ <u>C</u>olumns ⇒ <u>D</u>efine

   Move to the <u>S</u>pacing Between Columns text box.

4. Type `.25"`

5. Click on OK

6. Place the insertion point in the column headings line

7. Put the mouse pointer on the spacing bar between the first and second columns in the ruler bar. Click on the mouse button to display two dashed lines as shown in Figure 9-6

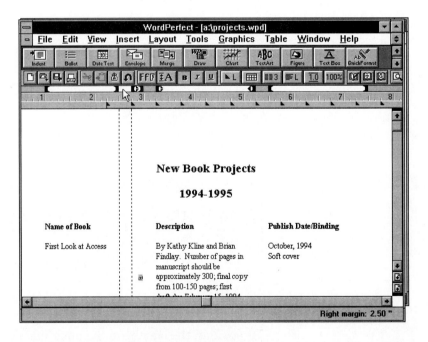

Figure 9-6

8. Drag the spacing bar to the left until the status bar reads "Right margin 2.5"" and release the mouse button

9. Following the same procedure, move the spacing bar between the second and third columns to the right to a right margin position of 5.44"

   The second column is now wider, and the text automatically adjusts to the new width.

10. Save the project2 file and print it

Compare your file to that in Figure 9-7.

New Book Projects

1994-1995

Name of Book	Description	Publish Date/Binding
First Look at Access	By Kathy Kline and Brian Findlay. Number of pages in manuscript should be approximately 300; final copy from 100-150 pages; first draft is due February 15, 1994.	October, 1994 Soft cover
Using CorelDraw	By Mike Williams and Sharon Lewis. Number of pages in manuscript approximately 600; final copy not more than 450. First draft is due by April 30, 1994.	December, 1994 Spiral
Working with Focus	By Gayle Allen, Linda Evans, and Vu Nguyan. Number of pages in manuscript should be approximately 450; final copy not more than 375. First draft is due by August 1, 1994.	February, 1995 Comb

Figure 9-7

If you were to check, you would notice that the column width box from the Columns Define dialog box looks similar to that in Figure 9-8.

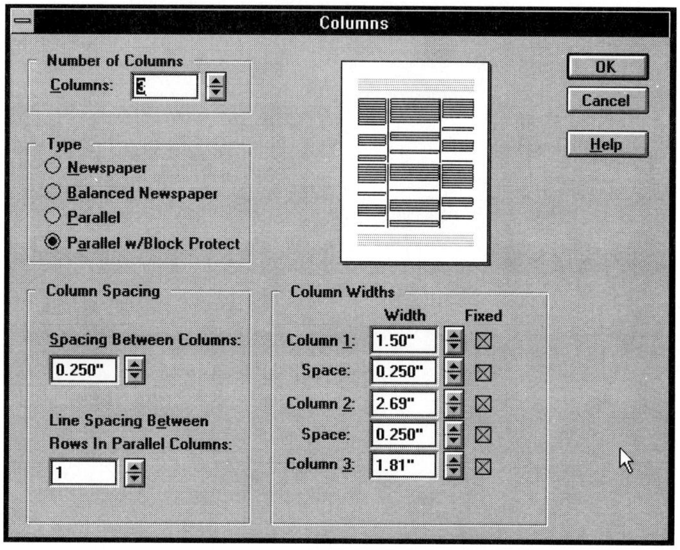

Figure 9-8

In this exercise you will move the last block, the one for Working with Focus, and make it the first block in the document. Before you begin this exercise, save your document in case you are unsuccessful in the cut/paste procedure. If that happens, close the file without saving the changes, then open it again.

Make sure the Reveal Codes screen is displayed.

1. Position the insertion point in front of the "W" in the title "Working with Focus"

2. Press (F8) and select the text, moving the (↓) to a position just in front of the Col Def code box

3. Click on Cut in the power bar or choose Edit ⇒ Cut

   ✓ Press (Ctrl) + (X)

4. Position the insertion point at the beginning of the line that reads "First Look at Access"

5. Click on the Paste icon or choose Edit ⇒ Paste

   ✓ Press (Ctrl) + (V)

6. Save your document

In this exercise, you will convert your parallel columns to a table. Save project2 first as projtabl.

1. Select all three columns, including the column headings, but excluding the title and subtitle. (Don't forget to make sure that selection stops *before* the Col Def:Off code.)

2. Click on T_able ⇒ _Create

   The Convert Table dialog box appears, as shown in Figure 9-9.

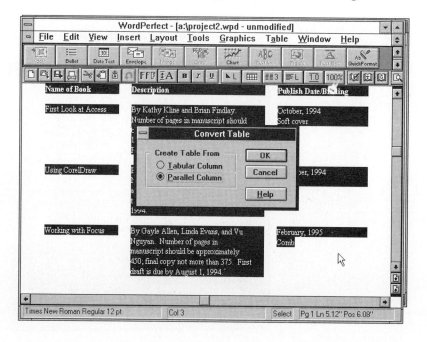

Figure 9-9

3. Click on <u>P</u>arallel Column (if not already marked)

4. Click on OK

5. Save and print the file

Compare your document to the one shown in Figure 9-10. Notice that your title and subtitle are also included.

New Book Projects

1994-1995

Name of Book	Description	Publish Date/Binding
Working with Focus	By Gayle Allen, Linda Evans, and Vu Nguyan. Number of pages in manuscript should be approximately 450; final copy not more than 375. First draft is due by August 1, 1994.	February, 1995 Comb
First Look at Access	By Kathy Kline and Brian Findlay. Number of pages in manuscript should be approximately 300; final copy from 100-150 pages; first draft is due February 15, 1994.	October, 1994 Soft cover
Using CorelDraw	By Mike Williams and Sharon Lewis. Number of pages in manuscript approximately 600; final copy not more than 450. First draft is due by April 30, 1994.	December, 1994 Spiral

Figure 9-10

6. Close the document

Creating Newspaper Columns

Creating newspaper columns requires the same basic steps as does creating parallel columns.

- Choose <u>L</u>ayout ⇒ <u>C</u>olumns ⇒ <u>D</u>efine.
- Select Number of Columns desired.
- Select Newspaper or Balanced Newspaper.
- Select OK.

You can also click on the Columns icon from the power bar; however, the maximum number of columns that can be specified is five. If more than five columns are required, you must use the Define Columns dialog box. Since you already know how to define columns using the Define Columns dialog box, we will use the power bar method.

To create newspaper columns using the Columns icon, put the insertion point in the document where you want columns to start (after any titles or subtitles). Then put the mouse pointer on the columns icon, drag the pointer to the desired number of columns, and release the mouse button. WordPerfect automatically allows ½" of space between columns. A Col Def code box is placed at the beginning of the current paragraph.

When you are typing text in newspaper columns, a new column is automatically started when the insertion point reaches the bottom of a column. To move text to the next column manually, put the insertion point before the text that you want in the next column, and press Ctrl + Enter. If you want the columns to be even on the page, select Balanced Newspaper.

It is possible to put a border around the columns and have a percentage of shading. The border goes around only the columns, not text before the columns start. The same options are available that you saw in the tables feature. To include a border and fill:

- Choose Layout ⇒ Columns ⇒ Border/Fill.
- Select border style.
- Select Fill option.
- Click on OK.

Retrieving a File into an Open Document

When you open a file, WordPerfect automatically places the file into an empty document window. To retrieve a file into an existing file:

- Choose Insert ⇒ File.
- Select the file to be retrieved.
- Choose Insert.
- A message box appears, asking if you want to insert the file into the active document; choose Yes.

The retrieved document is then inserted at the position of the insertion point.

The newsletter document is supplied on a data disk. Insert the data disk into a floppy drive. In this exercise, we will refer to the drive as A; if you are using a different drive, substitute that drive's letter.

You will create a two-column newsletter. You will be told when to retrieve the newsletter document.

1. Using the Layout ⇒ Margins feature, change the left and right margins to .5"

2. Centered, and in bold, extra large, type `The Chronicle`

3. Press Enter twice

4. In centered, bold, italic type, and Very Large format, type `Bookworm Computer Publishing Company`

5. Press Enter twice

6. Choose a small font and type `Winter, 1994`

7. Click on Layout ⇒ Line ⇒ Flush Right

   ✓ Press Alt + F7

8. Type `Volume 15, Issue 2`

9. Press (Enter) three times

You are now ready to define your newspaper columns. First, save and name the file newsltr.

10. Position the mouse pointer on the Columns icon and drag the mouse to select the 2 Columns option

To insert the news.wpd file into your newsletter:

11. Click on Insert ⇒ File

The Insert File dialog box appears, as shown in Figure 9-11, with the insertion point blinking in the Filename text box.

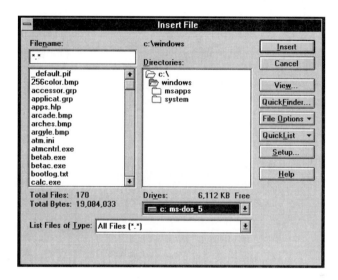

Figure 9-11

12. Type `a:news.wpd`

13. Click on Insert

14. Click on Yes at the prompt to insert the file into the current document

Notice that the text automatically wraps into two columns. To turn the columns off:

15. Position the insertion point at the bottom of the document

16. Click on the Columns icon

17. Click on Columns Off

Add a border around your columns.

18. Click on Layout ⇒ Columns ⇒ Border/Fill

The Columns Border/Fill dialog box displays as shown in Figure 9-12.

19. Click on the ⊙ beside the Border Style text box to get the drop-down box shown in Figure 9-13.

20. Click on Shadow ⇒ OK

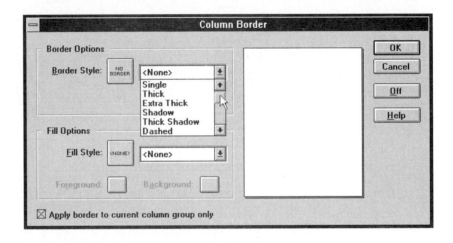

Figure 9-12

Figure 9-13

21. Print the file

    It should be similar to the one in Figure 9-14.

    You aren't pleased with the way it looks. The columns are not even and the border does not go around the entire newsletter.

22. With the insertion point at the beginning of the column, click on Layout ⇒ Columns ⇒ Define

23. Click on Balanced Newspaper ⇒ OK

24. Click on Layout ⇒ Columns ⇒ Border/Fill

25. Click on the Description box and select the picture that shows a line between columns (called Column Between in the arrow drop-down box) shown in Figure 9-15

26. Save again, print, and close

    Your document should look similar to the one in Figure 9-16. The only problem with it now is that it has one line all by itself at the top of column 2. You will learn how to prevent that in Lesson 10.

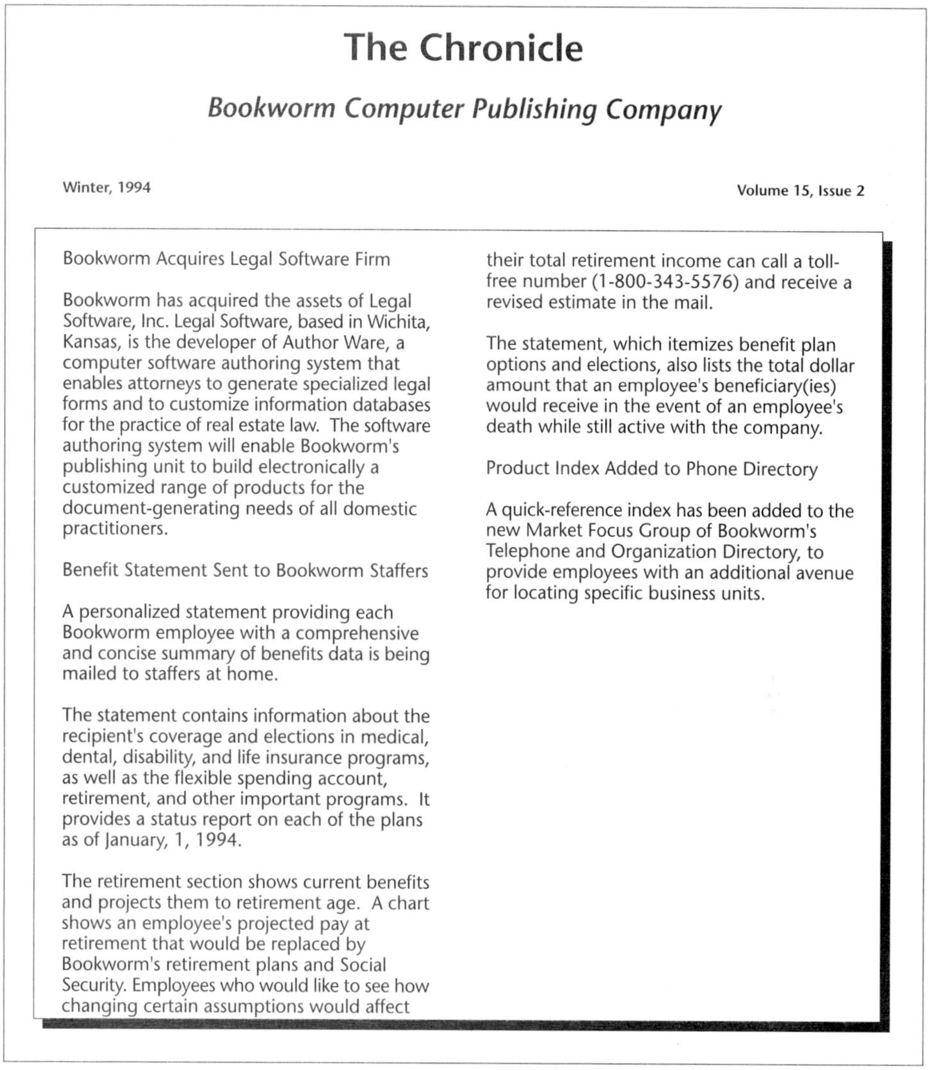

The Chronicle

Bookworm Computer Publishing Company

Winter, 1994   Volume 15, Issue 2

Bookworm Acquires Legal Software Firm

Bookworm has acquired the assets of Legal Software, Inc. Legal Software, based in Wichita, Kansas, is the developer of Author Ware, a computer software authoring system that enables attorneys to generate specialized legal forms and to customize information databases for the practice of real estate law. The software authoring system will enable Bookworm's publishing unit to build electronically a customized range of products for the document-generating needs of all domestic practitioners.

Benefit Statement Sent to Bookworm Staffers

A personalized statement providing each Bookworm employee with a comprehensive and concise summary of benefits data is being mailed to staffers at home.

The statement contains information about the recipient's coverage and elections in medical, dental, disability, and life insurance programs, as well as the flexible spending account, retirement, and other important programs. It provides a status report on each of the plans as of January, 1, 1994.

The retirement section shows current benefits and projects them to retirement age. A chart shows an employee's projected pay at retirement that would be replaced by Bookworm's retirement plans and Social Security. Employees who would like to see how changing certain assumptions would affect

their total retirement income can call a toll-free number (1-800-343-5576) and receive a revised estimate in the mail.

The statement, which itemizes benefit plan options and elections, also lists the total dollar amount that an employee's beneficiary(ies) would receive in the event of an employee's death while still active with the company.

Product Index Added to Phone Directory

A quick-reference index has been added to the new Market Focus Group of Bookworm's Telephone and Organization Directory, to provide employees with an additional avenue for locating specific business units.

Figure 9-14

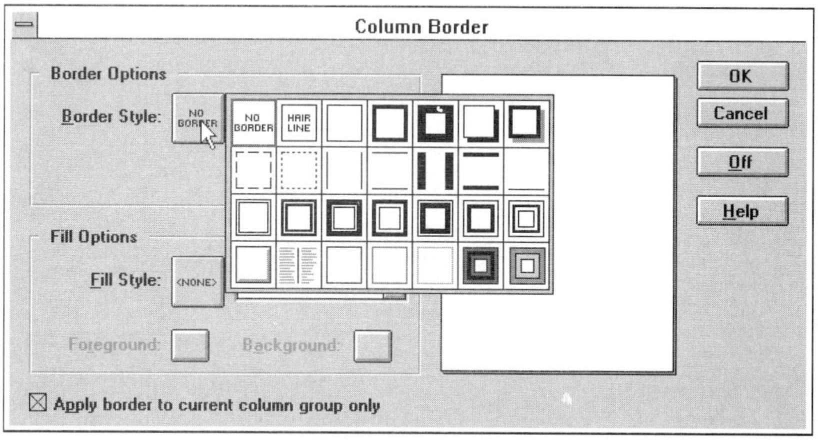

Figure 9-15

The Chronicle

Bookworm Computer Publishing Company

Winter, 1994   Volume 15, Issue 2

Bookworm Acquires Legal Software Firm

Bookworm has acquired the assets of Legal Software, Inc. Legal Software, based in Wichita, Kansas, is the developer of Author Ware, a computer software authoring system that enables attorneys to generate specialized legal forms and to customize information databases for the practice of real estate law. The software authoring system will enable Bookworm's publishing unit to build electronically a customized range of products for the document-generating needs of all domestic practitioners.

Benefit Statement Sent to Bookworm Staffers

A personalized statement providing each Bookworm employee with a comprehensive and concise summary of benefits data is being mailed to staffers at home.

The statement contains information about the recipient's coverage and elections in medical, dental, disability, and life insurance programs, as well as the flexible spending account, retirement, and other important programs. It provides a status report on each of the plans as of January 1, 1994.

The retirement section shows current benefits and projects them to retirement age. A chart shows an employee's projected pay at retirement that would be replaced by Bookworms retirement plans and Social Security. Employees who would like to see how changing certain assumptions would affect their total retirement income can call a toll-free number (1-800-343-5576) and receive a revised estimate in the mail.

The statement, which itemizes benefit plan options and elections, also lists the total dollar amount that an employee's beneficiary(ies) would receive in the event of an employee's death while still active with the company.

Product Index Added to Phone Directory

A quick-reference index has been added to the new Market Focus Group of Bookworm's Telephone and Organization Directory, to provide employees with an additional avenue for locating specific business units.

Figure 9-16

On Your Own

Review of Commands

Description	Menu Commands	Function Keys
Set up columns	_____	_____
Turn columns on	_____	_____
Turn columns off	_____	_____
Insert manual column break	_____	_____
Convert parallel columns to a table	_____	_____
Right-align text (flush right)	_____	_____
Retrieve a file into a document	_____	_____

Lesson Review

1. What is the difference between newspaper-style and parallel columns?

2. What is the purpose of the Parallel Block Protect feature?

3. What keystrokes move the insertion point from the end of one parallel column to the beginning of the next?

4. When is it necessary to enter a Column Off code?

5. What two keys do you press to move the insertion point horizontally within a column?

6. How do you move to the next column?

7. How do you move to the previous column?

8. What are the steps in copying a column?

9. What steps create a table from a document with parallel columns?

10. What is the maximum number of columns possible when you create columns using the power bar?

11. What is the amount of spacing between columns automatically set in WordPerfect?

12. What command will bring a selected file into an existing document?

▌ Assignments

9-1 Directions

1. Create the document at the top of the next page with three parallel columns using the default settings.
2. Leave one blank line after the title and one after the column headings.
3. Type in the information shown, using boldface and all capital letters for the title and column headings.
4. Change the spacing between columns to .3".
5. Save the document as handout.wpd.
6. Print the document and close it.

9-2 Directions

1. Open handout.wpd.
2. Save it as table201.wpd.
3. Convert the parallel columns into a table.
4. Save the document again, print it, and close the file.

9-3 Directions

1. Bold centered, and in a very large font size, type the title MODERN DATABASES.
2. Add two blank lines after the title.
3. Define two newspaper-style columns.
4. Insert the file database.wpd from your work disk.

HANDOUT FOR CMS 201 CLASS

LANGUAGE	PRIMARY USERS	COMMENTS
Assembler	Systems	Highly efficient; system-dependent; difficult to read and understand
BASIC	Education; simple programs	Simple to learn; limited functions
C	Systems	Developed by Bell Laboratories as part of the UNIX operating system
COBOL	Business	Old language; word; extensive file-handling capability; durable
FORTRAN	Scientific	Old language; has limitations, but very popular in science
Pascal	Education Systems, Scientific	Excellent structured language; limited I/O

5. Save the document as dbnewslt.wpd.

6. Print and close the document.

9-4   Directions

1. Open dbnewslt.wpd.

2. Change the column definition to Balanced Newspaper.

3. Compare the document to the printout from the previous exercise.

4. Save, print, and close the document.

9-5   Directions

1. Open dbnewslt.wpd.

2. Place a vertical line between the newspaper columns.

3. Create a horizontal line below the title and above the Column Definition.

4. In a small font, boldfaced, type:

(today's date)	Volume 1, Issue 1

5. Save, print, and close the document.

9-6 Directions

1. Open dbnewslt.wpd.

2. Place a border of your choice around the *entire* document. Experiment with a number of borders until you find one to your liking.

3. Save, print, and close the document.

9-7 Directions

1. Create a newsletter containing two columns.

2. Name the newsletter "Modern Data Processing" or some other appropriate title.

3. Insert the document internet.wpd from your data disk into the current document.

4. Format the newsletter using borders, different fonts, and so on until you feel you have an attractive document.

5. Save the file under a name of your choice.

6. Print and close the document.

9-8 Directions

1. Create a class schedule with three parallel columns.

2. Make the first column the name of the course, the second column a description of the course, and the third column the time the course meets.

3. Adjust the widths of the columns appropriately.

4. Assign a title and column headings.

5. Save the file under a name of your choice.

6. Print the document.

7. Covert the document to a table.

8. Print, save, and close the document.

10 Enhancing Documents with Graphics

Objectives

After completing this lesson, you will be able to:

- Define WordPerfect's graphic boxes
- Create and edit a graphic box
- Create a text box
- Create and delete user and table boxes
- Resize a graphic box
- Edit and rotate a graphic image
- Change a border style
- Add a caption to a box
- Create, edit, and move graphic lines
- Activate the Widow/Orphan feature

Graphics

WordPerfect's graphic feature is sophisticated and complex. In fact, word processing packages in general are acquiring more **desktop publishing** (DTP) capabilities, such as inserting graphs and logos into columns of text, inserting horizontal and vertical lines, and easily changing specific types of text throughout a document. Many of the documents previously done only in DTP packages, such as letterheads, newsletters, forms, simple brochures, and so on, can be done in a good word processing package. WordPerfect has a very wide range of font styles and sizes and allows you to add clip art images, logos, charts, or drawings to your documents. Those graphics can then be sized, moved, rotated, and edited; the borders and background patterns can be changed; and a Draw feature is available within WordPerfect to add text, draw freehand, and so on. WordPerfect has some graphic files built in, or you can use a graphic image from one of the software packages supported by WordPerfect. Finally, it is much easier to see what your document looks like as you are creating it with WYSIWYG (What You See is What You Get). WYSIWYG shows onscreen the document exactly as it will print.

When working with graphics, there are four basic steps: (1) type your text, (2) enter it in columns if desired, (3) insert graphics, and (4) edit the graphics and borders, if necessary.

The graphic can be enlarged or reduced, moved horizontally or vertically, and rotated any number of degrees. You can change the way the text flows around the inserted graphic. Also, you have many options for the borders surrounding the graphic and the background pattern or shading of the graphic. The graphic is visible on the screen in all views.

Types of Graphic Boxes

When you insert a graphic, it is contained in a box. The borders of the box depend on what kind of graphic you selected. There are eight different graphic box styles: Figure, Text, Equation, Table, User, Button, Watermark, and Inline Equation. Although these boxes are designed to hold specific contents, the contents and the types of box borders can be interchanged. You can put an image, text, or an equation into any graphic box style.

By default, the Figure, Text, and Equation styles are on the Graphics menu and can be accessed as follows:

- Select Graphics.
- Select Type of Box.
- Name of file, if any.

The other styles that are not on the Graphics menu—Table, User, Button, Watermark, and Inline Equation—must first be assigned to the Graphics menu.

- Select Graphics ⇒ Graphics Styles ⇒ Menu ⇒ Select style ⇒ OK.

They can then be accessed as described above.

Figure Box

The Figure box style is the most appropriate for images, charts, and drawings. The border of a figure box is a single narrow line. To insert a graphic image, first place the insertion point where you want the figure to appear.

- Select Graphics ⇒ Figure.

Text Box

The Text box style is useful for quotes, annotations, and any other text-type material. The length cannot exceed one page. You can use any of WordPerfect's features, including type size and appearance, centering, tabs, tables, and even columns. Choosing the Rotate button allows you to rotate text in the text box. Text boxes have a thick line on the top and bottom of the box. To insert a Text box:

- Select Graphics ⇒ Text.

The box appears onscreen with the insertion point inside. You can then either type text directly into the Text box or insert a file containing the text by selecting Insert ⇒ Filename.

If you want to go back into a Text box to add or edit information, you must:

- Select the Text box.
- Select Content from the feature bar.
- Select Edit.

Your insertion point will go into the Text box and you can edit the text.

Equation and Inline Equation Box

The Equation box style is used for lengthy scientific and mathematical equations and formulas. The Inline Equation box can be used to insert an equation in a single line of text. There are no visible borders on either type of equation box. To create an Equation box:

- Select Graphics ⇒ Equation.

The Inline Equation box is not on the Graphics menu. To create an Inline Equation:

- Select Graphics ⇒ Custom Box ⇒ Inline Equation.

Table Box

A Table box is most appropriate for tables, spreadsheets, and statistical types of data. A Table box has a thick line at the top and bottom. The Table box is not on the Graphics menu. To create a Table box:

- Select Graphics ⇒ Custom Box ⇒ Table ⇒ OK.

User Box

You can create a User box to insert a figure, drawing, chart, table, or anything else around which you want no border. A User box has no frame or shading; in fact, it is invisible until it is assigned contents. The User box is not on the Graphics menu. To create a User box:

- Select Graphics ⇒ Custom Box ⇒ User ⇒ OK.

Button Box

A Button box can be used for a keystroke or an icon. Some of the content possibilities are text, clip art images, or drawings. To create a Button box:

- Select Graphics ⇒ Custom Box ⇒ Button ⇒ OK.

Watermark Box

A watermark is a drawing, logo, or clip art image printed behind the text in your document. It can be printed on every page or on odd and even pages just like a header or footer. There is no border. You can add Watermark to the Graphics menu, but you can also insert one from the Layout menu. To insert a watermark:

- Select Layout ⇒ Watermark ⇒ Create.
- Select Figure from the feature bar.
- Select file name ⇒ OK.

The watermark covers most of the center of your document and is faded so the text can be read over it.

Numbering Boxes

Each box type is numbered consecutively by WordPerfect. That is, if you have both table and figure boxes, the table boxes are numbered separately from the figure boxes. If a box is deleted or added, the remaining boxes of that type are automatically renumbered. Box numbers are not displayed unless a caption is added to the box.

▌ Creating a Graphic Box

WordPerfect has provided more than 100 clip art images, border styles, and short notes, such as "Confidential" and "Draft," for your use. These files are in the WPWIN60\GRAPHICS directory and have a .WPG file extension. For example, the full path for the file golf.wpg would be c:\wpwin60\graphics\golf.wpg. Graphic images can also be imported from other software programs into your WordPerfect document. Table 10-1 lists formats currently supported by WordPerfect.

Extension	File Format
.BMP	Windows 3.x and OS/2 Presentation Manager bitmap
.CGM	Computer Graphics Metafile
.DRW	Designer
.DXF	AutoCAD format
.EPS	Encapsulated PostScript
.HPG	Hewlett-Packard Graphics Language
.PCX	PC Paintbrush
.PIC	Lotus 1-2-3 PIC
.PICT	Macintosh
.TGA	True Vision Targa
.TIF	Tag Image File
.WMF	Windows Metafile
.WPG	WordPerfect Graphics

Table 10-1

If you have a graphic image in the Windows Clipboard, it can be pasted directly into a document by choosing Edit ⇒ Paste. No other steps are required.

When a graphic box is created, WordPerfect automatically inserts a Box code. When activated it shows the type of the box and name of the file, if any. To delete a graphic box, simply delete the code.

In the following exercises, you will bring up your newsletter (newsletr.wpd) from the last lesson, update the date and issue number, delete the text, insert two images in Figure boxes, insert a quotation in a text box, and an image in a user box. You will edit the boxes later in the lesson. Refer to the completed newsletter in Figure 10-21 to see what the final version will look like.

1. Open newsletr.wpd

2. Change the date to `Spring, 1995` and the Volume to `16, Issue 1`

3. In the Reveal Codes screen, delete the Col Def code box

   Be sure to leave the Col Border code box.

4. Delete the rest of the text

5. Select Layout ⇒ Columns ⇒ Define ⇒ Newspaper ⇒ 2 ⇒ OK

   Be sure the red cursor bar falls immediately after the Col Def code box.

6. Click on Insert

   The Insert menu displays as shown in Figure 10-1.

   Note the cursor bar position in the Reveal Codes screen.

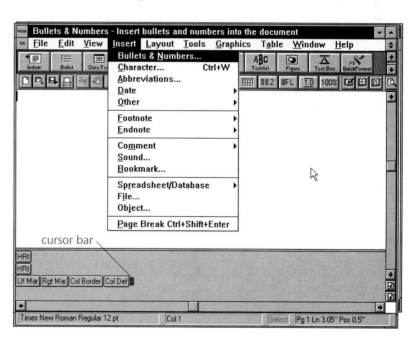

Figure 10-1

7. Click on File

   You will now insert a file from your data disk. Be sure your disk is in the drive.

8. Select interfac.wpd ⇒ Insert ⇒ Yes

   You document should be displayed in two columns.

9. Save your file as `internew`

   Save the file frequently throughout this lesson.

10. Position the insertion point (after Col Def code) at the beginning of the first line of the first paragraph, which reads "Author Guidelines . . ."

11. Click on <u>G</u>raphics

    The Graphics menu displays as shown in Figure 10-2.

Figure 10-2

12. Click on <u>F</u>igure

    The Insert Image file box appears, as shown in Figure 10-3.

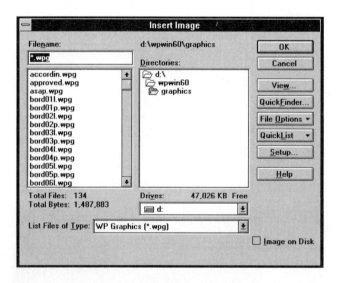

Figure 10-3

You want to select the graphic file called pencilbr.wpg.

13. Click on pencilbr.wpg ⇒ OK or double-click on the file name

    The pencil figure is inserted in your document and the box is "selected"—black sizing points surround it. Also, note that the Graphic feature bar is displayed. Your screen should look similar to the one in Figure 10-4.

    You want to make sure the graphic is anchored to the paragraph, that is, that if the paragraph's text shifts, the graphic will move with it.

14. Click on <u>P</u>osition in the feature bar

    The Box Position dialog box displays as shown in Figure 10-5.

feature bar ———

sizing point ———

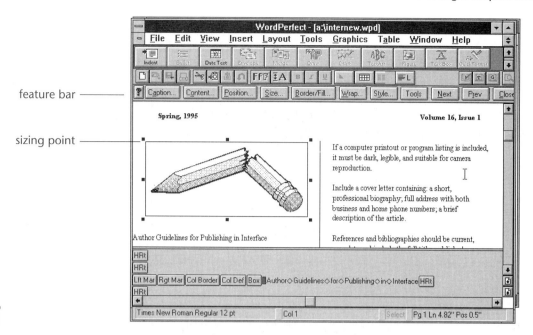

Figure 10-4

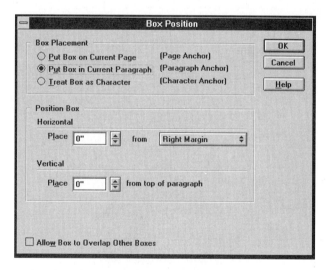

Figure 10-5

15. Click on the radio button Put Box in Current Paragraph (if not already marked)

16. Click on OK and deselect the box (click the mouse pointer somewhere outside the box)

 You will place another Figure box beneath the heading "International Interface Institute."

1. Move the insertion point below the line that reads "International Interface . . ." (first page, second column)

2. Click on Graphics ⇒ Figure

3. Click on world.wpg ⇒ OK

The image is larger than you want, but you will size it later. Next, insert a Text box and put a quotation in it.

4. Position the insertion point on the line "Microcomputer Applications . . ." (second page, column two)

5. Click on <u>G</u>raphics ⇒ <u>T</u>ext

The Text box displays with the insertion point inside the borders. You are now ready to begin typing the text in the Text box. You must not move the insertion point out of the box before you finish typing your text or you will have to edit it to get back in the box. To do so, click on the right mouse button and select Edit.

6. Type the following in bold and italic (make the errors):

```
"The 1994 Institute was one of the best lerning
experiences I've ever had. Count on my for next year."
Elaine Eggers
```

7. Click outside the box to move the insertion point

You are going to insert an image in a Figure box and later change the Figure box to a User box. You'll also add a User box to the Graphics menu for future use.

1. Move the insertion point to the line below "Golf Tournament" (page two, column two, last paragraph)

2. Click on <u>G</u>raphics ⇒ <u>F</u>igure

The clip art image you want is on your data disk.

3. Type `a:golf.wpg` and click on OK

The selected box displays in your document and moves to page three, along with the golf paragraph.

4. Deselect the box

5. Click on <u>G</u>raphics ⇒ <u>G</u>raphics Styles

The Graphics Styles option box displays as shown in Figure 10-6.

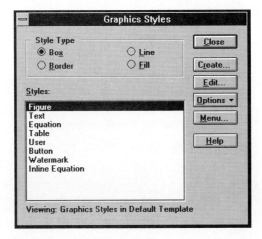

Figure 10-6

6. Click on <u>M</u>enu

The Edit Graphics Menu box displays as shown in Figure 10-7.

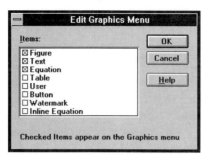

Figure 10-7

7. Click on <u>U</u>ser ⇒ OK ⇒ <u>C</u>lose

Editing Graphic Boxes

Once you have inserted a graphic box, both the contents of the box and the border can be edited. You can use the commands on the Graphic feature bar or, with the mouse pointer in the graphic box, click the right mouse button to display the commands of a drop-down menu. The available commands are Caption, Content, Position, Size, Border/Fill, Wrap, Style, and Tools. When you first insert a graphic, the feature bar is displayed. To edit an image if the feature bar is not displayed, select the graphic and click on the *right* mouse button to get a drop-down menu. Click on feature bar.

If you click on the *right* mouse button while in the graphic box, the box will be selected and a drop-down menu of the graphic functions will display, including the option to either display or hide the feature bar. Depending on what has already been done to the graphic, it may also give you the options to Create Caption and Edit Figure. If you check Create Caption, WordPerfect will number the figure and put your insertion point beside the figure number for you to space once and type in the caption text.

If you select Edit Figure, WordPerfect moves your figure into WP Draw, which has paint and draw program functions. You will use only one of these features in your exercises, but you can experiment further on your own. You can also activate WP Draw by double-clicking while in the graphic box.

Caption

You can create a caption that includes the number of the graphic box and some brief, descriptive text. If you do not want the caption to be numbered, simply delete the number. You can type the caption, edit the caption, and specify the position—top, bottom, left side, right side—and set the width and style of the caption. The graphic's number will display in bold. If you do not wish to have the graphic numbered, press (Backspace) to delete the number. Then type the caption and choose <u>C</u>lose.

Content

You can specify what the content in the graphic box is to be, and you can move the contents in the box horizontally and vertically.

Position

A graphic can be placed in a document in one of three ways: (1) anchored to a page, (2) anchored to a paragraph, or (3) anchored to a character. For example, if the graphic is anchored to a paragraph and that paragraph is moved to another page, the graphic goes with it. The default anchor is to a paragraph. If a graphic box is inserted into a blank, whole page, it is placed at the right margin and begins at the same vertical position as the insertion point. If a graphic box is inserted into empty columns, it is placed in the same vertical position and column as the insertion point. Otherwise, the position is dependent upon the paragraph next to it. The position can be changed by selecting the Position dialog box from the feature bar. When you first insert a graphic, the feature bar is displayed. When you edit a box after the feature bar is gone, click on the right mouse button to get a drop-down menu to show the feature bar.

Size

The size of the graphic will depend on the specific image selected. In most cases it is approximately 3.5" wide, with the height depending on the graphic. The size and width can be changed by selecting Size from the feature bar and entering specific measurements for the box or by dragging the sides with the mouse (the latter will be explained later).

Border/Fill

WordPerfect offers more than 20 different styles of borders, such as thin single line, double, thick single, thick double, shadow, and so on. It is also possible to select more than 20 different patterns within the box, and if you are working with color, a different foreground and background color. These options are accessible from the Border/Fill command on the Graphics feature bar. If you choose Customize Styles from the Border dialogue box, you can change the style of the inside border and depth of inside and outside border space, among other features.

Wrap

The manner in which text is arranged around a box is known as *wrap*. Text can be on either side of the box, on both sides of the box, top and/or bottom of the box, or on all sides. Choose the way you want your text to wrap from the Graphics feature bar.

Box Type

Once you have chosen a box type for a figure or a drawing, you can change that type by selecting Style from the Graphics feature bar.

Tools

By using Tools from the Graphics feature bar, you can rotate the image in the box, move the image, scale the image, and mirror it vertically or horizontally, among other choices. Selecting Tools will display an array of icons from which to choose.

▌Editing a Graphic Box with the Mouse

The easiest way to move or resize a graphic box is with the mouse. Before a graphic box can be moved, resized, or deleted, it must first be selected. To select a graphic box, position the mouse pointer anywhere inside the box and click the left mouse button once. WordPerfect shows that the box is selected by surrounding it with eight black boxes, called *sizing points*. To deselect a graphic box, position the mouse pointer outside the box and click once. You can change the size of the box by dragging any of the sizing points in or out. Put the pointer on one of the sizing points to get a double-headed arrow, then drag the side to the correct location.

Moving a Graphic Box

To move a graphic box with the mouse, first select the box, position the mouse inside it (the mouse pointer changes to a four-headed arrow), press the left mouse button, and drag the graphic to the new location. Release the mouse button.

Resizing a Graphic Box

Before a graphic box can be resized, it must first be selected. To change a box's size, first position the mouse pointer on one of the sizing points (the mouse pointer changes to a double-headed arrow), press the mouse button, and drag the sizing point until the box is the desired size.

To change both the horizontal and vertical dimensions of the box simultaneously, use one of the sizing points at the corner of the box. To change only one side (dimension) of the box, use the sizing handle in the middle of that side.

▌Deleting a Graphic Box

Delete a graphic box by first selecting it, then pressing (Del). If you inadvertently delete a box, you can immediately restore it by choosing either Edit ⇒ Undo or Edit ⇒ Undelete.

In this exercise, you are going to move the first Figure box, which contains the broken pencil image. You'll also enter a caption with the figure number. The first step is to select the box. Go to the beginning of your columns.

1. With the mouse pointer inside the pencil graphic box, click the left mouse button once

   The box is selected and the pointer becomes a cross of double-headed arrows.

2. Holding down the mouse button, drag the graphic box to the middle of the page, and release the mouse button

   Compare the placement of your graphic box to that shown in Figure 10-8.

3. Drag the box back to its original position and deselect it

   Remember, to deselect a graphic box, simply click the mouse anywhere outside the box. Now, let's add the caption.

4. Select the pencil Figure box

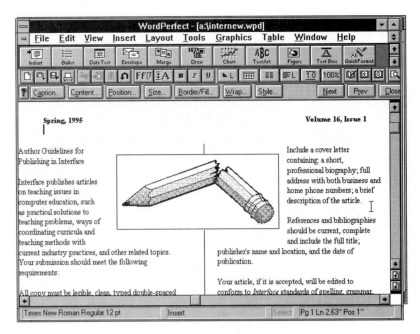

Figure 10-8

5. With the pointer inside the box click the *right* mouse button

The drop-down menu shown in Figure 10-9 appears.

Figure 10-9

6. Select Create Caption

7. After "Figure 1," space once, click on bold, and type `Don't give up!`

8. Deselect the figure

You are going to make the World graphic smaller, change the border, and add a caption.

1. Select the World graphic

2. Drag to size it to approximately 1.90" by 1.30"

   If you aren't sure how to get that size, click on the right mouse button and select Size. You can mark Set and type in the Width and Height you want.

3. Click on the right mouse button and select Border/Fill

   The Box Border/Fill Styles dialog box displays as shown in Figure 10-10.

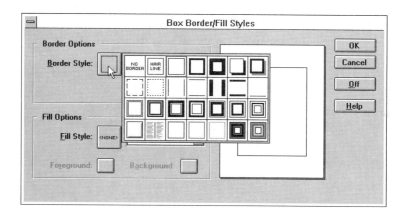

Figure 10-10

4. Click on Border Style

The border options display as shown in Figure 10-11.

Figure 10-11

5. Select the sixth one on the top row (Shadow) and click OK

6. Click on Caption in the feature bar

The Box Caption dialog box displays as shown in Figure 10-12.

Figure 10-12

7. Click on Edit

8. After the caption "Figure 2," type `It's Worldwide!`

You want to correct the errors in the Text box and add a background pattern.

1. Select the Text box

2. Click the right mouse button

3. Click on Edit Text

The insertion point is in the text box. Be careful not to click outside the box until after you are finished.

4. Correct "lerning" and change "my" to "me"

5. Click on Border/Fill

6. Click on Fill Style

The patterns shown in Figure 10-13 display.

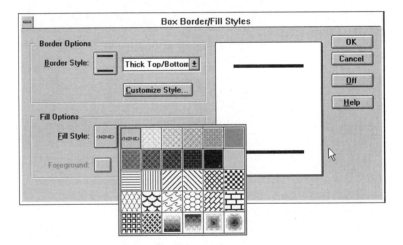

Figure 10-13

7. Click on the second pattern from the left in the top row

8. Click on OK

9. Deselect the Text box and select the golf graphic

You will change the box type to a User box, make the image smaller, and practice using the scale and rotate features. Display the Graphics feature bar if it is not displayed.

1. Click on Style

The Box Style dialog box displays as shown in Figure 10-14.

2. Click on User ⇒ OK

3. Click on Size

The Box Size dialog box displays as shown in Figure 10-15.

4. Under Width, Click on Set

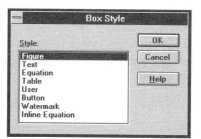

Figure 10-14

Figure 10-15

5. Type `1.80"`

6. Under Height, Click on S<u>e</u>t, then type `1.97"` and click on OK

7. If the golf image is not about one line below the title "Golf Tournament," click on the image and drag it there

8. Click on <u>W</u>rap

   The Wrap Text option box displays as shown in Figure 10-16.

Figure 10-16

9. Under Wrapping Type, click on <u>C</u>ontour

10. Under Wrap Text Around, click on <u>R</u>ight Side ⇒ OK

11. Double-click on the golf club

    The WP Draw screen opens with the graphic enlarged.

You want to type some words next to the club, but first you have to make a box to allow you to insert the text.

1. Click on the "A" in the tool box on the left side of the screen

2. Move your pointer, which changes to a cross, to the top of the box

3. Hold down the left mouse button and use the cross to drag and release, defining a box about ½" by 2" as shown in Figure 10-17

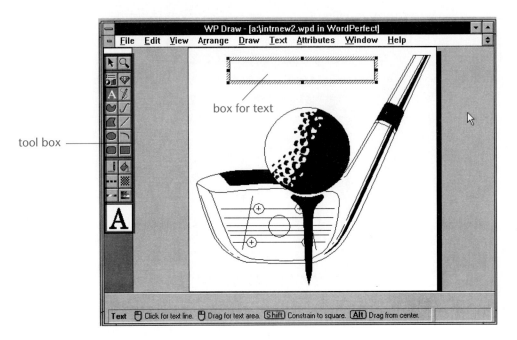

Figure 10-17

The insertion point is in the box.

4. Type `Bring Your Clubs`

5. Deselect the box, then click on File

6. Click on <u>C</u>lose and Return to (your document)

7. Answer the prompt "Save Changes?" with <u>Y</u>es

   You want to change the scale and rotate the image in the box.

8. Click on the right mouse button and select <u>I</u>mage Tools

   The tools display as shown in Figure 10-18.

9. Click on the bottom right icon (where the pointer is in Figure 10-18)

   The Image Settings option box displays as shown in Figure 10-19.

10. Click on <u>S</u>cale Image

11. Change Scale <u>X</u> to .8

12. Change Scale <u>Y</u> to .8

13. Click on R<u>o</u>tate Image

14. Set <u>A</u>mount to 5.0 and click on OK

    You decide that you don't like the way the changes look.

15. Activate the tool box

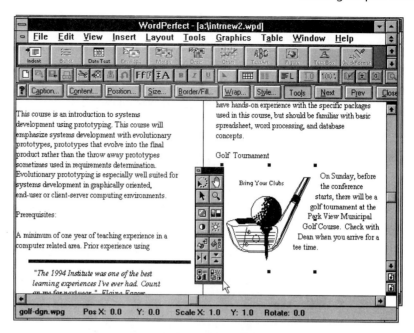

Figure 10-18

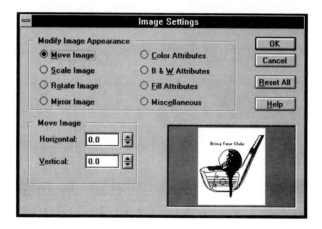

Figure 10-19

16. Click on the fifth icon down on the left side, Reset All Image Attributes

Your original settings are restored. Deselect the box.

Creating Graphic Lines

The Graphic Line feature allows you to insert horizontal and vertical lines in a document. Lines call attention to headlines, create borders at the top and bottom of a page, and separate columns. The lines can be in shades of gray or black and can vary in thickness. A GraphLine code box is inserted at the insertion point. When expanded, it shows the type and size of the line.

To create a horizontal or vertical line, first position the cursor where the line is to appear. Next, choose Graphics ⇒ Horizontal Line or Vertical Line. A narrow line appears. To change the length, thickness, style of the line, or spacing above or below the line, put the mouse pointer on the line and click the right mouse button. Select Edit from the drop-down menu to display the Edit Graphics Line dialog box. To save your settings and close the dialog box, choose OK.

▌ Editing Graphic Lines with the Mouse

Using the mouse is the easiest way to change the width, length, and position of a graphic line. As with graphic boxes, you must first select a line before it can be edited. To select a graphic line, position the mouse pointer somewhere on the line, then click the left mouse button once. To indicate that the line is selected, WordPerfect places sizing points around the line.

Changing Line Thickness and Length

To change the thickness of a line, position the mouse pointer on one of the sizing points in the middle of the line, click and drag the sizing point to the line's desired thickness, and release the mouse button.

To change the length of a line, position the mouse pointer on one of the sizing points at the end of the line, click and drag to the desired length, and release the mouse button. If you select a sizing point on any corner, it changes the height and width of the line at the same time.

Moving Graphic Lines

To move a graphic line, first select the line, then position the mouse pointer on the line, but not on a sizing point. The pointer changes to a four-headed arrow. Click and drag the mouse to the desired location, and release the mouse button.

▌ Widows and Orphans

You are already familiar with one of the parts of the Keep Text Together feature—Protect a Block. Another option is called Widow/Orphan, a term that defines a single line or part of a line alone at the top or bottom of a page. If you select the Widow/Orphan feature, single lines will not be left so. The exception to this is the one-line heading. Because that heading line is actually a separate paragraph, the Widow/Orphan feature will ignore it. When you've finished formatting a document, you still must read through it to be sure you don't have any heading lines in inappropriate places. To activate the Widow/Orphan feature, choose:

- <u>L</u>ayout ⇒ <u>P</u>age ⇒ <u>K</u>eep Text Together ⇒ Widow/Orphan ⇒ OK.

The last things you are going to do to your document are to add horizontal lines in the heading and prevent the first and last lines of a paragraph from being left alone on a page. Now you will add the finishing touches to your newsletter.

1. Scroll to the subtitle "Bookworm . . ."

2. Put the insertion point about halfway between "Bookworm" and the Issue line

3. Click on <u>G</u>raphics ⇒ <u>H</u>orizontal Line

    ✓ Ctrl + F11

    A narrow line is inserted from margin to margin.

4. With the mouse pointer on the line, click to select it

    Sizing points are shown around the line.

5. Put the pointer on one of the sizing points to get the double-headed arrow

6. Click and drag the line to widen it to about ¼"

7. Put the insertion point at the left margin on the line directly below "Spring, 1995"

8. Click on <u>G</u>raphics ⇒ <u>H</u>orizontal Line

✓ Ctrl + F11

Another narrow line is inserted.

9. With the mouse pointer on the line, click the right mouse button

A drop-down menu displays.

10. Click on <u>E</u>dit ⇒ Horizontal Line

The Edit Graphics Line dialog box displays as shown in Figure 10-20.

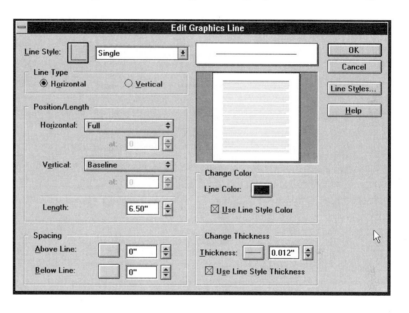

Figure 10-20

11. Click on <u>L</u>ine Style

12. Click on the third choice from the left, bottom row

13. In the Change Thickness box, change Thickness to .045". Check to see that the following are set: Line Type to Horizontal, the Position/Length to (Horizontal) Full, (Length) 7.50"

14. Click on OK

15. Click on <u>L</u>ayout ⇒ <u>P</u>age ⇒ <u>K</u>eep Text Together ⇒ Widow/Orphan ⇒ OK

To make sure your newsletter looks right, look at it in the Two Page mode (<u>V</u>iew ⇒ <u>T</u>wo Page). You can't read it, but you can see if your graphics and lines look well-placed. If not, while in this mode you can select the graphic or line and drag it to make it look better on the page. Don't forget to save any changes.

16. Save and print your newsletter

It should look similar to Figure 10-21.

object-oriented programming using C++. It will feature extensive hands-on program development using Turbo C++ or Borland C++ on an IBM-compatible system. Course materials will provide useful examples for those who plan to teach this subject in the future.

Prerequisites:

Participants should have studied at least one other programming language or be familiar with programming concepts. A knowledge of C programming is not absolutely necessary but would be helpful. A knowledge of MS/PC DOS would also be helpful.

Local Area Networks

This course is designed for the beginning user of data communications products. It is a practical, hands-on approach to data communications including LANs. The class will set up and install Novell NetWare. Use of public and remote dial-in facilities and considerations for setting up a lab will be included.

Systems Development with Prototyping

This course is an introduction to systems development using prototyping. This course will emphasize systems development with evolutionary prototypes, prototypes that evolve into the final product rather than the throw away prototypes sometimes used in requirements determination. Evolutionary prototyping is especially well suited for systems development in graphically oriented, end-user or client-server computing environments.

Prerequisites:

A minimum of one year of teaching experience in a computer related area. Prior experience using Microsoft Windows applications is helpful but not required.

Microcomputer Applications Using Windows 3.1

Participants in this course will develop teaching strategies for popular application programs: word processing, spreadsheet and database software within Microsoft's Windows 3.1 environment. Participants will have the option of working with the latest Windows applications including Word, WordPerfect, Excel, Quattro Pro, Lotus and Paradox. Special consideration will be given to integrating applications using Object Linking and Embedding (OLE) techniques and other Windows features. Strong emphasis will be placed on developing teaching methodologies for the utilization of cutting edge software in course development and personal use.

Prerequisites:

Teaching experience and knowledge of popular application packages. Participants do not need to have hands-on experience with the specific packages used in this course, but should be familiar with basic spreadsheet, word processing, and database concepts.

Golf Tournament

Bring Your Clubs

On Sunday, before the conference starts, there will be a golf tournament at the Park View Municipal Golf Course. Check with Dean when you arrive for a tee time.

"The 1994 Institute was one of the best learning experiences I've ever had. Count on me for next year." Elaine Eggers

Figure 10-21

Page 1

Creating a Letterhead

You will now create a letterhead for the Bookworm Computer Publishing Company to be used in a later lesson. The letterhead you will create is shown in Figure 10-22.

1. Select the typeface of your choice using the Font menu option, and select a font size of 64 points

   If you do not have a 64-point size available, choose the largest proportional font you have.

2. Click on Graphics ⇒ User

3. Click on Content from the feature bar

object-oriented programming using C++. It will feature extensive hands-on program development using Turbo C++ or Borland C++ on an IBM-compatible system. Course materials will provide useful examples for those who plan to teach this subject in the future.

Prerequisites:

Participants should have studied at least one other programming language or be familiar with programming concepts. A knowledge of C programming is not absolutely necessary but would be helpful. A knowledge of MS/PC DOS would also be helpful.

Local Area Networks

This course is designed for the beginning user of data communications products. It is a practical, hands-on approach to data communications including LANs. The class will set up and install Novell NetWare. Use of public and remote dial-in facilities and considerations for setting up a lab will be included.

Systems Development with Prototyping

This course is an introduction to systems development using prototyping. This course will emphasize systems development with evolutionary prototypes, prototypes that evolve into the final product rather than the throw away prototypes sometimes used in requirements determination. Evolutionary prototyping is especially well suited for systems development in graphically oriented, end-user or client-server computing environments.

"The 1994 Institute was one of the best learning experiences I've ever had. Count on me for next year." Elaine Eggers

Prerequisites:

A minimum of one year of teaching experience in a computer related area. Prior experience using Microsoft Windows applications is helpful but not required.

Microcomputer Applications Using Windows 3.1

Participants in this course will develop teaching strategies for popular application programs: word processing, spreadsheet and database software within Microsoft's Windows 3.1 environment. Participants will have the option of working with the latest Windows applications including Word, WordPerfect, Excel, Quattro Pro, Lotus and Paradox. Special consideration will be given to integrating applications using Object Linking and Embedding (OLE) techniques and other Windows features. Strong emphasis will be placed on developing teaching methodologies for the utilization of cutting edge software in course development and personal use.

Prerequisites:

Teaching experience and knowledge of popular application packages. Participants do not need to have hands-on experience with the specific packages used in this course, but should be familiar with basic spreadsheet, word processing, and database concepts.

Golf Tournament

Bring Your Clubs

On Sunday, before the conference starts, there will be a golf tournament at the Park View Municipal Golf Course. Check with Dean when you arrive for a tee time.

Figure 10-21
Page 2

Bookworm
Computer Publishing Company

Figure 10-22

The Box Content dialog box displays as shown in Figure 10-23. Next, get an image file from your data disk.

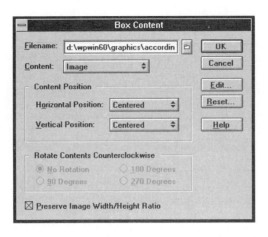

Figure 10-23

4. In the Filename text box, type `a:bookworm.wpg`

5. Click on OK twice

6. Click on Size

7. In the Width text box, click on Set and type `1.15"`

8. In the Height text box, click on Set, type `1"` and click OK

9. Move the graphic box to the upper left margin of your document

The next step will add additional space between the graphic box and the text.

10. Click on Border/Fill

11. Click on Customize Style

The Customize Border dialog box displays as shown in Figure 10-24.

12. In the Outside Space text box, type `0.467"` and click on OK

13. Click on OK again to return to your document screen

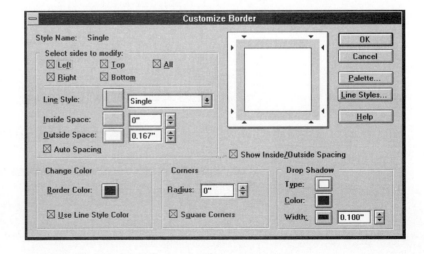

Figure 10-24

14. In boldface, type `Bookworm`

    If you do not have a 64-point font available, select the word "Bookworm" and choose <u>L</u>ayout ⇒ F<u>o</u>nt ⇒ Relative <u>S</u>ize: <u>E</u>xtra Large ⇒ OK.

15. Press (Enter)

16. Choose a 24-point, bold, italic and type `Computer Publishing Company`

    If you do not have a 24-point font available, type the text, select it, and choose <u>L</u>ayout ⇒ F<u>o</u>nt ⇒ Relative <u>S</u>ize: <u>V</u>ery Large ⇒ OK, and deselect the text.

17. Press (Enter) twice

    Now you will create the graphic line.

18. Click on <u>G</u>raphics ⇒ <u>H</u>orizontal Line

    ✓ Press (Ctrl) + (F11)

    A narrow line is inserted. Select it and click on the right mouse button to get a drop-down menu.

19. Click on <u>E</u>dit ⇒ Horizontal Line

    The Edit Graphics Line dialog box displays.

20. Click on <u>L</u>ine Style

    The Line Style choices display as shown in Figure 10-25.

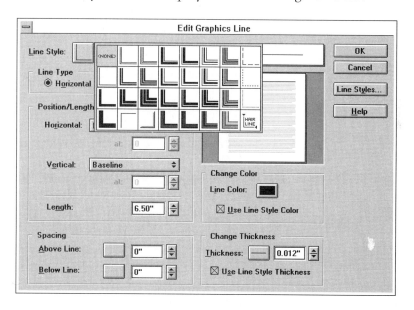

Figure 10-25

21. Click on the style on the third row, sixth one from the left. Check to see that the following are set: Position/Length to (Horizontal) Full, Length to 6.50", Thickness to .012", and place a checkmark in Use Line Style Thickness box

22. Click on OK

    NOTE: You may need to adjust the space between the text and your graphic line.

Now change the font back to its original size.

23. Click on <u>L</u>ayout ⇒ F<u>o</u>nt ⇒ Times New Roman 12 pt ⇒ OK

24. Close the file and save it as letrhead

25. Exit WordPerfect

On Your Own

Review of Commands

Description	Menu Commands	Function Keys
Create a Figure box	_____	_____
Create a Text box	_____	_____
Create a User box	_____	_____
Edit graphic image	_____	_____
Enlarge or reduce graphic size	_____	_____
Move an image	_____	_____
Reset image to original	_____	_____
Edit border style	_____	_____
Create caption	_____	_____
Create graphic line	_____	_____

Lesson Review

1. What are the four steps to create a graphic image?

2. How can you manipulate images?

3. What are the eight box types available in WordPerfect?

4. What are the distinguishing characteristics of each of the following box types: Figure, Table, Text, and User?

5. How are boxes numbered?

6. When a graphic box is created, what is the default size?

7. How do you select a box, and how does it appear after it is selected?

8. How do you move a box once it has been selected, and how does the pointer change?

9. What is a watermark?

10. What changes can be made to a border?

11. How do you include a caption with a graphic, and what types of lines can be inserted?

12. What characteristics of a line can be changed?

13. Explain the meaning of Widow/Orphan and describe the steps to invoke the command.

14. How do you delete a graphic box?

▌ Assignments

10-1 Directions

1. Retrieve dbnewslt.wpd, save it as dbgraph.wpd.

2. Using the default settings, insert a horizontal line between the title and the body of the newsletter.

3. Press (Enter).

4. Select a small font, bold, and type:

```
(today's date)                                          Volume I, Issue 1
```

5. Press (Enter).

6. Add another horizontal line below the date and volume.

7. Edit the second line. Choose Line Style: Thick/Thin 2 (second row, fourth from the left).

8. Save, print, and close the document.

10-2 Directions

1. Open dbgraph.wpd.

2. Position the insertion point in column 2, just above the second paragraph: "There are three types of . . ."

3. Insert group.wpg in a Figure box.

4. Save, print, and close the document.

10-3 Directions

1. Open dbgraph.wpd, and save it as dbgraph2.wpd. Edit the Figure box as follows.

2. Add the caption: `Databases help us communicate.`

3. Delete the figure number.

4. Change the size of the Figure box to approximately 2.5" by 2.5".

5. Move the Figure box near the center of the page.

6. Save, print, and close the document.

10-4 Directions

1. Open dbgraph.wpd and save it as dbgraph3.wpd.

2. At the end of the first column, create a Text box reading: `Setting up a database is expensive, but well worth the cost!`

3. Shade the Text box, bold the text, and choose any font style. Use a slightly larger font size than is used in your newsletter.

4. Save, print, and close the document.

10-5 Directions

1. Open database.wpd save as dbgraph4.wpd.

2. Format the document as a newsletter (choose a style that suits you).

3. Enhance the newsletter with graphics. Use the four basic steps of working with graphics to format graphics for the newsletter. Include an appropriate number of the different types of boxes.

4. Save, print, and close the document.

10-6 Directions

1. Open a new document and save it as assign.wpd.

2. Retrieve womdesk.wpg in a graphics box located at the top right of your document.

3. On the left side of the document, boldfaced, type:

```
(your name)
Class Title
Time class meets
Assignment:
```

4. Change the Border Style of the graphic to No Border and change the size to approximately 3" by 2".

5. Save, print, and close the document.

10-7 Directions

1. Open assign.wpd, save it as assign2.wpd.

2. Add a vertical line along the left margin.

3. Edit the line as follows. Choose Line Style: button at bottom right (third from left, bottom row). Increase the thickness of the line to approximately 1/10".

4. Save, print, and close the document.

10-8 Directions

1. Create a personal letterhead using a graphic from WordPerfect's clip art. Insert the graphic in the document at a location of your choice. It can be at the top, bottom, or somewhere along the margins.

2. Include your name and address, attractively placed, at the top of the page (use an expressive font and font size—be creative).

3. Remove the border from around the graphic.

4. Place a horizontal line in a style of your choice below your name and address.

5. Save, print, and close the document.

11 Merging and Importing Documents

Objectives

After completing this lesson, you will be able to:

- Define fields and records
- Define and create form and data files
- Merge form and data files
- Merge from the keyboard
- Import a file from a database or spreadsheet application

The Merge Feature

This lesson introduces you to the Merge feature, which is designed to combine a form document with a data document to create personalized letters, labels, envelopes, and so on. For example, if you need to send the same letter to several people, using the Merge feature will save you time. If you use other database programs such as dBase IV, it is possible to enter the data from selected fields into WordPerfect without typing them again.

To use the Merge feature, you must create two files: a **form file** and a **data file**. The form file contains the information and the formatting codes for the form letter, envelope, or label you want to send to each individual. The list of variables (such as names, addresses, and phone numbers for different individuals) is found in the data file. Compiling the data file involves two steps—naming the fields and entering the data. When Merge is executed, the specified variables in the data file are combined with the form file to produce an original document for each record in the data file.

A word processing program's merge feature is similar to a database, in that it uses records and fields. All the information pertaining to one individual or entity is called a **record**. Each record can contain as many units of information as needed; these are called **fields**. For example, some of the fields in one student's record might be name, address, telephone number, ID number, major, GPA, number of credit hours completed, and so on. WordPerfect makes the task of creating the files much simpler for you by entering most of the necessary commands, such as End Field and End Record. These codes are important when merging the two files so that the printer will know what information to put in which place.

The data file can hold as many records as required. You are limited only by how much disk space is available on your computer or network.

Creating a Data File

Before you create a data file, you need to determine what information should be included, such as addresses, employee information, inventory lists, and so on. You might also want to consider including information for future use that is not pertinent to the immediate project. For example, if you are creating a telephone list, you might not need the individuals' addresses. However, at a later time, you might want to send letters to those individuals, so it is efficient to create a data file that contained addresses *and* telephone numbers.

To create a data file:

- Choose <u>T</u>ools ⇒ <u>Me</u>rge.
- Choose <u>D</u>ata.
- Enter your first field name in the <u>N</u>ame a Field text box.
- Press (Enter).

The field appears in the <u>F</u>ield Name list and the insertion point moves back to the <u>N</u>ame a Field Box. The field names can be typed in either upper- or lowercase. Continue to add fields, pressing (Enter) after each field name. If you make a mistake, you can edit field names by selecting the field name from the Field Name list and choosing Delete or Replace. When you have entered all your field names, choose OK.

The Quick Data Entry Box appears, listing all the field names you have entered, each with a blank text box to receive information for each field. To enter information for each field:

- Type information in the first field of the first record (for example, type the name for the first person on your list).
- Press (Enter) or choose <u>N</u>ext Field.
- Enter the information for the next field (for example, a street address).
- Press (Enter) to go to the next field, and so on.

Quick Data Entry automatically brings up a blank record when you have filled in all the information for one record. Continue to fill in field information for each record. When you are finished entering information:

- Choose Close.
- You will be asked if you want to save the information; choose Yes.
- The Save Data File As dialog box will appear. Add a .dat extension to the data document to identify it as a data file.
- Name your file (for example, list.dat).

Your data file is now complete and ready to be used with a form document. An example of a data file is shown in Figure 11-1.

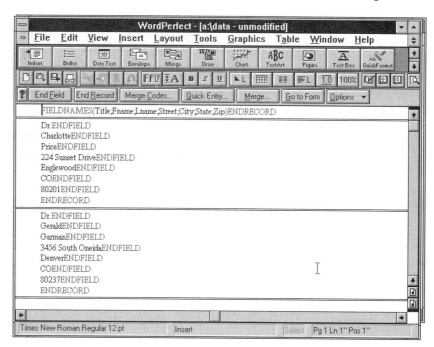

Figure 11-1

Creating a Form File

The form file is the skeleton for the merged output. It contains the text you want to appear in each merged document. It also contains merge codes, such as ENDFIELD and ENDRECORD, which control the merge and retrieve data information from the data files. To create a form file:

- Choose Tools ⇒ Merge.
- Choose Form.
- Type in the name of the file with the data to merge in the Associate a Data File name text box.
- Choose OK.

You can also select Go to Form from the Merge control bar and select Create from the Associate dialog box directly from the data file window.

A blank screen appears on which to create your Form document.

Type your document as you would any other document, with the exception of variable data placement. For each location, (for example, where you want a name or address to appear) select:

- Insert Field from the Merge feature bar that appears at the top of the screen. The Insert Field Name or Number Dialog box appears.
- Select the desired field name from the Field Names list.
- Choose Insert.

You can also double-click on the field name to insert it into your document.

When you have completed your form document, close the Insert Field Name or Number dialog box and save your form document with the .frm extension to identify it as a form. An example of a form file is shown in Figure 11-2.

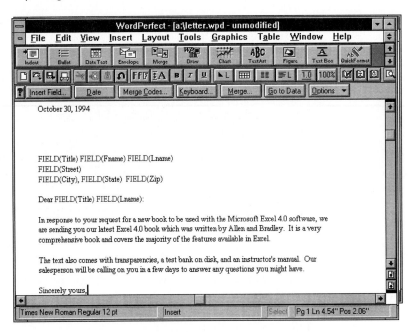

Figure 11-2

Performing the Merge

When both documents are complete, you are ready to merge the two together.

- Select Tools ⇒ Merge or select Merge from the Merge control bar to begin merging the form and data document you just selected.

- Select Merge from the Perform Merge Box.

The Perform Merge dialog box appears. From this dialog box, you can select any form and data document. Current Document appears in the Form File window. Pressing the arrow at the left of the window allows you to select another form by choosing Select File from the pop-up list.

The Data File window lists the associated data file. However, you can select any data file by choosing Select File from the pop-up list to the right of the Data File window.

The Output File window shows: <New Document>. This means the merged documents will display onscreen in a new document window. For other options, see the list of options displayed at the right of the window (press the arrow).

The data will merge and the merged documents will display on your screen. You can then review them, print them, and save them as individual files, if desired.

Merging from the Keyboard

It is sometimes convenient to have a form document with merge codes that allow variable information to be filled in directly from the keyboard. This is useful when data changes frequently or only a few forms need be filled out. For example, you may send out a memo to three or four members of your department each month. It may be more convenient to fill out the variable data from the keyboard than to create a data file.

To create a form document with keyboard merge codes:

- Choose Tools ⇒ Merge or click on the Merge button on the button bar ((Shift) + (F9)).

- Choose Form.
- The Create Form File dialog box will appear; select None (no data file is associated with this form).
- Select OK.

The document screen appears with the Merge feature bar at the top and you are ready to create your form document.

- Type your document as you would any other except where you wish to place a code for variable data.
- Select Keyboard from the Merge feature bar at the top of the document screen.
- The Insert Merge Code dialog box appears.

In the prompt window, name the type of information you wish to place at the code, such as "date" or "amount donated."

- Select OK or press (Enter).

The Keyboard (variable) code is placed at the insertion point in your document and a prompt tells you what kind of information to fill in. Continue creating your form document, repeating this procedure for each keyboard code. Save your document and use an extension such as .mrg or .frm to identify it as a keyboard merge file.

To perform the merge:

- Select Merge from the Merge feature bar.
- Select Merge from the Perform Merge box.
- Select OK.

The form document is displayed with the insertion point at the first keyboard code. A Merge Message dialog box is also displayed, prompting you with the data type to be entered.

- Type the data at the insertion point.
- Press Continue.

The insertion point moves to the next prompt. Enter information at each prompt and press Continue until the document is complete.

▌ Merging to Labels

WordPerfect's Label feature can be used to create mailing labels, file folder labels, and diskette labels. You can type the labels individually or merge them from a data file. A file containing preset label definitions comes with WordPerfect. To create a label form file, first place the insertion point on the page where you want labels to begin.

- Choose Tools ⇒ Merge ⇒ Form.
- Associate a data file that contains the information for the labels.
- Press OK.
- A blank document screen appears in which to set up your form document. Choose Layout ⇒ Labels.

- Select type of labels: Laser, Tractor Fed, or Both.
- Select label definition.

A preview box will show the labels as they would appear on a page, and the description of the labels will display in the Label Details text box.

- Choose Select.
- A blank label will show onscreen; choose Insert Field.
- Add the fields from the associated data file in the places they should appear on the label.
- Save the label file with an .frm extension.

You then merge the data file with the label form file to create the labels. Table 11-1 shows the keystrokes to use when moving around in labels.

Keystroke	Function
Ctrl + Enter	End text and move to next label
Enter	End a line of text in a label
Alt + PgDn	Move to next label
Alt + PgUp	Move to previous label
Ctrl + G	Move to a specific label number

Table 11-1

Moving in Labels

You can also print individual labels from a file of labels, much as you would print individual pages from a document.

- Choose File ⇒ Print ⇒ Multiple Pages ⇒ Print.
- Select the pages to print at the Page(s).
- Type number (see Table 11-2).
- Choose Print.

Keystroke	Label(s) Printed
3	Label 3
3,5,8	Labels 3, 5, and 8
3 8	Labels 3 and 8
3-	Label 3 through end of document
-3	Beginning of document through label 3
3-8	Labels 3 through 8
1-3 8	Labels 1 through 3 and label 8
3,5,9-15	Labels 3, 5, and 9 through 15

Table 11-2

Selecting Labels to Print

 In the next exercise you will create a data file. Make sure you have a blank document onscreen and that your WordPerfect button bar is displayed.

1. Press <u>T</u>ools ⇒ M<u>e</u>rge or choose Merge from the button bar

   ✓ Press (Shift) + (F9)

   The Merge dialog box displays as shown in Figure 11-3.

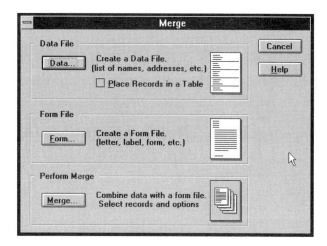

Figure 11-3

2. Click on <u>D</u>ata

   The Create Data File dialog box appears, with the insertion point in the <u>N</u>ame a Field window, as shown in Figure 11-4.

Figure 11-4

3. Type `Fname`

4. Press (Enter)

   The first field name appears under <u>F</u>ield Name List and the <u>N</u>ame a Field window is ready to enter the next field name.

5. Type `Lname`

6. Press (Enter)

   The second field name appears on the <u>F</u>ield Name List.

7. Type the following field names using the procedure demonstrated:

```
Street
City
State
Zip
```

8. Click on OK

The Quick Data Entry window opens as shown in Figure 11-5, and you are ready to enter information into your fields. With the insertion point positioned in the Fname field,

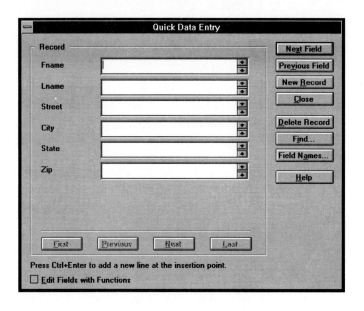

Figure 11-5

9. Type Susan

10. Click on Next Field (or press Enter)

11. Type Smith

12. Click on Next Field (or press Enter)

13. Type 210 S. Moore Avenue

14. Choose Next Field (or press Enter)

15. Type Denver

16. Choose Next Field (or press Enter)

17. Type CO

18. Choose Next Field (or press Enter)

19. Type 80010

20. Press Enter

A new record will appear. Enter the following information into the Quick Data Entry box using the procedure demonstrated.

21. Type:

```
Sara
Shaw
611 Dalton Road
Harrisburg
PA
17109

Thomas
Towerton
1234 Dentmire Court
Arlington
VA
22204

Benjamin
Bitterman
435 Elm Street
Columbus
OH
43211
```

If you make a mistake as you type in the names, move the insertion point to the error and correct it.

22. Click on Close

The Save Changes to Disk dialog box displays.

23. Click on Yes

The Save Data File As dialog box displays as shown in Figure 11-6 (your screen will look different).

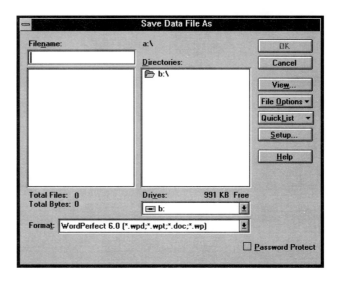

Figure 11-6

24. Name your file list.dat

25. Click on OK

Your screen should look similar to that in Figure 11-7.

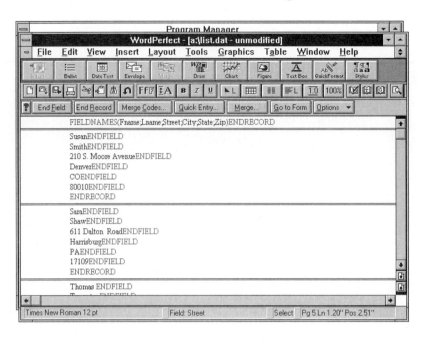

Figure 11-7

26. Close your file

 You will now create a form document. In this exercise you are creating a letter to send to the reviewers (whose names you've just typed in). You will use the letterhead you made in Lesson 10.

1. Open letrhead.wpd

2. Display the Reveal Codes screen

3. Move the red cursor to just after the Font Size:12 pt code box

4. Press (Enter) three times

5. Save the file as review.frm

6. Hide the Reveal Codes screen

 7. Click on Tools ⇒ Merge

   ✓ Press (Shift) + (F9)

8. Click on Form

9. Click on Use File in Active Window (if not already marked)

10. Click on OK in the Create Merge File dialog box

    The Create Form File dialog box appears as shown in Figure 11-8.

11. Type **list.dat** in the Associate a Data File text box (if the file name is not already shown)

    This step creates a link between your data file and the form file.

12. Click on OK

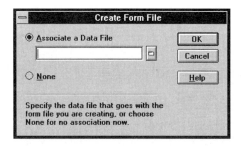

Figure 11-8

 You will now begin typing your form letter. Your screen displays the Merge control bar as shown in Figure 11-9, and many of the commands can be selected from there.

Figure 11-9

1. Click on Insert ⇒ Date ⇒ Date Code from the main menu

   ✓ Press (Ctrl) + (Shift) + (D)

2. Press (Enter) four times

3. Click on Insert Field from the Merge control bar

   The Insert Field Name option box displays as shown in Figure 11-10.

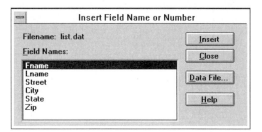

Figure 11-10

4. Click on Fname ⇒ Insert

5. Press (Spacebar)

6. Click on Lname ⇒ Insert

7. Press (Enter)

8. Double-click on Street

9. Press (Enter)

10. Double-click on City

11. Type a , (comma) and press the (Spacebar)

12. Double-click on State

13. Press (Spacebar) twice

14. Double-click on Zip

15. Press (Enter) twice

16. Type `Dear` (Spacebar)

17. Double-click on Fname

18. Type `:` and press (Enter) twice

19. Click on Close in the Insert Field Name or Number dialog box

20. Type the following text in bold:

    `RE: Review of WordPerfect for Windows 6.0: A Practical`
    `Approach`

21. Press (Enter) twice

22. Type the following text:

    `Enclosed with this letter are Chapters` (Spacebar)

    Here you will place a keyboard code that will cause WordPerfect to stop so you can enter data from the keyboard.

23. Click on <u>K</u>eyboard in the Merge control bar

    The Insert Merge prompt dialog box displays in Figure 11-11. To designate a prompt for the keyboard merge code at the insertion point:

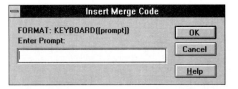

Figure 11-11

24. Type `Chapter Numbers` (Enter)

    A keyboard prompt is inserted as "Chapter Numbers."

25. Press (Spacebar) once and continue to type:

    `which the authors have recently sent me.`

26. Press (Enter) twice and type:

    `We would appreciate your reviewing these chapters and`
    `returning them to me by` (Spacebar)

27. Click on <u>K</u>eyboard

28. Type `Date` in the Enter Prompt text box and press (Enter)

29. Type a period, space twice, and continue:

    `I am enclosing more review forms for you to fill out`
    `concerning the questions asked. Continue to mark any`
    `pages and return the marked pages` <u>`plus your suggestions`</u>
    <u>`by chapter and page number`</u> `as you have done in the past.`

    `We all appreciate your help. I am sure the result will be`
    `a better book!`

30. Play your sign macro here, or type:

```
Sincerely,



your name
Acquisitions Editor
```

31. Spell check, and save your document as review.frm

Your document should look similar to the one in Figure 11-12.

32. Close the file

Bookworm

Computer Publishing Company

(today's date)

FIELD(Fname)FIELD(Lname)
FIELD(Street)
FIELD(City)FIELD(State)FIELD(Zip)

Dear FIELD(Fname):

Re: Review of <u>WordPerfect for Windows 6.0: A Practical Approach</u>

Enclosed with this letter are Chapters KEYBOARD(Chapter Numbers) which the authors have recently sent me.

We would appreciate your reviewing these chapters and returning them to me by KEYBOARD(Date). I am enclosing more review forms for you to fill out concerning the questions asked. Continue to mark any pages and return the marked pages <u>plus your suggestions by chapter and page number</u> as you have done in the past.

We all appreciate your help. I am sure the result will be a better book!

Sincerely,

your name
Acquisitions Editor

Figure 11-12

In this exercise you will merge the data file, list.dat, you just created with the form file, review.frm. At each keyboard code you will insert information as directed.

1. Click on <u>T</u>ools ⇒ <u>M</u>erge

   ✓ Press (Shift) + (F9)

2. Click on <u>M</u>erge

   The Perform Merge dialog box displays as shown in Figure 11-13.

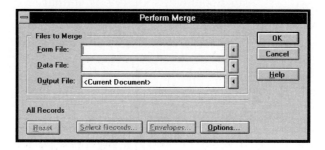

Figure 11-13

3. Click on the arrow box to the right of the <u>F</u>orm File window

4. Click on Select File from the pop-up list

5. Double-click on review.frm

6. Tab to <u>D</u>ata File

7. If list.dat is not shown in the file box, click on the arrow box to the right of the <u>D</u>ata File window

8. Click on Select File ⇒ list.dat

9. Click on OK

   The merge will begin to execute. It will stop at the first keyboard code. The Merge Message will prompt "Chapter Numbers."

10. Type 1, 2, and 3 (Spacebar)

11. Click on <u>C</u>ontinue from the Merge Control box

    The merge will stop at the second keyboard code, "Date."

12. Type August 28

13. Click on <u>C</u>ontinue

    The merge continues to the second document and stops at the keyboard merge.

14. Type the following information using the preceding procedure for the next three letters. Don't forget to click on <u>C</u>ontinue after each entry:

    4, 5, and 6
    September 1
    7, 8, and 9
    September 5
    10, 11, and 12
    September 10

Your merge is now complete. The three letters are in one file on the screen. They have not been saved. Scroll through the letters to see if they are correct, and if so, print them. Your letters should look similar to the one in Figure 11-14. Close the document without saving.

Computer Publishing Company

(today's date)

Susan Smith
210 S Moore Avenue
Denver, CO 80010

Dear Susan:

Re: Review of <u>WordPerfect for Windows 6.0: A Practical Approach</u>

Enclosed with this letter are Chapters 1, 2, and 3 which the authors have recently sent me.

We would appreciate your reviewing these chapters and returning them to me by August 28. I am enclosing more review forms for you to fill out concerning the questions asked. Continue to mark any pages and return the marked pages <u>plus your suggestions by chapter and page number</u> as you have done in the past.

We all appreciate your help. I am sure the result will be a better book!

Sincerely,

your name
Acquisitions Editor

Figure 11-14

In the next exercise you will create a data file and merge it with a form file of predefined labels. If you do not have labels available, simulate on paper.

1. Create a data file as you did at the beginning of the lesson using <u>T</u>ools ⇒ M<u>e</u>rge ⇒ <u>D</u>ata

2. Name the three fields Name; Street; and City,State,Zip

3. Enter the data shown in Figure 11-15

Larry and Susan Jenson 309 Hamilton Avenue Silver Spring, MD 20901	Gary and Sarah Foss 19619 Singing Hills Drive Northridge, CA 91326	Gary Downs 30 Winterberry Court Cumberland, ME 04021
Lee and Marla Nevers 31853 47th Avenue South Auburn, WA 98002	Al and Polly Williams 9705 Talleyran Cove Austin, TX 78750	Bill and Sue Stewart 254 S. Lakeview Blvd. Chandler, AZ 85225
Mildred Ward 2900 S. Valleyview Blvd. Las Vegas, NV 89102	Paul and Ruth Kindler 1437 Timberwood Lane St. Louis, MO 63146	Larry and Kristi Doneson 680 N. Range Colby, KS 67701

Figure 11-15

4. Save the file as newauthr.dat and close it

5. Click on Tools ⇒ Merge ⇒ Form

6. In the Associate a Data File box, type `newauthr.dat` and click OK

7. Click on Layout ⇒ Labels

The Labels dialog box displays as shown in Figure 11-16.

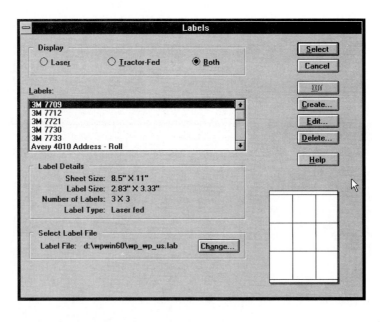

Figure 11-16

8. In the Display box, click on Both (if not marked)

9. In the Labels text box, select 3M 7730

The Label Details section should display as follows:

Sheet Size: 8.5" x 11"
Label Size: 2.63" x 1"
Number of Labels: 3/10
Label Type: Laser fed

A small preview screen will show how the labels will appear on the page.

10. Click on <u>S</u>elect

A blank label is displayed for you to add fields as desired.

11. Click on Insert Field

The fields of the newauthr.dat file are displayed.

12. Double-click on Name and press (Enter)

13. Double-click on Street and press (Enter)

14. Double-click on City,State,Zip and click on Close

Your screen should look similar to the one in Figure 11-17.

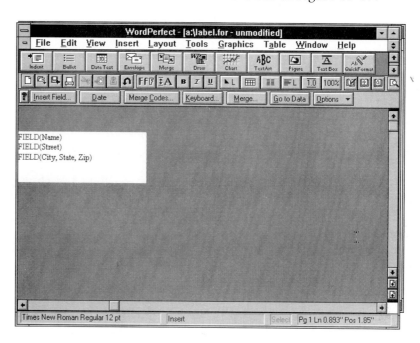

Figure 11-17

15. Save the file as labl7730.frm and close it

Next, you'll merge the data file with the labels.

1. Click on the Merge Icon

2. Click on M<u>e</u>rge from the dialog box

The Perform Merge dialog box displays.

3. Make sure labl7730.frm displays in the Form File text box and newauthr.dat displays in the Data File text box

4. Click on OK

The labels will display as was shown in Figure 11-15.

5. Save the file as labelsna (for "labels, new authors")

6. Print the file on regular paper and close it

Importing Spreadsheet and Database Files

You may want to use information from a database file or a spreadsheet in a word processing document. Two features allow you to do that: **importing** and **linking**. The importing feature copies information from the spreadsheet or database file one time only. The linking feature automatically updates the information in your WordPerfect document and keeps it current with any changes made in your original spreadsheet or database document. We will use only the importing feature. To import a file:

- Choose Insert ⇒ Spreadsheet/Database.
- Choose Import.
- In the Data Type drop-down list, choose the database or spreadsheet software from which you are importing.
- In the Filename text box, type the file name to be imported.
- In the Import As text box, choose Merge Data File, Table or Text.
- Choose OK.
- In the Field or Range text box, select the fields or ranges to be inserted.
- Click on OK.

Merging to Envelopes

You can create an envelope form file and merge it with a data file.

- Choose Tools ⇒ Merge ⇒ Form.
- Type in data file to associate and choose OK.
- Choose Layout ⇒ Envelope.
- Select or type a return address.
- Place the insertion point in Mailing Addresses text box.
- Choose Field.
- Select the field and choose Insert.
- Press (Enter) to end the line.
- Choose Field again, select the field, and choose Insert.
- Continue until all fields are chosen.
- Choose Append to DOC.
- Save, name, and close the form file.

After the envelope form file is completed:

- Choose the Merge icon from the button bar.
- Choose Merge.
- Specify the locations of form, data, and output files.
- Choose OK.

In the next exercise, you will import a dBase IV file stored on your data disk as a WordPerfect data file, then merge it with envelopes. (Again, use regular paper to print.)

1. Click on Insert ⇒ Spreadsheet/Database

The Spreadsheet/Database menu displays as shown in Figure 11-18.

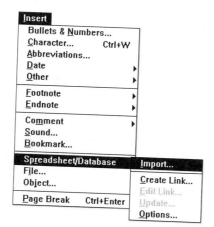

Figure 11-18

2. Click on Import

The Import dialog box displays as shown in Figure 11-19.

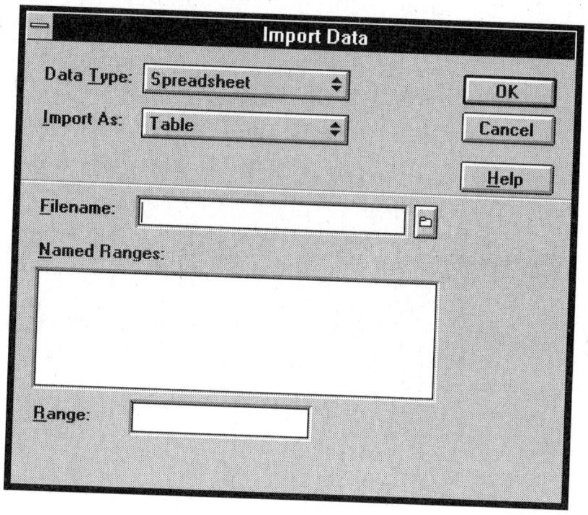

Figure 11-19

3. Click on Data Type: and use the pointer to select dBase

4. Click on Import As: Merge Data File

5. In the Filename text box, click to retrieve A:(or B:)dbnames.dbf

The file name dbnames.dbf should display in the text box.

6. For a list of the fields, press (Enter)

The database fields will display in the Fields text box as shown in Figure 11-20.

7. Make sure all the fields except "phone" are marked

8. Click on OK

The fields are brought in as a WordPerfect merge file. All the ENDFIELD and ENDRECORD codes are included in the document as shown in Figure 11-21.

9. Save the file as dbnames.dat

10. Close the file

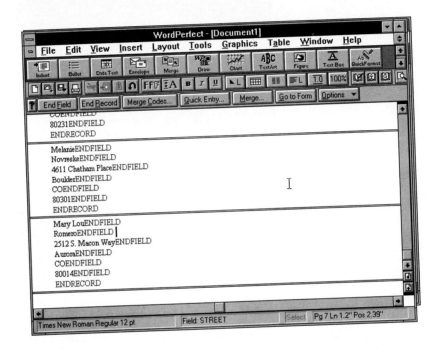

Figure 11-20

Figure 11-21

You will now merge the dbnames.dat file to envelopes. You must first create a form file to go with your dbnames.dat data file.

1. Click on <u>T</u>ools ⇒ <u>M</u>erge ⇒ <u>F</u>orm

2. Type **dbnames.dat** for your associated file

   Your insertion point is moved to a blank page.

3. Click on <u>L</u>ayout ⇒ En<u>v</u>elope

   The Envelope dialog box displays.

4. Type in your name and return address in the <u>R</u>eturn Addresses text box

5. Move the insertion point to the <u>M</u>ailing Addresses text box

6. Click on F<u>i</u>eld

   The fields for the dbnames.dat file are displayed.

7. Click on Fname, then click on Insert (don't forget to press (Spacebar))

8. Click on F**i**eld ⇒ Lname ⇒ Insert and press (Enter)

9. Continue to add all the fields, pressing (Enter) and typing appropriate commas and spaces

10. Click on Append _t_o Doc

Your envelope form should display onscreen as shown in Figure 11-22.

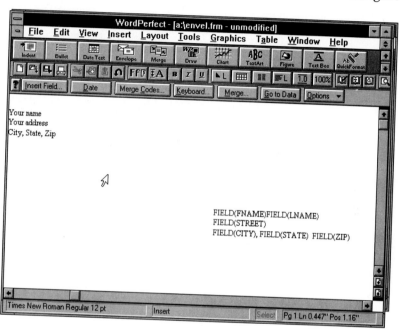

Figure 11-22

11. Save the file as envel.frm

12. Close the file

13. Click on the Merge icon

14. Click on _M_erge

The Perform Merge dialog box displays.

15. Type `envel.frm` in the _F_orm File text box and press (Tab)

16. Type `dbnames.dat` in the _D_ata File text box

17. Leave <current document> in the O_u_tput File text box

18. Click on OK

Your envelopes will appear on two pages on your screen.

19. Print them but do not save the file

 In the next exercise you will write a memo and insert an Excel spreadsheet (contained on your data disk) into the memo.

1. Play your Memo macro (it should be on your regular data disk) and fill it in to match the one shown in Figure 11-23

Bookworm Computer Publishing Company

Interoffice Memorandum

DATE: (today's date)

TO: Tony Martinez
                   Accounting Department

FROM: Your name
                   Acquisitions Editor

SUBJECT: Royalties on Computer Software Books

The following table shows the royalties for the period from July to December for our computer software books. Please let me know if you need any more information.

Figure 11-23

2. Save it as royalty

3. Press (Enter) three times

4. Click on Insert ⇒ Spreadsheet/Database

5. Click on Import

6. Click on Data Type and use the arrow to select Spreadsheet

7. Click on Import As: Table

8. In the Filename text box, click on A:(or B:)excel.xls

   The Excel spreadsheet is shown in Figure 11-24 for your reference.

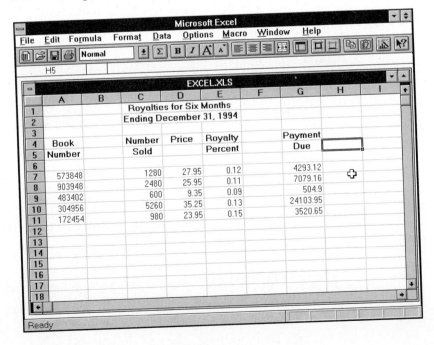

Figure 11-24

The range contained in the spreadsheet will display in the Named Ranges text box. The ranges can be edited, if desired.

9. Click on OK

The Excel spreadsheet information is now inserted in your memo as a table. You want to join the cells of the two title rows and center the title.

10. Move the insertion point to cell A1 and, with the mouse, select to cell G2

11. Click on T<u>a</u>ble ⇒ <u>J</u>oin ⇒ <u>C</u>ell

The cells are joined but the title is not centered.

12. Select the title row again

13. Click on <u>L</u>ayout ⇒ <u>L</u>ine ⇒ <u>C</u>enter

14. Save again and print the document

Your memo should look like the one in Figure 11-25.

15. Close the file and exit WordPerfect

Bookworm Computer Publishing Company

Interoffice Memorandum

DATE: (today's date)

TO: Tony Martinez
                    Accounting Department

FROM: Your name
                    Acquisitions Editor

SUBJECT: Royalties on Computer Software Books

The following table shows the royalties for the period from July to December for our computer software books. Please let me know if you need any more information.

Royalties for Six Months Ending (today's date)					
Book Number		Number Sold	Price	Royalty Percent		Payment Due
573848		1280	27.95	0.12		4293.12
903948		2480	25.95	0.11		7079.16
483402		600	9.35	0.09		504.9
304956		5260	35.25	0.13		24103.95
172454		980	23.95	0.15		3520.65

Figure 11-25

On Your Own

Review of Commands

Description	Menu Commands	Function Keys
Create a data file	_____	_____
Create a form file	_____	_____
Perform a merge	_____	_____
Import a data file	_____	_____

Lesson Review

1. In the Merge feature, what file contains the standard information?

2. What file contains the list of variables for each individual?

3. What is the term for information pertaining to one individual or one entity?

4. What is the term for one item of information about an individual or entity?

5. What kind of merge requires a form document but no data document?

6. How many fields and records can a data document hold?

7. Which merge document controls the merge? Why?

8. When is a keyboard merge useful?

9. List the steps to create a labels form document.

10. How do you print a single label from a file of labels?

11. You have created a number of labels. List the steps to print Labels 2–13.

12. Which WordPerfect feature imports information from a spreadsheet or database file once only?

13. Which WordPerfect feature automatically updates the imported information in your WordPerfect document from the source document?

14. List two ways an imported spreadsheet file can be displayed in WordPerfect.

Assignments

11-1 **Directions**

1. Create a data document. The field names are: Name, Address, Salutation, Course No., Course Name, Days, Time.

2. Make the following entries for the fields in the data file. Notice that the Address field consists of two lines. Use (Ctrl) + (Enter) after the first line of the Address field and (Enter) after the second line.

```
John M. Hunter                      Lois Hardin
135 Broadway                        1200 Logan
Denver, CO 80217                    Limon, CO 80828
John,                              Lois,
CMS 201                            CMS 323
Principles of Information Systems   Data Communications
MWF                                MW
930 TO 1145                        1400 to 1515


Mary Schaub                        Marc Lord
600 Locust                         3444 Pine
Aspen, CO 81611                    Byers, CO 80103
Mary,                              Marc,
CMS 211                            CMS 223
COBOL                              Word Processing
TR                                 MWF
1300 to 1350                       800 to 850
```

3. Save the file as partime.dat.

4. Show your completed data file to your instructor.

11-2 Directions

1. Create the following letter as a form document. Brackets show data document field names. Associate the file partime.dat.

2. Save the file as classes.frm. Print and close the document.

[Date Code]
[Name]
[Address]
Dear **[Salutation]**
Thank you for agreeing to teach **[Course No.]** **[Course Name]** for the CMS department this fall. Your class meets on **[Days]**, from **[Time]**. Classes start August 24, and we will have an orientation meeting sometime during the last week of August.
Sincerely,
Anne Rickard
Class Coordinator, CMS Department

11-3 Directions

1. Merge classes.frm and partime.dat.

2. Print the merged documents.

3. Do not save the documents.

11-4 Directions

1. Create a three-across-label form document for the names and addresses in partime.dat.

2. Save the file as labelspt.frm.

3. Merge labelspt.frm and partime.dat.

4. Print, simulating the labels on ordinary paper.

5. Do not save the merged file.

11-5 Directions

1. Create the data file below. Use Name, Street, Location, and Salute as the four field names.

```
Mrs. Susan Streis
1234 Smith Street
Xenberg, WI 55555
Susan

Mrs. Sara Manely
611 Dalton Road
Buchanan, MI 45369
Sara

Dr. Thomas Tarter
1224 Douglas Court
Appleton, CO 81178
Tom
```

2. Save the file as letter.dat.

3. Show the completed data file to your instructor.

11-6 Directions

1. Create the form document on the next page (again, brackets contain field names). Associate the data document letter.dat.

2. Save the file as letter.frm.

3. Print and close the document.

11-7 Directions

1. Merge letter.frm and letter.dat.

2. Print, but do not save the merged file.

Current Date
[Name]
[Street]
[Location]
Dear [Salute]:
Thank you, [Salute], for agreeing to sell 50 tickets to the Annual DPMA Ball
scheduled for the second Saturday night of next month.
Your pack of 50 tickets is enclosed. The price per ticket is $5. You might remind
folks who are hesitant to buy that the price at the door will be $6.
We really appreciate your willingness to help with this worthwhile project.
Sincerely,
Your name

11-8 Directions

1. Create the following form document using keyboard merge codes as
   indicated. Provide a suitable prompt for each keyboard merge code.

MEMORANDUM

TO: [Keyboard code]
FROM: your name
DATE: Date Code
SUBJECT: Department Goals

Congratulations! Your department has exceeded its fiscal goals for this quarter. This
makes your employees eligible for the cash drawing of [Keyboard Code]. Be sure to
check this week's newsletter for a list of the winners.

2. Save the file as memokey.frm.

3. Print the form document.

4. Perform a merge, typing the following information at the proper
   location:

Marian Seachrist	$25.00
Robert Aument	$25.00
Janet Nash	$50.00
Allen Mayfair	$75.00

5. Print, but do not save the merged documents.

12 Preparing Outlines

Objectives

After completing this lesson, you will be able to:

- Define and create an outline
- Collapse and expand an outline
- Edit an outline
- Move outline sections
- Change the outline numbering style

Creating an Outline

You may sometimes need text in outline form for a book, paper, or speech, or simply to make a list. Creating an outline with WordPerfect is easy, because the program automatically inserts the levels for you. When text is moved, added, or deleted, the outline levels are automatically renumbered.

Up to eight levels of numbering can be used. Each level is aligned under a tab stop. Therefore, if you plan to use eight levels, you must define eight tab stops. The first tab top is the first level of numbering. Each time (Tab) is pressed, the outline number changes to the next level.

Outline Family

An outline family includes the main level in an outline and all subordinate levels and text under it. For example, if the main level is I, then all the levels (A, B, C, 1, 2, 3, a, b, and so on) under it would be considered a family. The entire family can be moved and the rest of the outline will renumber.

You can also **collapse** the outline, or remove the subordinate levels. For example, if your outline is five levels deep, you could show only the first level; only the first and second levels; only the first, second, and third levels; or only the first, second, third and fourth levels. To show only the first level, select the "1" button on the feature bar; for only the first and second level, select the "2," and so on. You can also select all of a family or any number

267

of levels and click on the Minus icon on the feature bar (refer to Figure 12-1) to hide those levels; clicking on the Plus icon will redisplay the sublevels.

▌ Numbering Styles

WordPerfect offers seven predefined numbering styles. The default is Paragraph style. You can select any of the other six numbering styles, or you can create one of your own. The seven predefined styles are shown in Table 12-1.

Name	Example							
Bullets	●	○	-	■	*	+	•	x
Headings	Text (see explanation following)							
Legal (1.1.1)	1	.1	.1	.1	.1	.1	.1	.1
Legal 2 (1.0.0)	1	.0	.0	.0	.0	.0	.0	.0
Numbers	Same as Paragraph style numbers							
Outline	I.	A.	1.	a.	(1)	(a)	i)	a)
Paragraph	1.	a.	i.	(1)	(a)	(i)	1)	a)

Table 12-1
Numbering Styles

In the Headings style, the numbers are few. Level 1 text is bold and centered; level 2 is bold and flush with the left margin; and level 3 is flush with the left margin. Level 4 moves in one tab stop and is bold; level 5 moves in one tab stop and is italicized; level 6 moves in one tab stop and begins with arabic numerals followed by a period. Level 7 moves in one tab stop and begins with lowercase letters followed by a period. Level 8 moves in one tab stop and begins with an arabic numeral followed by a right parenthesis.

To create an outline:

- Choose <u>T</u>ools ⇒ <u>O</u>utline.

The Outline feature bar is displayed. The first level number appears at the first tab stop followed by a period, and the insertion point moves to the first tab stop. If you don't want that much space between the number and your text, change the spacing of your tab stops. As you type the outline the level number appears in the status bar to indicate your current level. Also, a symbol designating the level you are typing is displayed at the far left of the screen and remains there. These symbols will not be printed in your document. If you type text in the outline or enter blank lines, the symbol will be a large **T**. After you type the text for the first level, press (Enter) to go to the next level.

When you are typing an outline, the keys shown in Table 12-2 are used.

Keystroke	Action
(Enter)	Inserts a new number
(Tab)	Changes the indent and number to the next level
(Shift) + (Tab)	Changes the number and indent to the previous level

Table 12-2
Outline Keystrokes

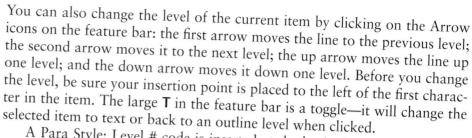

You can also change the level of the current item by clicking on the Arrow icons on the feature bar: the first arrow moves the line to the previous level; the second arrow moves it to the next level; the up arrow moves the line up one level; and the down arrow moves it down one level. Before you change the level, be sure your insertion point is placed to the left of the first character in the item. The large **T** in the feature bar is a toggle—it will change the selected item to text or back to an outline level when clicked.

A Para Style: Level # code is inserted at the beginning and end of each line in the outline.

If your document has regular text following the outline, you will need to turn off the Outline feature. To do so:

- Choose <u>O</u>ptions from the feature bar.
- Choose Outline Off or select OutlineEnd icon from the button bar.

An Outline code is inserted in the Reveal Codes screen. If your document does not have any regular text following the outline, the Outline feature does not need to be turned off.

You can also turn Outline off as you are typing the outline; when you want to begin the outline again, turn it back on. It will continue numbering with the next number. To turn Outline back on with a consecutive number:

- Choose <u>T</u>ools ⇒ <u>O</u>utline.
- Choose Options on the feature bar.
- Choose Set Number.
- In the Paragraph Number text box, type the starting number.
- Choose OK.

Editing an Outline

WordPerfect allows you to edit your outline by inserting and deleting items at any level and by moving items or entire sections. The renumbering is done automatically. To insert a new line, position the cursor at the end of the line that precedes the new line and press (Enter). The outline level of the inserted item will be the same as that of the preceding line. If necessary, you can press either (Tab) to use the next sublevel (or click on the left arrow icon on the feature bar), or (Shift) + (Tab) (or click on the right arrow icon on the feature bar) to use the previous one. If the remaining entries do not automatically renumber, press the (↓) key.

To change an item's level, position the insertion point before the outline character to be modified, then press (Tab) to use the next sublevel or (Shift) + (Tab) to use the previous one. Press (↓) to automatically renumber the outline.

Moving a Section of an Outline

You can move, copy, or delete individual levels of an outline or an outline family. Remember, a family consists of the line in which the insertion point is positioned, plus the numbers and text of any subordinate levels.

- Place the insertion point to the left of the first character in Level 1.
- Choose the SelFamily icon from the button bar.

- Click the right mouse button.
- Make desired choice from the drop-down list.

Moving an Outline Family

You can also move an outline family by clicking on the level number to select the family. You then click on the up or down arrows in the feature bar. The outline family will move one line at a time until you have it in the desired location. The family will automatically renumber in its new location. Deselect the family by clicking anywhere outside the outline.

Changing the Numbering Style

You can change the numbering style before or after you type your outline. The default outline-numbering style is called Paragraph. Six other predefined styles can be selected instead of Paragraph, or you can design your own numbering style. To change the numbering style, first be sure to place the insertion point where the new numbering is to begin.

- Choose Options from the feature bar.
- Choose Define Outline.
- Choose new style.
- Choose OK.

Additional editing features are available by clicking on the red question mark at the left end of the feature bar. Those features and their corresponding shortcut keys are shown in Table 12-3.

Feature	Shortcut keys
Previous level	Alt + Shift + P
Next level	Alt + Shift + N
Move up	Alt + Shift + U
Move down	Alt + Shift + W
Change to body text	Alt + Shift + T
Show family	Alt + Shift + S
Hide family	Alt + Shift + I
Show all	Alt + Shift + A
Options	Alt + Shift + O
Close	Alt + Shift + C

Table 12-3
Outline Editing Features

The Outline Button Bar

Because of the commands available on the Outline button bar, such as OutlineDef, SetPara#, Outline Level, SelPara, SelFamily, and OutlineEnd, this button bar should be retrieved whenever you work with outlines if it does not automatically appear.

Creating a New Style

You can create your own outline style, with each level marked by any character in the Custom Number box as follows:

- Choose Options from the feature bar.
- Choose Define Outline.
- Choose Create.
- Type a name in the Name text box.
- Type a description in the Description text box.
- Select Level 1 and its associated style.
- Click on the arrow in the Custom Number box.
- Select desired style from the drop-down list.
- Repeat until all levels are selected.
- Click on OK.

The style is saved with that file. To use it for another outline, you must first save it as a new style by using Tools ⇒ Outline ⇒ Options ⇒ Save As ⇒ Name; to later retrieve that style:

- Select Tools ⇒ Outline ⇒ Options.
- Select Define Outline.
- Select Options.
- Select Retrieve.
- Enter new style file name.
- Click on OK. The screen prompts: "Overwrite Current Style?"
- Answer Yes.
- Click on OK.

As an editor at Bookworm Computer Publishing Company, you have had several manuscript submissions for the Interface Quarterly Scholastic Journal. The document you will create in the following exercise is the outline for one of those manuscripts. (The finished outline is shown in Figure 12-2 for your reference.)

1. Centered and in boldface, type `Electronic Mail: The Privacy Issue`

2. Press (Enter) three times

NOTE: As you type your outline, if you somehow lose your automatic number, place the insertion point at the end of the last line containing a number and press (Enter).

Now turn the Outline feature on. The Outline feature bar and the outline button bar will display onscreen as shown in Figure 12-1.

3. Click on Tools ⇒ Outline

The number: "1." appears one tab stop in from the left edge and the insertion point appears on the second tab stop (the added space is thus automatic). The words "Level 1" appear in the status bar, indicating the current level.

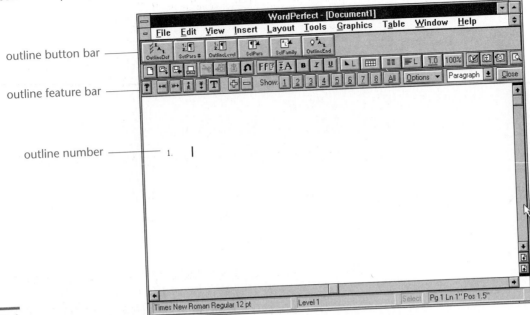

outline button bar

outline feature bar

outline number

Figure 12-1

4. Retrieve the Outline button bar if it does not appear: <u>F</u>ile ⇒ <u>P</u>references ⇒ <u>B</u>utton Bar ⇒ Outline

5. Type INTRODUCTION

6. Press (Enter)

A "2." appears under the "1." However, you want to go to the second level:

7. Press (Tab)

An "a." appears.

8. Type Cyberspace

9. Press (Enter)

10. Type Configurations

11. Press (Enter)

12. Type Software Available (Enter)

To go to the third level:

13. Press (Tab)

The correct level, "i." appears.

14. Type Higgins (Enter)

15. Type ccMail (Enter)

16. Type WordPerfect Office (Enter)

The Roman numeral "iv." appears. Move the outlining number to the previous level.

17. Press (Shift) + (Tab)

The correct outline level "(d)" appears.

18. Type `Privacy Issue` and press (Enter) twice

    You want to return to Level 1.

19. Press (Shift) + (Tab)

    A "2." appears.

20. Type `BACKGROUND AND LITERATURE REVIEW`

21. Add the levels shown below:

    a. `Legislation`
    b. `Productivity`
    c. `Privacy`
    d. `Pending Litigation`
    e. `Conflict`
    3. `CONCLUSION`
    a. `Awareness`
    b. `Available Laws`
    4. `RESEARCH STUDY`
    a. `Design`
    b. `Findings`

    Now turn the outline off.

22. Click on the OutlineEnd icon on the button bar

23. Save the file as `outline` and print it

    Your document should look similar to the one in Figure 12-2.

Electronic Mail: The Privacy Issue

1.   INTRODUCTION
       a.   Cyberspace
       b.   Configurations
       c.   Software Available
              i.   Higgins
              ii.   ccMail
              iii.   WordPerfect Office
       d.   Privacy Issue

2.   BACKGROUND AND LITERATURE REVIEW
       a.   Legislation
       b.   Productivity
       c.   Privacy
       d.   Pending Litigation
       e.   Conflict

3.   CONCLUSION
       a.   Awareness
       b.   Available Laws

4.   RESEARCH STUDY
       a.   Design
       b.   Findings

Figure 12-2

You decide to make some changes to your outline.

1. Place the insertion point at the end of the line "ccMail"

2. Press (Enter)

   An "iii." appears.

3. Type **Profs**

   The entries automatically renumber.

4. Position the insertion point at the beginning of the "P" in "Pending Litigation"

5. Click on SelPara on the button bar

   The whole line is selected.

   CAUTION: If you use any other method to select, the number is not included.

6. Press (Del)

   Now you want to move the family beginning "4. Research Study" to level 3, ahead of Conclusion.

7. Place the insertion point in the first level of "4. Research Study"

8. Click on the SelFamily icon on the button bar

   The first and second levels are selected.

9. Click on the Cut icon in the power bar

10. Place your insertion point in the line above "Conclusion"

11. Press (Enter)

12. Click on the Paste icon

    Your outline will renumber. It should look like the one in Figure 12-3.

13. Click on the level number to the left of "Software Available." Level 2 and its subordinate levels should be selected

14. Click on the up arrow on the feature bar until "Software Available" renumbers to the letter "a"

15. Click on the down arrow on the feature bar until you have returned "Software Available" to its original location (after letter "c." in the family)

16. Deselect the family by clicking anywhere outside the outline

17. Save the file as outline2

You now want to show only the first and second levels of your outline. The insertion point can be anywhere in the outline.

1. Click on the "2" button on the feature bar

   You should see only the first and second levels of your outline.

Electronic Mail: The Privacy Issue

1. INTRODUCTION
    a. Cyberspace
    b. Configurations
    c. Software Available
        i.   Higgins
        ii. ccMail
        iii. Profs
        iv. WordPerfect Office
    d. Privacy Issue

2. BACKGROUND AND LITERATURE REVIEW
    a. Legislation
    b. Productivity
    c. Privacy
    d. Conflict

3. RESEARCH STUDY
    a. Design
    b. Findings

4. CONCLUSION
    a. Awareness
    b. Available Laws

Figure 12-3

2. Click on the "1" button on the feature bar

Only the first level is shown.

3. Click on "All" on the feature bar

Your outline is intact again.

You can hide levels of selected families in your outline by using the Hide Family command from the red question mark on the feature bar. A drop-down list of commands appears as shown in Figure 12-4.

More Feature Bars	▶
Previous Level	Alt+Shift+P
Next Level	Alt+Shift+N
Move **U**p	Alt+Shift+U
Move Do**w**n	Alt+Shift+W
Change to Body **T**ext	Alt+Shift+T
Show Family	Alt+Shift+S
H**i**de Family	Alt+Shift+I
Show **A**ll	Alt+Shift+A
Options	Alt+Shift+O
Close	Alt+Shift+C
Help...	

Figure 12-4

4. Select the "Introduction" family

5. Click on the red question mark for the drop-down list of commands

6. Click on H**i**de Family

  ✓ (Alt) + (Shift) + (I)

All the sublevels below Introduction are hidden.

7. Click on <u>S</u>how Family

The sublevels are redisplayed.

You now want to change the outline style to the Outline numbering style.

1. Position your insertion point in front of the "I" in "Introduction"

2. Click on <u>O</u>ptions

The Options drop-down list appears as shown in Figure 12-5.

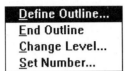

Figure 12-5

3. Click on <u>D</u>efine Outline

The Outline Define dialog box displays as shown in Figure 12-6. In the Name text box:

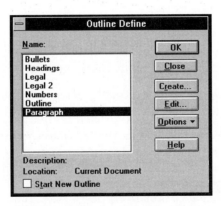

Figure 12-6

4. Select Outline

5. Click on OK

Your outline should now follow the Outline numbering style I., A., 1.

6. Do not save your outline in this style; on your own, change the numbering style to Bullets

Your screen should look similar to that of Figure 12-7.

7. Print and close without saving, which will leave your outline in the Paragraph numbering style

8. Exit WordPerfect

```
┌─────────────────────────────────────────────────────────┐
│              Electronic Mail: The Privacy Issue           │
│                                                           │
│   ●   INTRODUCTION                                        │
│       ○      Cyberspace                                   │
│       ○      Configurations                               │
│       ○      Software Available                           │
│              -      Higgins                               │
│              -      ccMail                                │
│              -      Profs                                 │
│              -      WordPerfect Office                    │
│       ○      Privacy Issue                                │
│                                                           │
│   ●   BACKGROUND AND LITERATURE REVIEW                    │
│       ○      Legislation                                  │
│       ○      Productivity                                 │
│       ○      Privacy                                      │
│       ○      Conflict                                     │
│                                                           │
│   ●   RESEARCH STUDY                                      │
│       ○      Design                                       │
│       ○      Findings                                     │
│                                                           │
│   ●   CONCLUSION                                          │
│       ○      Awareness                                    │
│       ○      Available Laws                               │
└─────────────────────────────────────────────────────────┘
```

Figure 12-7

On Your Own

Review of Commands

Description	Menu Commands	Function Keys
Create an outline		
Move to next sublevel		
Move to previous level		
Turn outline on		
Turn outline off		
Move family		
Copy family		
Delete family		
Change numbering style		

Lesson Review

1. How many outline levels are available?

2. What must be done before creating an outline?

3. How many predefined numbering styles are available, and what is the default?

4. What keystroke(s) takes you to the next sublevel?

5. What keystroke(s) takes you to the previous level?

6. Under what circumstances must you turn Outline off?

7. When editing an outline, what are the steps for inserting new items?

8. How do you delete one or more items?

9. What comprises an outline family?

10. Is it possible to change the numbering style after you've typed your outline?

▌ Assignments

12-1   Directions

1.   Type the outline shown below in the default numbering style.

CMS DEPARTMENT MEETING AGENDA

1.   Summer Class Schedule
    a.   Check to see if all days and times are correct
    b.   Check to see if all your rooms are assigned correctly

2.   Program Review
    a.   Reception for Dr. Pope, Thursday at 4:00
    b.   General Faculty meeting with him Friday at 2:30
        i.   Bring all your class syllabi
        ii.   Bring your class schedule
        iii. Bring your curriculum vitae

3.   Graduation
    a.   Attendance is required
    b.   Time: 2:00 Sunday, May 18
    c.   Place: Convention Hall
    d.   Order caps, gowns, and hoods May 1-4 in the Student Center

4.   Problems in Computer Labs
    a.   Viruses
        i.   Be sure to scan all floppy disks before using
        ii.   If you find a virus, see lab assistant
    b.   Scheduling
        i.   Do not schedule labs for lecturing
        ii.   If you are not using all computers, please allow other students to use them

5.   Reunion for Alumni
    a.   Saturday brunch, May 16, 10:00
    b   Department get-together, 12:30 to 1:30
        i.   Volunteers to bring alumni to our offices
        ii.   Show them new computers for student advising
        iii. Demonstrate new page scanner

---

2. Save the document as agenda.wpd.

3. Print and close the document.

12-2 Directions

1. Open agenda.wpd.

2. In the Program Review section, after "Reception . . . 4:00" type the following line on the same level: `Class visitations all morning on Friday`

3. After "General faculty . . ." in the same section, delete the line "2. Bring your class schedule"

4. Move the "Graduation" family to the end of the agenda.

5. Save, print, and close the document.

12-3 Directions

1. Open agenda.wpd and save it as agenda1.wpd.

2. Change the numbering style to Bullets. You may have to scroll through the document to get the new style applied.

3. Save, print, and close the document.

12-4 Directions

1. Open agenda.wpd and save it as agenda2.wpd.

2. Change the numbering style to Headings and make any necessary adjustments.

3. Save, print, and close the document.

12-5 Directions

1. Open agenda.wpd and save it as agenda3.wpd.

2. Click on the level number next to "Reunion for Alumni" to select the family.

3. Use the up arrow on the feature bar to move the family to the first position in the outline.

4. Change the numbering style to Legal.

5. Delete the "Program Review" family.

6. Save, print, and close the document.

12-6 Directions

1. Create an outline for this course or another course of your choice.

2. Use at least three levels.

3. Apply a numbering style other than the default.

4. Save the document as course12.wpd and print it.

5. Collapse the outline to its first level and print it.

6. Expand the outline to include all levels.

7. Close the document.

13

Working with Complex Documents

Objectives

After completing this lesson, you will be able to:

- Use the Indent feature
- Insert special characters
- Use the Conditional End of Page feature
- Create, edit, and delete footnotes and endnotes
- Use the page numbering feature
- Customize a header
- Use the Bookmark feature
- Insert a watermark
- Mark text for, define, and generate a table of contents
- Use the QuickFormat feature

Indenting Text

WordPerfect supports three different ways to indent text. First, the Indent feature indents a paragraph one tab stop from the left margin each time it is executed. This feature essentially sets a temporary left margin; the text automatically moves right, to the indent position, until (Enter) is pressed (at the end of the paragraph). The insertion point then returns to the original left margin. The Indent feature is useful when you want to line up a paragraph after a number. Second, the Double Indent feature, often used for quoted material, is similar except that it indents a paragraph one tab stop from *both* margins. Third, the Hanging Indent command moves all but the first line of a paragraph one tab stop to the right. The Hanging Indent feature is used in bibliographies.

To use any of the indenting features, tab stops must first be set for each indent level desired. For Indent:

- Choose <u>L</u>ayout ⇒ Pa<u>r</u>agraph ⇒ <u>I</u>ndent ((F7)) or click on the Indent icon on the button bar.

For Double Indent:

- Choose <u>L</u>ayout ⇒ Pa<u>r</u>agraph ⇒ <u>D</u>ouble Indent ((Ctrl) + (Shift) + (F7)).

For Hanging Indent:

- Choose <u>L</u>ayout ⇒ Pa<u>r</u>agraph ⇒ <u>H</u>anging Indent ((Ctrl) + (F7)).

A HdLeftInd code is entered for Indent; a HdLeft/RightInd code is entered into the text for Double Indent; and a HdBackTab code is inserted for Hanging Indent.

Inserting Special Characters

WordPerfect offers a wide variety of special characters, such as bullets (● and ■); copyright, paragraph, and section symbols (©, ¶, and §); and other characters such as ☜, ♦, and ♥, just for fun.

Over 1,600 of the characters—referred to as *WordPerfect characters*—are available, divided into different groups or **character sets**. Each set contains the characters of a particular type or alphabet. Some of the character sets available are Iconic and Typographic Symbols, Math/Scientific, Greek, Hebrew, and Japanese. You may or may not be able to print every character, depending on the printer you are using.

To insert a WordPerfect character, first position the insertion point where the character is to appear.

- Choose <u>I</u>nsert ⇒ Character ((Ctrl) + (W)).
- In the Character Set box, click on the arrow box to display all the different character sets.
- Select the desired character from the Characters Symbol box.
- Choose <u>I</u>nsert (Or <u>I</u>nsert and <u>C</u>lose).

Also, because both the character sets and individual characters in the sets are numbered, you can specify the numbers if you know them, such as "5, 1" for a diamond (the ♦ is character 1 of set 5). Consult your WordPerfect manual for the correct numbers.

Conditional End of Page

The Conditional End of Page feature protects a specified number of lines from being divided by a page break so that, for example, a heading will not appear by itself at the bottom of a page. WordPerfect will always keep the specified number of lines together, even if it has to place a page break before the lines to do so. To use this feature, position the insertion point one line above the first line to be affected, then:

- Choose <u>L</u>ayout ⇒ <u>P</u>age ⇒ Keep Text Together ⇒ Conditional <u>E</u>nd of Page.
- In the Conditional End of Page option box, click on Number of lines to keep together.
- Type the number of lines to be kept together.
- Choose OK.

A Cndl EOP:(number) code is inserted.

Working with Footnotes and Endnotes

Footnotes and endnotes are used to give the source for material provided in a document (such as the name of the book or periodical, the author and publisher, and the date of publication) or to give additional information. Footnotes are placed at the bottom of the page on which the material is referenced, and endnotes are placed at the end of the chapter or document on a separate page. WordPerfect automatically numbers each footnote or endnote sequentially.

Creating a Footnote or Endnote

To create a footnote or endnote, first position the insertion point where the footnote or endnote number is to be placed, then:

- Choose Insert ⇒ Footnote or Endnote ⇒ Create.

The footnote window opens with the divider line and the footnote reference number at the bottom of the page (the endnote window opens at the end of your document). The corresponding feature bar appears automatically.

- Type the footnote or endnote text.
- Choose Close from the feature bar.

The reference number appears in the body of the text.

Editing a Footnote or Endnote

The insertion point can be anywhere in the document. To edit a footnote or endnote:

- Choose Insert ⇒ Footnote or Endnote ⇒ Edit.
- Type the number of the footnote or endnote to be edited.
- Choose OK.
- Make the corrections.
- Choose Close from the feature bar.

Deleting a Footnote or Endnote

To delete a footnote or endnote, position the insertion point either just before or just after the reference number. If the insertion point is before the reference number, press (Del); if it is after the reference number, press (Backspace). Remember, if you delete a footnote or endnote by mistake, immediately use the Undo feature to restore it. If you add or delete a footnote or endnote, all are renumbered automatically.

Using Page Numbering

You can insert a page number in your header or footer and it will appear on every page displaying a header or footer. It is also possible to include additional text, such as "Page," with the page number. You can select the type of number you want, Arabic or Roman numeral.

You can place numbers in any of eight alternative places on the page, such as top right, top center, bottom right, and so on. To use Page Numbering, move the insertion point to the page on which you want numbering to begin, and:

- Select Layout ⇒ Page ⇒ Numbering.
- Select Position.
- Select location from pop-up list.
- Select Options.
- In the Format and Accompanying Text box, type any desired additional text in the appropriate position.
- Select OK.

Customizing a Footer

In Lesson 6, you learned about headers and footers. In this lesson you will learn how to add a graphic line to a header or footer.

- Choose Line from the Header/Footer control bar.

Bookmark

You can set a Bookmark or QuickMark to mark a place to which you want to return. Procedures for setting and finding both are similar. You can set only one QuickMark and the system marks its symbol, but you can set as many bookmarks as you like and name each one. Place the insertion point where you want the bookmark to be inserted. To set a QuickMark:

- Choose Insert.
- Choose Bookmark.
- Choose Set QuickMark.

A QuickMark or Bookmark code is inserted in the Reveal Codes screen. To find these, select GoTo and the name of the bookmark; a QuickMark cannot be named, as there can be only one. Follow the same procedure to set bookmarks, but create and name each bookmark. To find the QuickMark:

- Choose Insert.
- Choose Bookmark.
- Choose Find QuickMark.

Again, follow the same procedure for bookmarks, but select the name of the bookmark and choose Go To "name."

Inserting a Watermark

A watermark is a lighter figure or text that appears behind the darker, printed text. It usually covers most of the page. The watermark works as do headers and footers, in that you can select Watermark A or Watermark B and have it appear on every page, on odd pages, or on even pages. First place the insertion point in the first paragraph of the page on which you want the watermark to appear.

- Choose Layout.
- Choose Watermark.

- Choose Watermark <u>A</u> or Watermark <u>B</u>.
- Choose <u>C</u>reate.

The Watermark feature bar is activated, from which you can choose: <u>F</u>igure to insert an image; <u>F</u>ile to insert an existing file; <u>P</u>lacement to specify the pages on which the watermark will appear; <u>N</u>ext to go to the next watermark if there is one; <u>P</u>revious to go to the previous watermark; and <u>C</u>lose. A Watermark A or B code is inserted.

- Choose P<u>l</u>acement.
- Select the page configuration.
- Choose <u>F</u>igure or F<u>i</u>le.
- Specify path and file name of the image or text file.
- Choose OK.
- Choose <u>C</u>lose from feature bar.

Before you begin the exercises, open the document on your data disk named mail.wpd. Print the document for reference during the exercises. Before you begin, save it as a new document named mail2.wpd.

In the next exercise, you will use the Indent, Double Indent, and WP Character features, and you will insert three footnotes. Several bookmarks have been set to help you find the correct places in the document. Be sure that your tabs are set at the default setting of every five spaces. Activate the Bookmark feature.

1. Click on <u>I</u>nsert

2. Click on <u>B</u>ookmark

The Bookmark dialog box shown in Figure 13-1 appears.

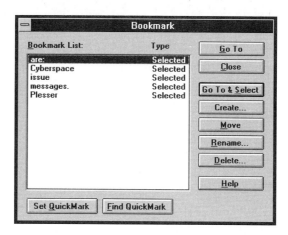

Figure 13-1

3. Click on "Cyberspace"

4. Click on <u>G</u>o To

Your insertion point should stop to the left of "Cyberspace" in the beginning of the second paragraph. You want to insert a footnote at this point.

5. Click on Insert ⇒ Footnote ⇒ Create

   The footnote screen opens and the insertion point is at the bottom of the screen followed by a superscript "1."

6. Including the error, type **A term invented by science function writer William Gibson.**

7. Click on Close on the feature bar

   You will now insert a WordPerfect Character from the Character set.

8. Go to the Bookmark "are:"

9. Move the insertion point after "are:" and press (Enter) twice

10. Press (Tab)

11. Click on Insert ⇒ Character

   ✓ Press (Ctrl) + (W)

12. In the Character Set box, click on the arrows

13. In the drop-down list, click on Iconic Symbols (if not already marked)

14. Scroll down until you see black circles with numbers as shown in Figure 13-2

select this character

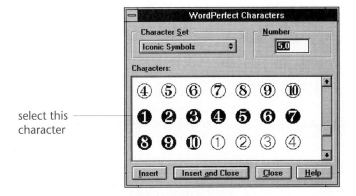

Figure 13-2

15. Click on the 1 displayed in reverse video

   Notice that WordPerfect places an outline box around the selected character.

16. Click on Insert and Close

   The number is inserted into your document. To position the insertion point at the next tab stop and set a temporary left margin using the Indent feature:

17. Click on Layout ⇒ Paragraph

   The Paragraph menu displays as shown in Figure 13-3.

18. Click on Indent

   ✓ Press (F7)

Layout
Font...	F9
Line	▶
Paragraph	
Pa**g**e	
Document	
Columns	
Header/Footer...	
Watermark...	
Margins... Ctrl+F8	
Justification	▶
Typesetting	▶
En**v**elope...	
La**b**els...	
QuickFormat	
St**y**les... Alt+F8	

Paragraph submenu:
F**o**rmat...	
Border/Fill...	
Indent	F7
Hanging Indent	Ctrl+F7
Double Indent	Ctrl+Shift+F7
Back **T**ab	

Figure 13-3

19. Type:

Can a company read the electronic files of an absent
employee to obtain vital company data?

Your text should be indented five spaces to the right of the number 1.

20. Press (Enter) twice

21. Press (Tab)

22. Insert a 2 from the Iconic Symbol character set

23. Press (F7)

24. Type:

Can a company legally intercept and read electronic mail
messages to ensure its electronic mail use policy is
being observed?

Be sure there is a blank line between the paragraph and the next heading.

You will go to the bookmark "Messages." and use the Double Indent feature.

1. Go to the end of the bookmark "Messages."

2. Press (Enter) twice

3. Click on **L**ayout ⇒ **P**aragraph ⇒ **D**ouble Indent

   ✓ Press (Ctrl) + (Shift) + (F7)

   This sets up temporary left and right margins five spaces in from the original margins.

4. Type:

One of the greatest advantages of E-Mail is that it
breaks down barriers between employer and employees and
enhances communication, providing a positive effect on
organizational productivity.

Your text should be indented five spaces on both sides.

5. Go to the bookmark "issue"

6. Click on <u>I</u>nsert ⇒ <u>F</u>ootnote ⇒ <u>C</u>reate at the end of "issue"

The Footnote window appears and displays a 2, indicating that WordPerfect is keeping track of your footnotes.

7. Type:

```
SPSS was used to summarize the data from the fifty usable
completed surveys.
```

8. Click on <u>C</u>lose

9. Go to the bookmark "Plesser"

10. Click on <u>I</u>nsert ⇒ <u>F</u>ootnote ⇒ <u>C</u>reate at the end of "Plesser"

11. Type:

```
Former general counsel of the US Privacy Protection Study
Commission.
```

12. Click on <u>C</u>lose

In the next exercise you will apply the Conditional End of Page feature to headings that appear near the end of a page. Start with your cursor at the beginning of the document (Ctrl + Home).

1. Use Find (F2) to find the heading "Privacy Issue"

2. Place the insertion point to the left of the "P" in "Privacy"

3. Click on <u>L</u>ayout ⇒ <u>P</u>age ⇒ <u>K</u>eep Text Together

4. Click on the box in front of Number of lines to keep together

5. In the Number box, type **4**

This will include the "Privacy Issue" line, one line after, and at least two lines of the next paragraph.

6. Click on OK

Scroll through your document to see if other headings are near the bottom of the page; if so, use Conditional End of Page.

In the next exercise you will create a header with a graphic line and use the Page Numbering feature to insert your page numbers. Page numbering could be done in the header, but we want to show you both features.

1. Press Ctrl + Home

2. Click on <u>L</u>ayout ⇒ <u>H</u>eader/Footer

3. Select Header A ⇒ Create

The header/footer feature bar appears below the power bar.

4. At the left margin in small capitals (<u>L</u>ayout ⇒ <u>F</u>ont ⇒ Small Cap), type
E-Mail Draft

5. Press (Enter)

6. Click on <u>G</u>raphics ⇒ Custom <u>L</u>ine

7. Change the <u>T</u>hickness to 0.040"

8. Click on OK

9. Click on <u>C</u>lose on the feature bar

10. Press (Ctrl) + (Home) twice (to go before all codes)

11. Click on <u>L</u>ayout ⇒ <u>P</u>age ⇒ <u>N</u>umbering

    The Numbering dialog box displays as shown in Figure 13-4.

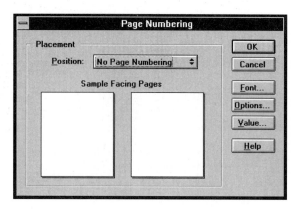

Figure 13-4

12. In the Placement box, click on the Position arrows and select Bottom Right

    The preview box shows the number as it will appear on your page.

13. Click on <u>O</u>ptions

    The Page Numbering Options dialog box opens.

14. Move the insertion point to the left of Pg # in the Format and accompanying Text box

15. Type **Page** and press (Spacebar)

16. Click on OK

    See if the format looks correct in the preview box at the bottom of the dialog box.

17. Click on OK

    If you scroll to the bottom of the page, you will see "Page 1."

    When typing documents containing several pages, it is good practice to activate the Widow/Orphan feature you learned about in Lesson 10 to ensure that at least two lines of any paragraph remain together on a page.

18. Press (Ctrl) + (Home)

19. Click on <u>L</u>ayout ⇒ <u>P</u>age ⇒ <u>K</u>eep Text Together ⇒ Widow/Orphan ⇒ OK

You must correct the mistake in the first footnote. (It does not matter where your insertion point is.) You'll also add a watermark.

1. Click on <u>I</u>nsert ⇒ <u>F</u>ootnote ⇒ <u>E</u>dit

2. Click on <u>F</u>ootnote Number 1 ⇒ OK

3. Change "function" to "fiction"

4. Click on <u>C</u>lose

   Now add a watermark.

5. Press (Ctrl) + (Home)

6. Click on <u>L</u>ayout ⇒ <u>W</u>atermark

   The Watermark dialog box displays as shown in Figure 13-5.

Figure 13-5

7. Select <u>W</u>atermark A ⇒ <u>C</u>reate

   The Watermark feature bar displays as shown in Figure 13-6.

Figure 13-6

8. Click on <u>F</u>igure on the feature bar

   The Image file name box displays.

9. Scroll down to buterfly.wpg and click on OK

   The Graphics feature bar appears, and you have all the standard graphic capabilities. You can see the butterfly behind your text. Unfortunately, it is much prettier in color than it will be when printed.

10. Click on Close twice

▌ Creating a Table of Contents

WordPerfect creates a table of contents from text that you mark. Five levels of headings and subheadings can be specified. Generally, you mark the title, headings, and subheadings of the document, and the marked text is placed into the table of contents along with the number of the page on which each entry appears. There are three basic steps used to generate a table of contents: (1) mark the text to be used in the table of contents; (2) define the number of levels and the page-numbering style of the table of contents; and (3) generate the table of contents.

Marking the Text

To mark the text for a table of contents:

- Choose Tools ⇒ Table of Contents.
- Select the text.
- Select Mark 1–5 on the feature bar.

A Mrk Txt ToC code is inserted before and after the marked text. When expanded, the code box shows the level selected. Mark all the headings you want to appear in your table of contents.

CAUTION: Work in the Reveal Codes screen and be careful to select only the text—no codes. If you include codes in your text selection, such as bold or underline, the text will appear formatted so in your table of contents. Also, if you include a hard return code, that will cause an extra blank line.

Defining the Table of Contents

Defining the table of contents tells WordPerfect how many levels you have marked in the text, the numbering style, and the location for the table of contents. To define the table, place the insertion point where you want the table of contents (usually at the beginning of the document on a page of its own). Proceed as follows at the beginning of your document.

- Press Ctrl + Enter.
- Move the insertion point into the new page.
- Type the title (Table of Contents).
- Choose Define from the feature bar.
- Specify the number of levels and the numbering format.
- Choose OK.

The default numbering style positions the page number on the right margin, with dot leaders running from the text to the number. The numbering style can be changed for a specific level by first clicking on the double-headed arrow in that level's list box to display the drop-down menu, then selecting the desired numbering format.

Generating the Table of Contents

The final step in creating the table of contents is to generate it.

- Select Generate from the feature bar.

If it does not look right, check in the Reveal Codes screen to see if any extra codes were included.

▌ QuickFormat

QuickFormat is a feature that copies the fonts, attributes, and paragraph styles used in one area of text to another. This feature is very useful when you want to change the way headings and subheadings look throughout a document. First place the insertion point in the text having the format you want copied.

- Choose <u>L</u>ayout.
- Choose QuickFormat.
- Designate fonts, attributes, and paragraph styles.

The mouse pointer becomes an I-beam with a roller.

- Place the I-beam to the left of the text and click.
- Drag the roller over the text you want changed.
- Choose <u>L</u>ayout ⇒ QuickFormat to turn feature off.

▌ Overstrike

The Overstrike feature allows you to combine existing characters on your keyboard to create composite characters—both characters will print in one space. This is useful for words such as "resumé" and names such as "Peña." Place insertion point where new character is to appear, then:

- Choose <u>L</u>ayout ⇒ <u>T</u>ypesetting ⇒ <u>O</u>verstrike.
- In the Characters text box, type the two characters.
- Choose OK.

Before you create the table of contents, you will type a bibliography of the sources in the manuscript. You will use the Hanging Indent feature as the first line, which must be five spaces to the left of the following lines. Start on a new page.

1. Press (Ctrl) + (End)

2. Press (Ctrl) + (Enter)

3. Center and type BIBLIOGRAPHY

4. Press (Enter) twice

5. Click on <u>L</u>ayout ⇒ <u>P</u>aragraph ⇒ <u>H</u>anging Indent

   ✓ (Ctrl) + (F7)

6. Type the following sources, pressing (Ctrl) + (F7) at the beginning of each one and double spacing between entries. Do not press (Enter) in the middle of a source; let the text wrap. Use the hard space code ((Ctrl) + (Spacebar)) to keep numbers together on a line.

Casatelli, Christine. "Setting Ground Rules for Privacy," <u>Computerworld</u>, 18 March 1991, 47-50.

——. "Addressing the New Hazards of the High Technology Workplace," <u>Harvard Law Review</u>, June 1991, 1909-1915.

LaPlante, Alice. "Is Big Brother Watching?," <u>Infoworld</u>, 22 October 1990.

Nash, Jim. "Who Can Open E-Mail?" <u>Computerworld</u>, 14 January 1991.

There is a diacritical mark in the next citation.

6. Type `Pe`

7. Click on <u>L</u>ayout ⇒ <u>T</u>ypesetting

The Typesetting menu displays as shown in Figure 13-7.

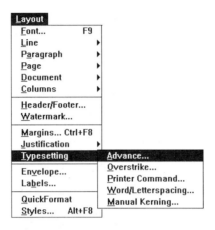

Figure 13-7

8. Click on <u>O</u>verstrike

9. Type `n~`

10. Click on OK

11. Type `a, Robert. "Using Electronic Mail."` <u>`The Education Quar-`</u>
<u>`terly`</u>`, March 1993.`

 In this exercise, you are going to mark the text to appear in the table of contents, specifying two levels. Refer to your document outline2.wpd from Lesson 12. Work in the Reveal Codes screen to prevent including codes in your selection.

1. Click on <u>T</u>ools ⇒ Table of <u>C</u>ontents

The Table of Contents feature bar displays as shown in Figure 13-8.

Figure 13-8

2. Select "INTRODUCTION"

A fast way to select text without codes is to move the insertion point to the left of the text, press (F8), then press (End).

3. Click on Mark <u>1</u>

4. Select "Cyberspace"

5. Click on Mark <u>2</u>

Continue marking all the headings as per your outline which are shown below. Hint: Use Find ((F2)) to locate the words.

6. For the following, choose Mark <u>1</u>: BACKGROUND AND LITERATURE REVIEW; RESEARCH STUDY; CONCLUSION; and BIBLIOGRAPHY

7. For the following, choose Mark <u>2</u>: Configurations; Software Available; Privacy Issue; Legislation; Productivity; Privacy; Conflict; Design; Findings; Awareness; and Available Laws

You will create a new page for the Table of Contents, define, and generate it.

1. Press (Ctrl) + (Home) twice

2. Press (Ctrl) + (Enter)

3. Move the insertion point to the top of the new page. Centered and in all caps, type `TABLE OF CONTENTS`

4. Press (Enter) three times

5. Click on <u>D</u>efine on the feature bar

   If the feature bar is not activated, click on <u>T</u>ools ⇒ Table of <u>C</u>ontents.

6. In the Number of Levels (1–5) box, type **2**

   The preview window shows how the outline will look.

7. Click on OK

   A message displays, stating that the Table of Contents will appear there.

8. Click on <u>G</u>enerate

   The Generate option box displays.

9. Click on OK

10. Close from the feature bar

    Your screen should look similar to the final document in Figure 13-10, which appears on pages 301–306. Because you put the Table of Contents at the top of the document before all codes, it will have neither the watermark behind it nor the header on the page.

The last thing before you are finished with your document is to change the formatting of the headings within the document. You would like to have the Level 1 headings in bold and the Level 2 headings in italics.

1. Select "TABLE OF CONTENTS"

2. Click on the Bold icon

3. Deselect, then put insertion point back in the title

4. Click on <u>L</u>ayout ⇒ QuickFormat or click on the right mouse button and select QuickFormat

   The QuickFormat option box displays as shown in Figure 13-9.

5. Click on Fonts and Attributes ⇒ OK

   The mouse pointer becomes an I-beam and a roller.

QuickFormat

Format other text based on the fonts/attributes or
paragraph styles in effect at the insertion point.

OK

Cancel

Help

QuickFormat Options

○ Fonts and Attributes

○ Paragraph Styles

◉ Both

Figure 13-9

6. Scroll to "INTRODUCTION" on Page 2 of the text

7. Place the I-beam to the left of the "I" in "INTRODUCTION" and drag the roller over the text; release the mouse button to apply the new format

8. Search for "BACKGROUND AND LITERATURE REVIEW"

9. Roll the unit over the text and release the mouse button

10. Repeat the process for "RESEARCH STUDY," "CONCLUSION," and "BIBLIOGRAPHY"

11. Turn off QuickFormat by pressing the QuickFormat button on the WordPerfect button bar

12. Select "Cyberspace"

13. Click on the Italics icon

14. Click on Layout ⇒ QuickFormat

15. Roll the roller over the rest of the level 2 headings

16. Turn off QuickFormat

17. Save and print your document

It should look similar to the one shown in Figure 13-10 (starting on page 301).

18. Exit the document

19. Exit WordPerfect

On Your Own

Review of Commands

Description	Menu Commands	Function Keys
Indent text	_____	_____
Double indent text	_____	_____
Use a hanging indent	_____	_____
Insert special characters	_____	_____
Insert conditional end of page	_____	_____
Protect widows/orphans	_____	_____
Create footnotes	_____	_____

Edit footnotes   _____   _____

Mark text   _____   _____

Define table of contents   _____   _____

Generate table of contents   _____   _____

Insert page numbers   _____   _____

Copy a format to other text   _____   _____

Use a bookmark   _____   _____

Create a Watermark   _____   _____

Use QuickFormat   _____   _____

▌ Lesson Review

1. Explain how the Indent feature works.

2. Name and describe three types of indents.

3. What are three of the available character sets?

4. What is the purpose of the Conditional End of Page feature?

5. What is a widow/orphan in WordPerfect?

6. What distinguishes footnotes from endnotes?

7. After inserting a footnote, can you see it on your document screen?

8. What happens to remaining footnotes when new ones are added or others deleted?

9. What are the three steps in creating a table of contents?

10. How do you delete a footnote?

11. What is a bookmark?

12. How do you find a bookmark?

13. What is a watermark?

14. How do you number pages in WordPerfect?

15. Describe the Overstrike feature. When would you use it?

16. What is a quick way to copy the format of a block of text to another block of text?

▌ Assignments

13-1   Directions

1. Retrieve the document called downsize.wpd from your data disk, and save it as downsz1.wpd to keep the original intact.

2. Create a title page with the following information in boldface, attractively spaced:

MOVING INFORMATION SYSTEMS APPLICATIONS FROM
LARGE SYSTEMS TO NETWORKED MICROCOMPUTERS
(DOWNSIZING)
The Association of Management Conference
Paris, France, 1994

---

3. In the Literature Review section, there are three citations by Eckerson, Bulkeley, and Sheier. Remove the last name and date from each citation, enter footnote numbers in the same location, and use the information below to create a footnote for each of the citations.

Bulkeley, William M. "PC Networks Begin to Oust Mainframes in Some Companies." The Computer Journal, May 1990.

Eckerson, Wayne. "Hospital to Replace Minis with Microcomputer LANS." Network World, 8 October 1990.

Schier, Robert L. "Local Area Networks Pull End Run on the Mainframe." PC Week, 10 September 1990.

---

4. At the end of the Research Design section, add the following text, using WordPerfect's character for the square bullet (or a similar character) and the Indent feature.

The questions asked of each of the companies were as follows:

Please describe the hardware in the company's information system at present.

What hardware was added to the above list in the last five years?

What hardware was eliminated, downgraded, upgraded, or used in a different manner in the last five years?

How many networks do you have?

---

5. To prevent any widows or orphans from occurring, at the beginning of your document implement the Widow/Orphan feature.

6. Save, print, and close the document.

13-2   Directions

1. Open the downsz1.wpd document, and save it as downsz2.wpd.

2. Following the title page, put in a header reading **Downsizing**, with an attractive horizontal line and page numbering.

3. Protect the table within the body of the report with Conditional End of Page.

4. Mark the following headings for a table of contents: "Abstract," "Introduction," "Review of Literature," "Research Design," "Research Findings," and "Conclusions."

5. Create a new page after the title page for the table of contents. (Be sure your insertion point is after the header code.)

6. Define the table of contents for one level.

7. Generate the table of contents.

8. Save the document again, print, and close the document.

13-3   Directions

1. Open downsz2.wpd and save it as downsz3.wpd.

2. Use QuickFormat to bold the section headings in the document.

3. At the end of the document, create a new page. Title the page **Bibliography.**

4. Using the Hanging Indent feature, compile a bibliography from the footnotes in the document. (Consult your instructor if you do not know how to set up a bibliography.) Select and mark the heading "Bibliography" for Table of Contents - Level 1.

5. Delete the table of contents (leave the title of the page).

6. Redefine and regenerate the table of contents.

7. Save, print, and close the document.

13-4   Directions

1. Open downsz3.wpd. Save it as downsz4.wpd.

2. Delete the second footnote and edit the third footnote as follows: replace the date of the article with October 7, 1990.

3. Save, print and close the document.

13-5   Directions

1. Open login.wpd on your data disk. Save it as login1.wpd to keep the original in tact.

2. Move to the bookmark: "netware." Bullet and indent the three paragraphs following the bookmark using WordPerfect's special characters. Select a bullet style of your choice.

3. Move to the following bookmarks: "scripts," "user," "end," "unit," and "commands." In order, at each bookmark, insert the following footnotes:

---

1 Charles Koontz, Netware 3.x: A Do-it-Yourself Guide Charles Koontz (San Rafael: Prima Computer Books, 1991).
2 Ibid., 186.
3 Ibid., 188.
4 Ibid., 189-90.
5 Ibid., 192.

---

4. Move to the bookmark "conventions." Indent the five paragraphs that follow the bookmark.

5. Edit the footnotes so that the title of the book (<u>Netware 3.x: A Do-It-Yourself Guide</u>) is underlined.

6. Use QuickFormat to bold the headings: "Introduction," "Types of Login Scripts," "Definitions," "Variables," "Conventions," and "Conclusion."

7. Save, print, and close your document.

13-6 Directions

1. Open login1.wpd. Save it as login2.wpd.

2. Move to the bookmark "correct." Make each of the 21 definitions that follow the bookmark into hanging indents.

3. Search for the word "Attach:" and select it to apply italics.

4. Use QuickFormat to apply the italics format to the first word in each of the 20 definitions following "*Attach:*". (Each definition word is followed by a colon.)

5. Move to the bookmark "author." Apply a double indent to the paragraph following the bookmark.

6. Save, print, and close the document.

13-7 Directions

1. Open login2.wpd. Save as login3.wpd.

2. Create a header that reads:

Login Scripts for Networks   December 1994

---

3. Insert a horizontal line in the header beneath the text. Use the default line thickness.

4. Number the pages of the text at the bottom right of each page.

5. Implement the Widow/Orphan feature. Examine the document and place a Conditional End of Page command wherever needed.

6. Move to the end of the document. Make an additional page. Title the page **BIBLIOGRAPHY**. Type the following bibliography entry in proper format:

Koontz, Charles. <u>Netware 3.x: A Do-It-Yourself Guide</u>. San Rafael: Prima Computer Books, 1992.

---

7. Save, print, and close the document.

13-8 Directions

1. Open login3.wpd save as login.4.

2. Move the insertion point to the top of the document before all codes.

3. Create a title page in an appropriate format using the following information:

SYSTEM LOGIN SCRIPTS
Prepared for CMS 327
December 1994

---

4. Mark for Table of Contents each of the headings: "Introduction," "Types of Login Scripts," "Definitions," "Variables," "Conventions," and "Conclusion." Do not include the bold codes. Mark for one level only.

5. Create and title a table of contents page between the title page and the body of the report. Make sure your insertion point is before the header code and page numbering code when you create the page.

6. Position the insertion point at an appropriate location on the new page. Define and generate a table of contents.

7. Move to the first page of the document. Insert a watermark. Select the image Copyrite.wpg.

8. Save, print, and close the document.

TABLE OF CONTENTS

Figure 13-10
Page 1

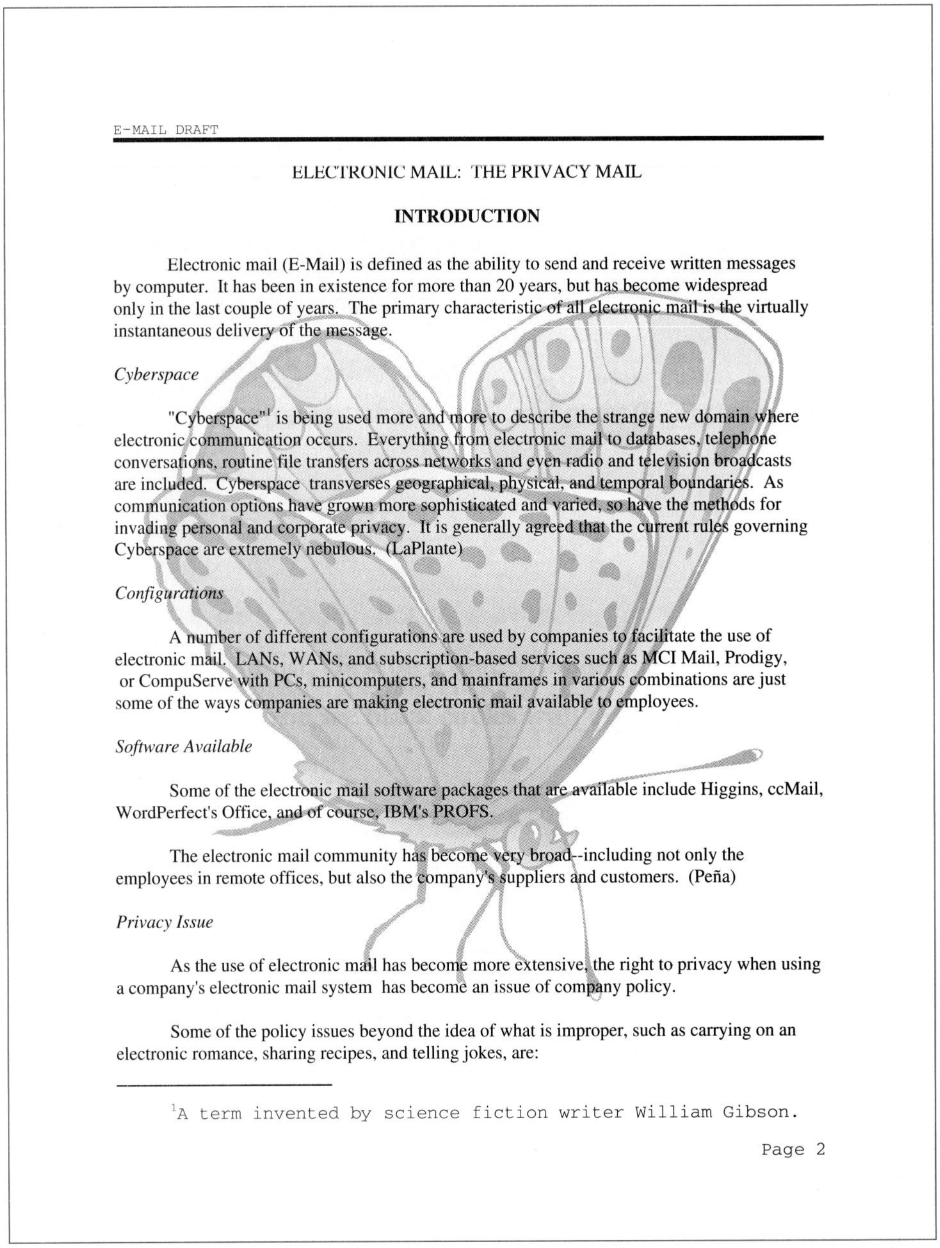

E-MAIL DRAFT

ELECTRONIC MAIL: THE PRIVACY MAIL

INTRODUCTION

Electronic mail (E-Mail) is defined as the ability to send and receive written messages by computer. It has been in existence for more than 20 years, but has become widespread only in the last couple of years. The primary characteristic of all electronic mail is the virtually instantaneous delivery of the message.

Cyberspace

"Cyberspace"[1] is being used more and more to describe the strange new domain where electronic communication occurs. Everything from electronic mail to databases, telephone conversations, routine file transfers across networks and even radio and television broadcasts are included. Cyberspace transverses geographical, physical, and temporal boundaries. As communication options have grown more sophisticated and varied, so have the methods for invading personal and corporate privacy. It is generally agreed that the current rules governing Cyberspace are extremely nebulous. (LaPlante)

Configurations

A number of different configurations are used by companies to facilitate the use of electronic mail. LANs, WANs, and subscription-based services such as MCI Mail, Prodigy, or CompuServe with PCs, minicomputers, and mainframes in various combinations are just some of the ways companies are making electronic mail available to employees.

Software Available

Some of the electronic mail software packages that are available include Higgins, ccMail, WordPerfect's Office, and of course, IBM's PROFS.

The electronic mail community has become very broad--including not only the employees in remote offices, but also the company's suppliers and customers. (Peña)

Privacy Issue

As the use of electronic mail has become more extensive, the right to privacy when using a company's electronic mail system has become an issue of company policy.

Some of the policy issues beyond the idea of what is improper, such as carrying on an electronic romance, sharing recipes, and telling jokes, are:

---

[1]A term invented by science fiction writer William Gibson.

Page 2

Figure 13-10
Page 2

E-MAIL DRAFT

❶ Can a company read the electronic files of an absent employee to obtain vital company data?

❷ Can a company legally intercept and read electronic mail messages to ensure its electronic mail use policy is being observed?

BACKGROUND AND LITERATURE REVIEW

Legislation

In 1986 Congress passed the Electronic Communication Privacy Act, which extends existing privacy protection for oral and wire communications to electronic communications. The Act prevents government agents and third parties from intercepting electronic mail, but it has not been held to cover the interception of business electronic mail messages by private parties. (Harvard Law Review)

Productivity

Many companies feel that it is important for the employees to have the confidence of privacy when sending messages.

One of the greatest advantages of E-Mail is that it breaks down barriers between employer and employees and enhances communication, providing a positive effect on organizational productivity.

People should feel comfortable using their E-mail system. When employees feel secure they are motivated to do a better job. There is a definite time and money savings in using E-mail instead of telephone calls especially when dealing on an international basis. However, if employees cannot be assured that their E-mail is confidential, much of the benefit will be lost.

Privacy

Many employees may consider electronic mail to be the same kind of private property as personal letters. They use it to write notes to their co-workers about their personal lives or to make derogatory remarks about their supervisors. Some companies believe that employees should realize that E-mail messages generated from company computers and stored on company media are company property.

Some companies remind employees on their computer screens that they should use the system for business only, and that the company retains the right to monitor messages. One large corporation's manual states that the 110,000 users may "communicate matters of opinion and common interests."

Page 3

Figure 13-10
Page 3

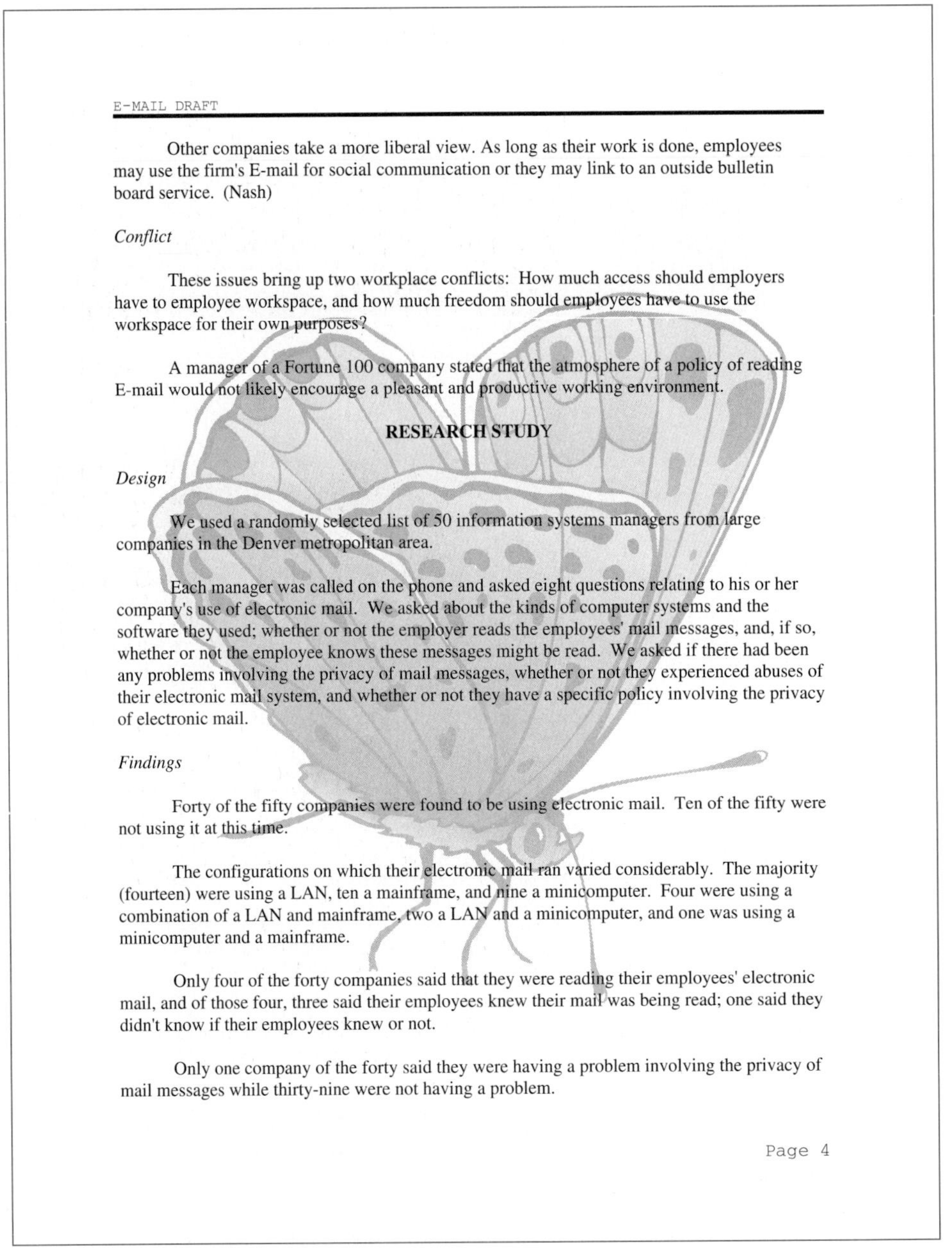

E-MAIL DRAFT

Other companies take a more liberal view. As long as their work is done, employees may use the firm's E-mail for social communication or they may link to an outside bulletin board service. (Nash)

Conflict

These issues bring up two workplace conflicts: How much access should employers have to employee workspace, and how much freedom should employees have to use the workspace for their own purposes?

A manager of a Fortune 100 company stated that the atmosphere of a policy of reading E-mail would not likely encourage a pleasant and productive working environment.

RESEARCH STUDY

Design

We used a randomly selected list of 50 information systems managers from large companies in the Denver metropolitan area.

Each manager was called on the phone and asked eight questions relating to his or her company's use of electronic mail. We asked about the kinds of computer systems and the software they used; whether or not the employer reads the employees' mail messages, and, if so, whether or not the employee knows these messages might be read. We asked if there had been any problems involving the privacy of mail messages, whether or not they experienced abuses of their electronic mail system, and whether or not they have a specific policy involving the privacy of electronic mail.

Findings

Forty of the fifty companies were found to be using electronic mail. Ten of the fifty were not using it at this time.

The configurations on which their electronic mail ran varied considerably. The majority (fourteen) were using a LAN, ten a mainframe, and nine a minicomputer. Four were using a combination of a LAN and mainframe, two a LAN and a minicomputer, and one was using a minicomputer and a mainframe.

Only four of the forty companies said that they were reading their employees' electronic mail, and of those four, three said their employees knew their mail was being read; one said they didn't know if their employees knew or not.

Only one company of the forty said they were having a problem involving the privacy of mail messages while thirty-nine were not having a problem.

Figure 13-10
Page 4

E-MAIL DRAFT

Three of the forty companies said their company had experienced abuse(s) of their electronic mail system.

Only eight of the forty companies said they had a specific written or unwritten policy involving the privacy issue.[2]

CONCLUSION

Awareness

We found a lack of awareness regarding every facet of the electronic mail privacy issue among our survey companies. They were not generally aware of abuses of their electronic mail system, and reported almost no problems involving privacy of mail messages. Among the few companies with a specific policy involving the privacy issue, few managers know any details of the company policy.

Available Laws

There is currently no federal law that addresses the rights of E-mail users and owners. Ron Plesser[3] suggests that companies make sure the "ground rules are explicitly clear." If a company intends to monitor E-mail, the employees must be notified of that intention from the beginning. (Castaletti)

There seems little that employees can do to defend their right to privacy in electronic communications in the workplace. Employers can institute their rights because of the use of business resources and to guard against computer crime.

At issue is whether or not the employer makes it clear that your communications are subject to routine supervision. If so, then management has the right to monitor those communications. If not--and the employee believes that their communications are private--then the employer may have violated the law.

The people caught in the middle are the MIS, PC, and communications managers. Even if they are not in favor of a policy to read the E-mail, they are likely to be the ones involved if it is carried out.

---

[2]SPSS was used to summarize the data from the fifty usable completed surveys.

[3]Former general counsel of the US Privacy Protection Study Commission.

Page 5

Figure 13-10

Page 5

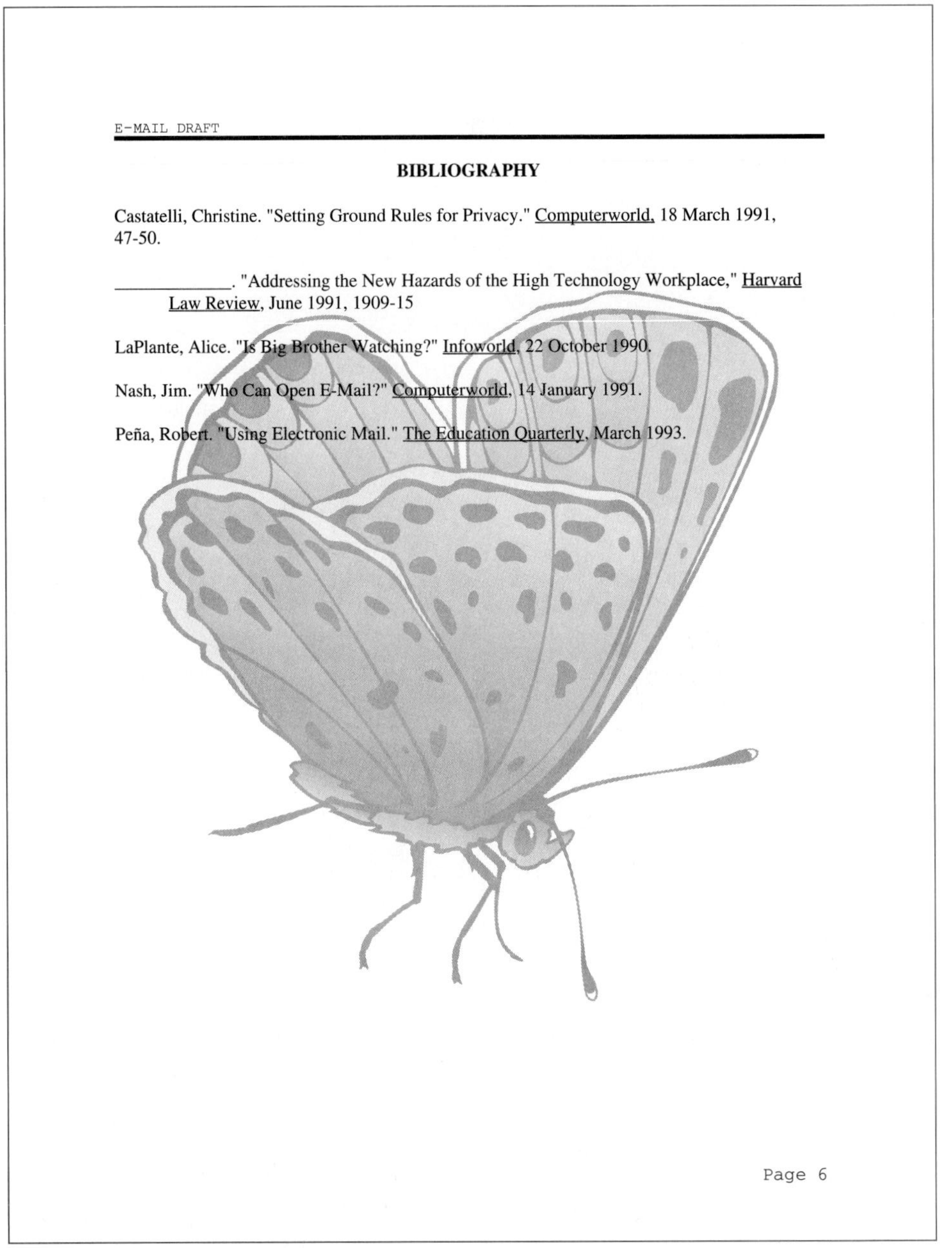

E-MAIL DRAFT

BIBLIOGRAPHY

Castatelli, Christine. "Setting Ground Rules for Privacy." Computerworld, 18 March 1991, 47-50.

____________. "Addressing the New Hazards of the High Technology Workplace," Harvard Law Review, June 1991, 1909-15

LaPlante, Alice. "Is Big Brother Watching?" Infoworld, 22 October 1990.

Nash, Jim. "Who Can Open E-Mail?" Computerworld, 14 January 1991.

Peña, Robert. "Using Electronic Mail." The Education Quarterly, March 1993.

Page 6

Figure 13-10
Page 6

14

Sorting and Selecting Records

Objectives

After completing this lesson, you will be able to:

- Identify fields, lines, words, and keys in the Sort feature
- Sort lines, paragraphs, and merge records
- Sort within a table
- Set up text correctly for Sort to work
- Select text based on specified criteria

Sort Procedures

When you are using WordPerfect, you might want to alphabetize a list of names, sort zip codes in numerical order, or list only those individuals who live in a certain zip code area. The Sort feature allows you to do that.

WordPerfect enables you to sort lines, paragraphs, merge records, and items in a table. To do so, you must have the file open. However, when the sort procedure is complete, the file onscreen is replaced with the sorted one; if you wish to keep the original, unsorted file intact, you must enter a new file name in the output file text box.

Review the following definitions before proceeding with the Sort exercises.

Records

As you learned in Lesson 11, a record is a body of information relating to one individual or entity. Assume you are working with an address list. All the information (name, address, city, state, zip code, and so on) about one individual, for example, Mr. Jones, is a record. All the information about another person, Ms. Smith, is another record. In a sort (or selection) procedure, records are the units that are sorted (or selected).

Five types of records can be sorted or selected: **merge records, line records, paragraph records, column records,** and **table records.** In a line sort, each line constitutes a record and must end with a hard return. In a paragraph sort, each paragraph constitutes a record and must end with two or more hard returns. In a merge record, as you recall, the variables separated by the {END RECORD} merge code are records. In a parallel column, each record is a row of columns, and in a table, each row of cells comprises a record.

Fields

As you remember from Lesson 11, each record is divided into fields. A particular field will have the same type of information from one record to the next. For example, a city name in an address list is considered a field. You can have any number of fields in a record.

In doing a sort, you will need to specify the field number on which to sort. Fields are numbered sequentially in WordPerfect. In lines or paragraphs, fields are separated by tabs or indents. In merge records, fields are separated by {END FIELD} merge codes in the secondary file.

Lines

In a line sort, each line is a record. Lines are counted from top to bottom, and fields are separated by tabs or indents. However, merge records and paragraph records can have multiple lines, each of which is *not* a record. For these types of sorts, a line number must be specified.

Words

Words are separated by spaces, forward slashes (/), and hard hyphens within a line or field and are usually counted from left to right. Because a field may contain several words, the number of the word must be specified. Words *can* be counted from right to left by using negative numbers. For example, if you want to sort a list of names, such as John M. Thomas, George Jones, and Mary S. Ramirez, by last name, you would select a -1. If you were to use a 3 for the last name, it would be incorrect if some had a middle initial. Also, if you had names such as Lucille M. Piedmont III, you would use a hard space between the name and the "III" so it would be counted as one word. You could also use a hard space if some people had titles and others didn't in a sort on first names.

Keys

A key is an item (word or number) on which you want to sort (or select) records. You can sort records in a file on up to 9 keys. Key 1 has the first priority, key 2 has second priority, and so on. For example, if you have a list of names, and you want to sort them first by surname and second by given name (when there is more than 1 record with the same surname), key 1 is assigned to the surname and key 2 is assigned to the given name. For example, to sort Mary Brown, George Brown and Sam Brown by surname, key 1 would be word 2 (or -1) and key 2 would be word 1 (or -2). Most of the time you will sort on only key 1.

Cells

Table rows are divided into cells. Each record is a row of cells, and cells are numbered from left to right, starting with cell 1.

▌ Using Sort

In a sort, keys are defined as alphanumeric (containing letters and/or numbers) and numeric (containing numbers only). Both can be sorted in ascending order (from A–Z and 1–10) or descending order (from Z–A and 10–1). Unless you want to sort everything contained in the document, select the specific text to sort. To sort a table or parallel column, place the insertion point inside the table or column. To perform a sort:

- Choose Tools ⇒ Sort ((Alt) + (F9)).
- The Sort dialog box displays; specify the Input File (usually the current document).
- Specify the Output File.
- Choose Line, Paragraph, or Merge Record.
- Designate the Key number.
- Designate the Type (Alpha or Numeric).
- Designate the Sort Order (Ascending or Descending).
- Designate Field, Line, if any, and Word.
- Choose OK.

NOTE: *In an alphanumeric sort, characters are evaluated from left to right, and each numeral is treated as a separate character. In a numeric sort, numbers are treated as numeric values instead of as a string of characters.*

Table 14-1 illustrates the difference between an alphanumeric and a numeric sort.

Alphanumeric Sort	Numeric Sort
1	1
10	2
11	3
12	10
2	15
21	20
3	30

Table 14-1

If the key consists of both numbers and letters, choose Alpha. If the key consists of numbers of the same length (such as account numbers, zip codes, or Social Security numbers) either Alpha or Numeric can be chosen. If the numbers are uneven in length, always choose Numeric. This differs from most database programs. In database programs, a field is alphabetic if you do not intend to perform calculations on it, such as addition, subtraction, and so on.

When you want to perform a line sort, be sure that only one tab stop is defined between columns in the file you are sorting and that each line ends with a hard return. If more than one tab stop is present or the hard return is missing, the sort will be unsuccessful.

If the file contains text that is not to be included in the sort procedure (such as a title or heading), be sure to select only the text that is to be sorted, or your heading will be sorted into the data.

In the following exercises, you'll be using the authors.wpd file on your data disk. This file contains a list of the authors to whom you are assigned. The list includes the authors' names, their cities and states, the number of books each has written, and the amount of royalties each has earned. First, you will sort the list by surname and given name. Key 1 will be the surname (field 1, word -1) and key 2 will be the given name (field 1, word 1).

1. Open the authors.wpd file on your data disk

   In the Reveal Codes screen, you will notice that fields are separated by single tabs and records are separated by hard returns (HRt codes). Therefore you will instruct WordPerfect to sort by line.

2. Click on <u>T</u>ools ⇒ So<u>r</u>t

   ✓ Press (Alt) + (F9)

   The Sort dialog box appears, as shown in Figure 14-1. The I<u>n</u>put File will remain as <Current Document>.

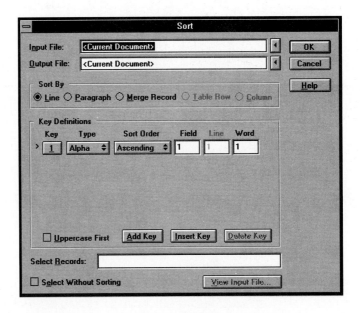

Figure 14-1

3. In the <u>O</u>utput File type `autname`

4. Select <u>L</u>ine in the Sort By box, if not already selected

   Since you are going to sort on two keys, you must insert a second key.

5. Click on <u>I</u>nsert Key

   A second key is inserted. You want key 1 to sort on the surname. Notice that the surname is the last word of the first field. Because some names are three words, you need to sort on the last word in the field by specifying -1. Use (Tab) to go to the text boxes.

6. In Key 1, click on Alpha under Type

7. Click on Ascending under Sort Order

8. Insert 1 in Field text box (for first column)

9. Insert -1 in Word text box (for last word of first field)

10. Make the following changes to the Key Definition section of the dialog box for key 2:

Type: Alpha
Sort Order: Ascending
Field: 1
Word: 1

Compare your dialog box to the one shown in Figure 14-2. Now begin the sort.

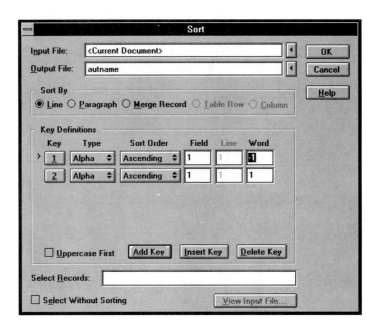

Figure 14-2

11. Click OK

12. Open autname

Compare your document to the one shown in Figure 14-3. Notice that when two same surnames occur, the entries are also sorted by first name (Cheryl Anne Thomas, Courtney Thomas).

13. Print and close autname

 Now you will sort the list by the amount of royalties earned (field 4), in descending order—the highest-earning authors will be listed first. Authors.wpd should still be on the screen. There is only one word in the fourth field, so 1 is correct.

Donna Flanders	Salt Lake City, Utah	1	15,000
James Jordan	Boulder, Colorado	4	56,000
George L. Kingman	Santa Cruz, California	4	73,000
Anita Majore	Atlanta, Georgia	5	77,000
Mary Norblom	Bangor, Maine	9	220,000
Cheryl Anne Thomas	Lakewood, Colorado	6	92,000
Courtney Thomas	Sierra Madre, California	1	15,000
Jim Witherspoon	Tampa Bay, Florida	7	133,000
Tom Yoder	Littleton, Colorado	2	30,000

Figure 14-3

1. Click on <u>T</u>ools ⇒ So<u>r</u>t

   ✓ Press (Alt) + (F9)

2. Name the output file authroy

   Make sure <u>L</u>ine is selected. Since you are sorting on one field only, you need to delete the second field.

3. Click on <u>D</u>elete Key

4. Set the information in the Sort box as follows:

   Type: Numeric
   Sort Order: Descending
   Field: 4
   Word: 1

   Compare your dialog box to the one shown in Figure 14-4.

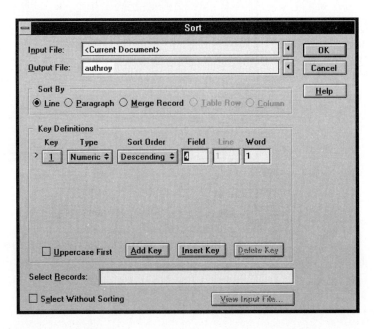

Figure 14-4

5. Click on OK

6. Open authroy

   Compare your document to the one shown in Figure 14-5.

Mary Norblom	Bangor, Maine	9	220,000
Jim Witherspoon	Tampa Bay, Florida	7	133,000
Cheryl Anne Thomas	Lakewood, Colorado	6	92,000
Anita Majore	Atlanta, Georgia	5	77,000
George L. Kingman	Santa Cruz, California	4	73,000
James Jordan	Boulder, Colorado	4	56,000
Tom Yoder	Littleton, Colorado	2	30,000
Courtney Thomas	Sierra Madre, California	1	15,000
Donna Flanders	Salt Lake City, Utah	1	15,000

Figure 14-5

7. Print and close the file

▌ Performing Merge Sorts

In this exercise, you are going to sort a secondary merge file called speakrs.wpd, which is on your data disk. You will sort that file by zip code. Open this file. You will change the document only onscreen and will not create an output file.

For your reference, the first record is shown following.

Dr. Tom Westcott{END FIELD}
Healthcare Computer System{END FIELD}
7455 W. Elm Drive
Trumbull, CT 06111{END FIELD}
(203) 533-4499{END FIELD}
Dr. Westcott{END FIELD}
Computers in Healthcare{END FIELD}
Thursday{END FIELD}
March 14{END FIELD}
10:00 a.m. - 3:00 p.m.{END FIELD}
{END RECORD}

You will see that the zip code is the third field, the second line, and the last word from the right.

1. Click on <u>T</u>ools ⇒ So<u>r</u>t

   ✓ Press (Alt) + (F9)

2. Click on <u>M</u>erge Record

3. In the Key Definitions box, set:

   Type: <u>N</u>umeric
   Sort Order: A<u>s</u>cending
   Field: 3
   Line: 2
   Word: 1

   Compare your dialog box to that in Figure 14-6.

4. Click on OK

   The records should be sorted by zip code in ascending order.

Sort

Input File:	\<Current Document\>	◀		**OK**	
Output File:	\<Current Document\>	◀		**Cancel**	

Sort By
○ **Line** ○ **Paragraph** ◉ **Merge Record** ○ Table Row ○ Column

Help

Key Definitions

Key	Type	Sort Order	Field	Line	Word
▶ **1**	Numeric ⬍	Ascending ⬍	3	2	1

☐ **Uppercase First**   [**Add Key**] [**Insert Key**] [Delete Key]

Select Records: [   ]

☐ **Select Without Sorting**   [View Input File...]

Figure 14-6

5. Print and close the file *without* saving the changes

In the next exercise, you will sort the secondary merge file first by state and then by city. The state will be specified as key 1 and the city as key 2. Open the speakrs.wpd file again and stay in the current document.

1. Click on <u>T</u>ools ⇒ So<u>r</u>t

   ✓ Press (Alt) + (F9)

2. Make the changes in your dialog box to reflect the following:

   Key 1
   Type: <u>A</u>lpha
   Sort Order: Ascending
   Field: 3
   Line: 2
   Word: -2

   Key 2
   Type: <u>A</u>lpha
   Sort Order: Ascending
   Field: 3
   Line: 2
   Word: 1

3. Click on OK

   Check to make sure your sort is successful. The file should be sorted by state and then by city in ascending order.

4. Print and close the file without saving the changes

Performing Paragraph Sorts

In this exercise, you are going to perform a paragraph sort. The file you will be working with, para.wpd, is on your data disk. Open it now, and notice that each paragraph of this document has a heading. You want to have the paragraphs appear in alphabetical order by heading.

1. Click on <u>T</u>ools ⇒ So<u>r</u>t

   ✓ Press (Alt) + (F9)

2. Set the following information in the Sort box:

   Sort By: <u>P</u>aragraph
   Type: Alpha
   Sort Order: A<u>s</u>cending
   Field: 1
   Line: 1
   Word: 1

3. Click on OK

   Compare your file to the one shown in Figure 14-7.

CALENDARING - A calendaring package is software that is loaded on a workstation, or on a host computer if workstations are networked together. The simpler packages will allow you to keep track of all the meetings and appointments made for one day, one week, or one month.

ELECTRONIC MAIL - An electronic mail package allows the user to send a message via computers within the same room, within the same building, across a campus, or across the ocean. A software package is loaded on some type of computer, and every person at a workstation attached to that computer has the capability of sending a message to every other person at a workstation.

SPREADSHEETS - Spreadsheet software is probably the package most widely used by business decision-makers today. A spreadsheet is a tool for analyzing data. It is a problem solver, an instrument to assemble data into a logical format. It is used to measure, analyze, and project.

TIME MANAGEMENT - Of all the resources available to professionals, time is the most valuable because it is a fixed quantity. It cannot be increased; it can only be managed by judicious planning, by prioritizing tasks, and then by working efficiently, effectively, and creatively within the constraints of the calendar.

WORD PROCESSING - One of the most obvious time-savers is word processing. Instead of typing slowly and being very careful not to make mistakes, users can type at rough-draft speed, not being concerned about mistakes. They can then correct errors; insert, delete, move, and copy blocks of text; and print the document out in a few minutes.

Figure 14-7

4. Print and close the file without saving the changes

Performing Table Sorts

In this exercise you will sort a table. The table is on your data disk, is called seminar.wpd, and is shown in Figure 14-8.

Interface Seminar Speakers		
Mr. Don Daniels	Windows Training	Tuesday 7:30 a.m. - 4:30 p.m.
Dr. Susan Jackson	OS/2 Installation	Friday 3:00 p.m. - 5:30 p.m.
Mr. Al Thompson	Purchasing a PC	Wednesday 4:30 p.m. - 7:00 p.m.
Dr. Tom Westcott	Computers in Healthcare	Thursday 1:00 p.m. - 3:00 p.m.
Mr. Kirk Jackson	PC Peripherals	Monday 3:30 p.m. - 6:00 p.m.
Dr. Lea Albergetti	Bytes in Banking	Wednesday 1:30 p.m. - 3:30 p.m.

Figure 14-8

You are going to sort the table by surname and then by given name. Because you don't want the title included in the sort, you will select the rest of the table. Be sure your pointer is positioned in a column in the table.

1. Select the table, excepting the title row

2. Click on <u>T</u>ools ⇒ So<u>r</u>t

   ✓ Press (Alt) + (F9)

   The Sort dialog box appears, with <u>T</u>able Row already selected as the record type. You need two keys for the sort. Tables and columns cannot be output to a file, so you will sort the original document.

3. Click on <u>I</u>nsert Key

4. Make the following changes to the Key Definitions section of the dialog box:

   Key 1
   Type: Alpha
   Sort Order: Ascending
   Cell: 1
   Line: 1
   Word: -1

   Key 2
   Type: Alpha
   Sort Order: Ascending
   Cell: 1
   Line: 1
   Word: 2

   Compare your dialog box to the one shown in Figure 14-9.

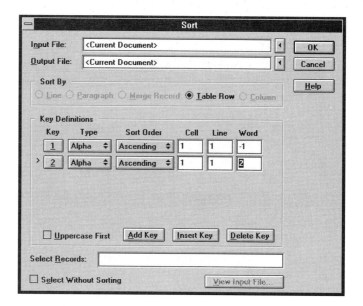

Figure 14-9

5. Click on OK

The names should be in alphabetical order, with Kirk Jackson before Susan Jackson.

6. Print and close your file without saving it

Using Select

There will be occasions when you do not want to use an entire list of records. You might instead want to have a sublist that contains records meeting a specific criterion, for example, a list of individuals who live within a specific zip code or who have an annual income of more than a specified amount.

To select certain records from a file, use **logical symbols** to see if the fields meet the criteria you specify as the key or keys. The logical symbols are listed in Table 14-2.

Symbol	Function
¦ (OR)	Selects records that meet condition of either key
& (AND)	Selects records that meet conditions of both keys
=	Selects records that have *exactly* the same information as key
<>	Selects records that do not match (are not equal to) key
>	Selects records that are greater than key
<	Selects records that are less than key
>=	Selects records that are greater than or equal to key
<=	Selects records that are less than or equal to key

Table 14-2

Logical Symbols

To use the Select feature, first specify the desired keys in the Key Definitions section of the Sort dialog box. Next, in the Select Records text box, type the condition. For example, suppose you want to select all the records for Denver. In that case, you would define key 1 as the city, and in the Select Records text box, you would type Key 1=Denver.

In this exercise, you will select all the authors who live in Colorado. Key 1 will be the state and key 2 the city, so that the records will appear in alphabetical order by city. Open the authors.wpd file.

1. Click on <u>T</u>ools ⇒ So<u>r</u>t

    ✓ Press (Alt) + (F9)

2. Name the output file sortcolo

3. Click on <u>I</u>nsert Key if two fields are not already showing

4. Make the following selections:

    Sort By: Line

    Key 1
    Type: Alpha
    Sort Order: Ascending
    Field: 2
    Word: -1

    Key 2
    Type: Alpha
    Sort Order: Ascending
    Field: 2
    Word: 1

5. Move to the Select <u>R</u>ecords text box and type `Key 1=Colorado`

    Compare your dialog box to the one shown in Figure 14-10.

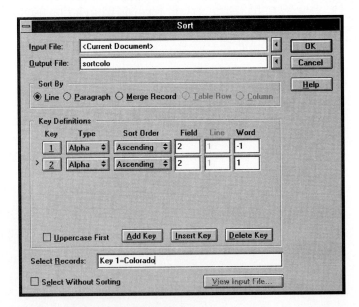

Figure 14-10

6. Click on OK

7. Open sortcolo

The sublist appears on your screen. There are three authors who live in Colorado. Compare your screen to the one shown in Figure 14-11.

James Jordan	Boulder, Colorado	4	56,000
Cheryl Anne Thomas	Lakewood, Colorado	6	92,000
Tom Yoder	Littleton, Colorado	2	30,000

Figure 14-11

8. Print and close the file

In the following exercise, you are going to create a sublist of all your high producers—authors who have written more than 4 books and have made more than $60,000—in descending order. The Royalty field is 4 and the Number of Books field is 3.

1. Open authors.wpd if it is not already displayed on your screen

2. Click on <u>T</u>ools ⇒ So<u>r</u>t

   ✓ Press (Alt) + (F9)

3. Name the output file sorthigh

4. Make the following selections:

   Sort By: Line

   Key 1
   Type: Numeric
   Sort Order: Descending
   Field: 4
   Word: 1

   Key 2
   Type: Numeric
   Sort Order: Descending
   Field: 3
   Word: 1

5. Move to the Select <u>R</u>ecords text box and type `key 1>60,000 & key 2>4`

   Remember, the "&" specifies that both conditions must be met.

   Compare your dialog box to the one shown in Figure 14-12.

6. Click on OK

7. Open `sorthigh`

   The sublist appears on your screen. There are five authors who meet these criteria. Compare your screen to the one shown in Figure 14-13.

8. Print sorthigh and close both documents without saving them

9. Exit WordPerfect

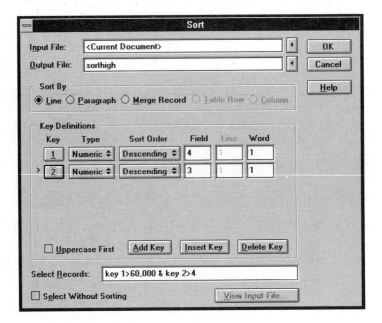

Figure 14-12

Mary Norblom	Bangor, Maine	9	220,000
Jim Witherspoon	Tampa Bay, Florida	7	133,000
Cheryl Anne Thomas	Lakewood, Colorado	6	92,000
Anita Majore	Atlanta, Georgia	5	77,000

Figure 14-13

On Your Own

Review of Commands

Description	Menu Commands	Function Keys
Begin sort or selection	_____	_____

Lesson Review

1. What are two of the four record types that can be sorted?

2. What comprises a record in a merge record?

3. What denotes a record in a table?

4. How are words defined in a sort?

5. How are keys defined, and how many keys can be used in a sort?

6. What is the essential formatting criteria for a line sort?

7. How would you sort only on the state in the following record? Specify alpha or numeric, and the field, line, and word of the key.

Name [end field]
Street [end field]
City/State/Zip [end field]

8. What logical symbol denotes greater than or equal to?

9. What symbol do you use when selecting on more than one condition?

10. Assuming key 1 and key 2 are correctly defined, what would you type in the Record Selection box to select all the Smiths who live in Denver?

11. When do you use negative numbers in a sort?

12. How do you sort records in a table without sorting the title and column headings?

13. What is descending order?

14. What is ascending order?

15. Compare an alphanumeric sort and a numeric sort on the numbers 1–10.

Assignments

14-1 Directions

1. Type a three-line title, boldface and centered:

THE UNIVERSITY OF LEARNING
CMS Department
Fall Semester

2. Set up headings for the following five columns (remember to use only one tab between each column).

Student Name	City & State	Age	GPA	Scholarship Amount

3. Enter the following information:

Cathy Ward	Denver, Colorado	24	3.2	1,000
Linda A. Werner	Arvada, Colorado	26	2.9	900
Boyd G. Rivera	Denver, Colorado	18	2.0	00
Charles Dysert	Aurora, Colorado	39	1.5	600
Wendy Pope	Arvada, Colorado	45	3.7	1,200
Laurie Wright	Arvada, Colorado	20	3.5	1,100

4. Save the file as finaid.wpd and print it.

14-2 Directions

1. Open the file finaid.wpd.
2. Save the file as finaid2.wpd.
3. Line sort the file on the students' surnames, in ascending order.
4. Save the file, print it, and close it.
5. Open finaid.wpd.
6. Save the file as gpa.wpd.
7. Line sort on the students' GPAs in ascending order.
8. Save the file again, print, and close it.

14-3 Directions

1. Open the file finaid.wpd.
2. Save the file as finaid25.wpd.
3. Select all students older than 25 with a GPA greater than 3.0.
4. Save the file, print, and close it.
5. Open finaid.wpd.
6. Save it as finamt.wpd.
7. Select students with a GPA above 3.0 and a scholarship amount greater than or equal to $600.
8. Save the file and print it.
9. From the original file, create and print a list of all students who live in Arvada. Save it as arvada.wpd.

14-4 Directions

1. Open letter.dat from your data disk and save it as letter1.dat.
2. Sort on surname in ascending order.
3. Print, but do not save the document.
4. From the same file, sort on zip code in descending order.
5. Print, but do not save the document.
6. From the same file, sort on state in ascending order.
7. Print, but do not save the document.

14-5 Directions

1. Open partime.dat from your data disk. Save as partm2.dat.
2. Do an alphabetic sort by Surname in ascending order, print, and do not save the document.

3. Perform a numeric sort by course number in descending order, and print, but do not save the document.

4. Do an alphanumeric sort by zip code in descending order, and print, but do not save the document.

5. Select all records with a course level greater than or equal to 300. Print, but do not save the document.

14-6 Directions

1. Open font.wpd on your data disk.

2. Perform a paragraph sort on the second through the last paragraphs.

3. Sort in ascending order.

4. Print, but do not save the document.

14-7 Directions

1. Open interfac.wpd from your data disk. Save as inter2.wpd.

2. Select the table, excepting the title row.

3. Sort the table in alphabetical order by last name, and print, but do not save the document.

4. Open inter2.wpd again. Select the Wednesday speakers' names.

5. Make sure the Wednesday speakers are listed in alphabetical order by surname.

6. Print, but do not save the document.

14-8 Directions

1. Open student.wpd on your data disk. Save it as student1.wpd.

2. Select the table, excepting the title and header rows. Sort by surname in ascending order. Print, but do not save the document.

3. Open student1.wpd again.

4. Select all married students. Sort in descending order by income. Print, but do not save the document.

5. Open student1.wpd again.

6. Select all married, female students. Sort them in ascending order by income. Print, but do not save the document.

7. Open student1.wpd again.

8. Select all students who have children. Sort them numerically, in descending order *and* alphabetically within each number. Print, but do not save the document.

15

Implementing

Styles

LESSON

Objectives

After completing this lesson, you will be able to:

- Define the Styles feature
- Create and use styles in document formatting
- Save styles in a style document
- Retrieve a style
- Edit a style
- Use a template to format a document
- Modify a WordPerfect template
- Use the TextArt feature within a document

■ About Styles

If you use a consistent format for various documents, WordPerfect allows you to save the format in a **style** so that you can easily apply it to any document. A style is usually a group of stored formatting codes which can also contain text. Using this powerful feature, you can designate a set of formats for longer documents such as reports or books. For example, one style might control the margins, the widow/orphan control, page numbering, and the justification. Another style could designate the font size and alignment of the main heading. A third style might apply special emphasis to certain paragraphs by indenting and italicizing them. After you build the styles, attach the style document to your text document. Your styles can also be saved as a separate document, and then retrieved and used in any document.

Another advantage of using styles is that if you wish to change a style, all the text formatted with that particular style will be automatically changed. Thus, if you change your mind about the way a particular heading should appear, you do not have to search the entire document to locate all the headings that use that particular formatting. Instead, you simply edit the style, and all the text with that style format is changed at once.

325

You should be aware, however, that using styles increases the size of your document because the styles are saved with the document. This makes formatting a document that has several styles run more slowly than formatting a document that has none.

A related feature of WordPerfect for Windows 6.0 is a series of preformatted documents called templates. A **template** document can be used repeatedly to create documents of the same type. An example of a template document might be a memorandum heading that has all the formatting and standard text in place. All you need do is enter the variable information that changes from memo to memo. WordPerfect has created interactive template documents called **Expressdocs.**

In this chapter you will learn to apply and create styles, as well as use a template document. You will also be introduced to **TextArt,** a very easy-to-use graphics program that allows you to jazz up your documents.

▌ Using Styles

Styles are most useful when you create them yourself because you can tailor them to your own preferences. However, WordPerfect has created a few styles for you. You will work with these styles first to familiarize yourself with the styles concept; then you will go on to create and use styles of your own. To use a style:

- Choose Layout ⇒ Styles (⟨Alt⟩ + ⟨F8⟩).
- Select a style from the Style List dialog box.
- Choose Apply.

▌ Creating Styles

You have the option to either create your styles before typing your document, or type the document and then create and apply the styles. To create a style:

- Choose Layout ⇒ Styles (⟨Alt⟩ + ⟨F8⟩).
- Choose Create.
- Type a name in the Style Name text box.
- Type a description in the Description text box.
- Choose Type and select Paragraph, Character, or Document.

Paragraph (Paired)

This style formats the entire paragraph in which the insertion point is placed. Paragraph styles are useful for formatting items such as titles and headings. Remember that a paragraph is any text that ends with a hard return code.

NOTE: *The words "paired" and "open" refer to the placement of the style codes. Paired styles have a style on and a style off code enclosing the text to be affected. Open styles have only one code to mark the beginning of the text to be affected.*

Character (Paired)

This style formats all text from the insertion point forward until you turn it off by choosing the None style. Character styles are useful for formatting text within a paragraph. Some common usages might be bolding, changing font size, and so on.

Document (Open)

This style has only a beginning. In other words, it is in effect from the position of the cursor forward until another code of the same type is encountered, instructing a change. This style is used to set the format for a document or page, such as top and bottom margins, or for the paragraph, such as the left and right margins. An open style cannot be turned off.

Turning Styles On and Off

When a style is turned off, the text you are typing returns to its original format. To turn a style off:

- Choose Layout ⇒ Styles.
- Select None from the Styles List.

You can also have the (Enter) key turn off a style. The Enter Key will Chain to: option determines what the (Enter) key will do when you are using a paired style. There are three choices available.

First, deselecting the Enter Key will Chain to: option causes (Enter) to operate in its normal manner without turning off the style.

Second, selecting the Enter Key will Chain to: None option moves the insertion point, when (Enter) is pressed, past the style code, thus turning it off. In other words, the "None" option causes (Enter) to deactivate the style. This option is useful when typing a heading, for example; turn the style on, type the text, and then turn the style off by pressing (Enter).

Third, selecting the Enter Key will Chain to: Same Style option causes (Enter) to turn off a paired style, and then turn it on again. For example, you might use this option for a list of bulleted items. Each item is preceded by an indent, a bullet, and another indent, with a hard return at the end of each item. To use this option, you would turn the style on (the style includes an indent, bullet, and another indent), type the text, and press (Enter). The hard return that was included at the end of the style is inserted, the style is then turned off and back on again for the next item—including the indents and bullet.

Building the Style

There are two ways to create a style. You can build a style from scratch, the method discussed here, by inserting desired codes into the style editor. Second, you can create a style using QuickCreate, a method discussed in the next section.

The Contents window, which appears at the lower half of the Styles Editor, is where the style contents are placed. Reveal Codes is turned on so that you can see the codes as they are inserted. Insert the codes for the desired formats and enter text if you desire. You can use the menu at the top of the Style Editor to select the formatting codes you desire, or you may use shortcut commands from the keyboard. Once your style is complete and all your options are selected, choose OK.

Using QuickCreate

Using QuickCreate has advantages over building the style from scratch. You can create a style "by example" from text that has already been formatted. Doing so is both faster and less prone to error. To create a style from formatted text, first place the insertion point in the formatted text.

- Choose Layout ⇒ Styles.
- Choose QuickCreate.
- Enter a name and description of the style.
- Choose OK.

▌ Saving Styles in a Style Document

The styles you create for a document are saved automatically *only* with that document. However, WordPerfect also lets you save these styles in a **style document** so that you can use the same styles in other documents. To save a style document:

- Choose Layout ⇒ Styles.
- Choose Options ⇒ Save As.
- Name the style document.
- Select User Styles.
- Choose OK.

Be sure to put an extension on the file name such as ".sty" to identify the document as one containing styles. Style documents are automatically saved in WordPerfect's Template directory.

▌ Retrieving a Style Document

Once a style document has been saved, it can easily be retrieved and attached to another text document so that the styles listed can be used to format the new document. To do so:

- Choose Layout ⇒ Styles ⇒ Options ⇒ Retrieve.
- Type the directory and name of the style document.
- Choose OK.

After the style document has been retrieved, you can either create a new text document or open an existing one.

▌ Editing Styles

Once a style is created, it can easily be edited. When you do so, all text marked with that style is automatically changed. To edit a style:

- Choose Layout ⇒ Styles.
- Select the style to be edited.
- Choose Editor.
- Make the desired changes.
- Choose OK.

You are reviewing and editing an article for publication in the *Interface* newsletter. The document is a report with several sections divided by headings and subheadings. You will apply a style to each heading.

1. Open oapaper.wpd and immediately save as oapaper2.wpd

2. Place the insertion point in the title

3. Click on <u>L</u>ayout ⇒ <u>S</u>tyles

   ✓ Press (Alt) + (F8)

   The Style List dialog box appears as shown in Figure 15-1. You can see several style names in the <u>N</u>ame text box.

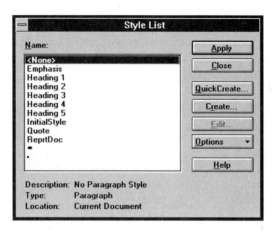

Figure 15-1

4. Select Heading 1

   The description at the bottom of the dialog box changes to "Title."

5. Click on <u>A</u>pply

   The title of the report becomes centered, boldfaced, and in a larger font.

6. Place the insertion point in the word "BACKGROUND"

7. Click on <u>L</u>ayout ⇒ <u>S</u>tyles, select Heading 2, and click on <u>A</u>pply

   Notice that the description changes to Main Heading.

8. Click on <u>A</u>pply or double-click on Heading 2

   The main heading becomes boldfaced in a slightly larger font.

9. Apply the Heading 2 style to the remaining main headings: LITERATURE SEARCH, ORIGINAL RESEARCH, and REFERENCES

10. Place your insertion point in the Automated Office Systems subheading on page 1

11. Apply the Heading 3 style

12. Use QuickFormat from the button bar, or double-click on the right mouse button, and apply the **Heading 3** style to the remaining subheadings in the document

13. Save and close the document; do not print it

In the following exercises you will use both methods to create three styles. You will first build a style to format an entire document by selecting a Document Initial Code, specifying double-spacing, and turning on the Widow/ Orphan feature. The second style is a paragraph format for quotations. You will use QuickCreate to create it. You will build the third style, a character format style designed to emphasize text within a document. Do not close the document until the end of the exercises. Name and save it if you need to exit before you are finished.

1. Choose <u>L</u>ayout ⇒ <u>S</u>tyles

   ✓ Press (Alt) + (F8)

   The Style List dialog box appears.

2. Click on C<u>r</u>eate

   The Styles Editor dialog box appears with the insertion point in the <u>S</u>tyle Name window as shown in Figure 15-2.

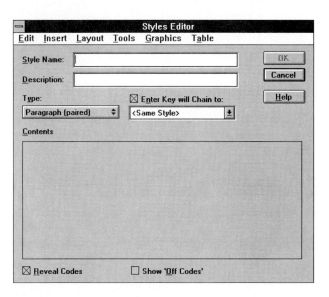

Figure 15-2

3. Type `ReprtDoc`

4. Tab to the <u>D</u>escription window and type `Courier New 10 pt, 2 spacing, and W/O on`

   Now you will specify a document style. Remember, a document style is an open style that has only a beginning and takes effect from the cursor forward.

5. Click on T<u>y</u>pe ⇒ Document (open)

   Move the insertion point to the <u>C</u>ontents area of the dialog box. It should have a flashing cursor bar at the top left corner. This is where you will insert the formatting codes for the style.

6. Click on <u>L</u>ayout ⇒ <u>F</u>ont ⇒ Courier New ⇒ 10 pt ⇒ OK

7. Click on <u>L</u>ayout ⇒ <u>L</u>ine ⇒ <u>S</u>pacing ⇒ 2 ⇒ OK

8. Click on <u>L</u>ayout ⇒ <u>P</u>age ⇒ <u>K</u>eep Text Together ⇒ Widow/Orphan ⇒ OK

Compare your screen to Figure 15-3.

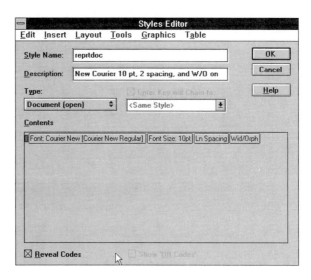

Figure 15-3

9. Click on OK

The Style List dialog box reappears and the ReprtDoc style is listed with the description shown below the list box.

10. Click on <u>C</u>lose

 Now you will use QuickCreate to create a paragraph style that can be used for quotations. It will be indented five spaces from both sides, italicized, and in boldface.

1. Type the following, using bold, italic, Helvetica 14 pt, and double indent (all of these can be found on the power bar)

   `"There has been a lot of confusion about where and how to educate office automation systems professionals."`

2. Click on <u>L</u>ayout ⇒ <u>S</u>tyles

   ✓ Press (Alt) + (F8)

   The Style List dialog box appears.

3. Click on QuickCreate

   The Styles QuickCreate dialog box appears as shown in Figure 15-4 with the insertion point in the Style <u>N</u>ame window.

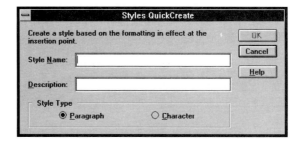

Figure 15-4

4. Type `Quote`

5. Move to Description and type `dbl indent, italics, bold, Helve 14pt`

6. Make sure that <u>P</u>aragraph is the Style Type button selected

7. Click on OK

   The Style List window appears with "Quote" listed as a style name; the description appears at the bottom of the screen. This is by far the fastest and easiest way to create a style.

8. Click on <u>C</u>lose in the dialog box

Now you are ready to create the last style. It is a character style that you can use to bold and double underline text within a document wherever you want emphasis. The (Enter) key will turn this style off.

1. Click on <u>L</u>ayout ⇒ <u>S</u>tyles ⇒ <u>C</u>reate

   The Styles Editor dialog box appears, with the insertion point in the <u>N</u>ame text box.

2. Type `Emphasis`

   Move to the <u>D</u>escription text box.

3. Type `Bold, dbl underline`

   You want to specify a character style:

4. Click on <u>T</u>ype ⇒ Character (paired)

   Now specify that the style be turned off with (Enter).

5. Select E<u>n</u>ter Key will Chain to: (the box may already be selected) and select None

6. Move to the <u>C</u>ontents area of the screen

7. Select <u>L</u>ayout ⇒ Font from the Styles Editor menu

8. Select Bold and Double Underline from the Appearance list

9. Click on OK

   The Styles Editor box displays the codes in the <u>C</u>ontents area.

10. Click on OK

    The Style List box appears. Make sure "Emphasis" is listed among the style names.

11. Click on <u>C</u>lose to close the Style List Dialog Box

    Do *not* close the document.

    NOTE: You could also have created the Emphasis style by using QuickCreate.

In this exercise, you are going to save the styles you created so that they can be used in other text documents. You will give the style document the name manscrpt.sty.

1. Choose <u>L</u>ayout ⇒ <u>S</u>tyles

The Style List dialog box appears with the styles you just created still listed.

2. Click on <u>O</u>ptions ⇒ Save <u>A</u>s

The Save Styles To dialog box appears, as shown in Figure 15-5.

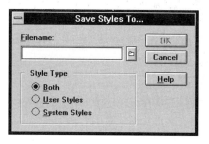

Figure 15-5

3. Type `manscrpt.sty`

Make sure to add the .sty extension. Remember, the style document will be stored in the Template directory.

4. Select <u>U</u>ser Styles from the Style Type box

5. Click on OK

6. Close the Style List dialog box

7. Close your original document without saving

In this exercise, you will retrieve the style document manscrpt.sty and then retrieve the text file located on your data disk called oapaper.wpd. Make sure you have a clear document window.

1. Click on <u>L</u>ayout ⇒ <u>S</u>tyles ⇒ <u>O</u>ptions ⇒ <u>R</u>etrieve

The Retrieve Styles From dialog box appears as shown in Figure 15-6.

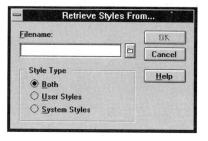

Figure 15-6

2. Type `c:\wpwin60\template\manscrpt.sty`

3. Click on OK

4. Click on Close

You will now see your styles listed whenever you access Styles. You are going to retrieve the oapaper.wpd document.

5. Click on <u>F</u>ile ⇒ <u>O</u>pen

6. Select oapaper.wpd

7. On your own, position the insertion point after the title at the top of the document and apply the ReprtDoc style

8. Scroll down through your document until you come to the second paragraph under "Curriculum Deficiencies:" beginning "These programs . . ."

9. Apply the Quote style to the two paragraphs that are direct quotes in this section

10. Scroll down to the end of the document just above "REFERENCES"

You are going to add a concluding paragraph using your Emphasis style. You will turn off the style using the (Enter) key.

11. Press (Enter) twice and type the following text:

    `We believe this new emphasis fulfills a`

12. Apply the emphasis style and type:

    `largely unmet need for office information systems`
    `graduates.`

13. Press (Enter) to turn off the style and continue typing:

    `We invite your comments and suggestions on our`
    `implementation of this area of study.`

14. Save and close the document

In this exercise, you are going to edit the ReprtDoc style so that the text is single-spaced.

1. Open oapaper.wpd

2. Choose Layout ⇒ Styles

   The Style List dialog box appears.

3. Select ReprtDoc

4. Click on Edit

   The Styles Editor window appears.

5. Move the insertion point to the Description window and replace the number 2 in front of spacing with number 1

6. In the Contents area, use the left mouse button to "grab" the Ln Spacing 2.0 code. Drag the code out of the Styles Editor Box and release the mouse button

7. Click on OK

8. Click on Close

   You are returned to the document. Notice that the report is now single spaced.

9. On your own, put in page numbering and Conditional End of Page commands where necessary

10. Save, print, and close the document

Your document should look similar to that in Figure 15-7.

▌ Using a Template

You have learned to use styles to format text. Now you are ready to use an entire preformatted document called a template.

A template is like a stencil that you use repeatedly to create documents. It can be used for documents, such as memos, that are used often. All the formatting for the memo is already completed. You need only fill in the needed information.

MODERN OFFICE INFORMATION SYSTEMS

BACKGROUND

In 1981 the CMS Department (Computer Information Systems and Management Science) at MSCD (Metropolitan State College of Denver) offered only two courses which related to office automation: word processing and automated office systems.

Automated Office Systems

When the automated office systems course was first offered in 1981, there was little information available in books. Most of the material taught was obtained from articles in periodicals such as <u>Computer World</u>, <u>Modern Office Technology</u>, and <u>The Office</u>. The emphasis of the course was on word processing, describing stand-alone systems such as Micom, CPT, NBI, and Lanier. Teleconferencing, voice mail, OCR and facsimile were also discussed.

Students were required to complete a major project concerning some issue involving office automation. Most of their material was obtained through secondary sources. The course was taught from the clerical point of view emphasizing how to use the various office systems.

Word Processing

The word processing course was also begun in 1981. There was no equipment available at the college, so the concepts were taught in the classroom, and students were taken on tours to word processing vendors and centers in the Denver area so they could see what word processing looked like.

In 1984, after the advent of the microcomputer, the college decided to offer a course on microcomputer hardware and software. A small lab was equipped with 10 personal computers, and a generic package called MicroUse was chosen to teach word processing, spreadsheet and database applications.

At that time, the CMS department was primarily a mainframe and minicomputer-oriented department which stressed data processing applications. The three areas of emphasis for the student to choose from were Systems Development and Design, Management Information Systems, and Decision Science. The curriculum committee became concerned that there was no area of emphasis for students who wanted to specialize in microcomputer training and support, information centers, and other careers in the office systems area; a study to determine the advisability of implementing an office systems emphasis was undertaken.

LITERATURE SEARCH

Curricula Deficiencies

As far back as 1984, experts were calling for the replacement of clerical/secretarial programs. Old stereotyped clerical/secretarial programs needed to be replaced by new information processing programs which combined word processing and data processing. (Regan, 1984)

In 1988, Khosrowpour noted a stereotyping similar to that reported by Regan. He said:

-1-

Figure 15-7

Page 1

"These programs view OA applications as solely useful to clerical people, not as a managerial tool. These limited programs do not focus on the behavioral aspects of OA technology and its impact on typical office personnel."

He continues:

"Most curricula used for training systems professionals have been overwhelmed with technical and programming language courses, with insufficient concentration on the organizational behavior and management of computer systems and their applications." (Khosrowpour, 1988)

In the case of OA education, there has been a lot of confusion about where and how to educate office automation systems professionals. In most information systems curricula, there are no courses covering the depth of OA or its possible applications and management.

Textbook Deficiencies

Curriculum deficiencies are compounded by textbook deficiencies. It is not surprising to find that the overwhelming majority of textbooks used in computer information systems or management information systems courses for business programs have little or no emphasis in the area of office automation. At the same time, the graduates of these programs would be the very ones who would benefit the most from knowing OA applications. (Khosrowpour, 1988)

Mulder found a similar situation in European schools. Texts are made up of programming, system analysis and of preparing flowcharts. As a result, schools offer too few opportunities to practice applications of information technology in an office context. Being able to imagine a company's structure and organization are not being sufficiently emphasized. (Mulder, 1987)

Required Competencies - General

In 1983, Disney found that business and industry were involved in an increasingly rapid change toward new equipment, and that the distinctions between office, communications, and computer equipment were disappearing. More skills were needed by staff members, especially more in-depth knowledge of office systems based on integrated new technology. (Disney, 1983)

In 1984, Regan called attention to the importance of office automation. At first, office automation was targeted for clerical tasks. Today, the emphasis has switched to tasks performed by professional and managerial personnel. Indeed, the impact is being felt all the way to the executive suite. (Regan, 1984)

Required Competencies - Specific

According to Graves (1985), required competencies of managerial personnel in automated offices include the use of: dictating machines,electronic keyboards,computer graphics, magnetic media storage, electronic mailsystems, facsimile, teleconferencing, executive workstations, distributed logic, decision support systems. (Graves, 1985)

A different view of specific skills is offered by Hosler. Recent studies have

-2-

Figure 15-7
Page 2

To create a template document:

- Select <u>F</u>ile ⇒ <u>T</u>emplate (Ctrl + T).
- Choose Options ⇒ Create Template.
- Type a name and description for the template as if it were a style.

You can then insert any information you want in the template, such as titles, headings, graphics, and so on. You can also create a template based on another template. Choose a template that has many of the formatting features you desire from the Template to Base On window, then simply modify it by adding text or formatting features. Save the modified template under a new name.

A different view of specific skills is offered by Hosler. Recent studies have shown that the four major uses of the microcomputer in business are spreadsheets, graphics, word processing, and database management. Faculty must prepare students to become familiar with each of these business applications of software. (Hosler, 1988)

Literature Review in Perspective

Everett puts our literature review into perspective. The forces in office automation focus on significant technological developments, such as the integration of the personal computer, communication networks, and information handling tools. These tools together comprise an integrated office system, designed to deliver information to the right person at the right time for effective decision making. (Everett, 1988)

In office automation, similar to other areas of business operations such as finance or marketing, management is needed. Few schools have begun to respond to this need. (Khosrowpour, 1988)

In the literature, we found support for the following:

a move away from the stereotypical office automation course designed for secretaries

a move away from a few stand-alone courses such as word processing and data processing

a move toward the use of office automation as a system

a move toward the use of office automation as an integral part of a company information system

ORIGINAL RESEARCH

Design

In 1988, a survey instrument was constructed and sent to a randomly selected sample of Denver information systems managers. The survey asked: "How important will each of the following be to your employees three years from now--in 1991?"

Our paper focuses upon the data received on the information center, office automation, and business graphics areas.

Managers were asked to check one of the following: very important, somewhat important, not very important, not at all important, or not applicable.

The mean was computed for each question based upon a value of 5 assigned to very important, 4 to somewhat important, 3 to not very important, 2 to not at all important, and 1 to not applicable. Thirty-two surveys were usable.

Findings

Table one below summarizes the responses given by the thirty-two information systems managers as to the projected importance of each skill for their employees by 1991. These responses are arranged from highest to lowest mean. The higher the mean, the more importance these managers attached to the skill.

-3-

Figure 15-7
Page 3

WordPerfect has designed a number of interactive templates called ExpressDocs. These include many types of business, education, and home-use documents. You can use these documents as they are or modify them to your specifications, save them under a new template name, and use the modified template. Take some time to explore your template directory and become familiar with the different templates.

▌ Using TextArt

TextArt is a graphics program that allows you to create type images in the shape of waves, pennants, circles, bow ties, and so on. TextArt is quite simple to use and can improve the appearance of your documents. To create a

> The student in this area of study learns about the technologies available for an office system such as personal computers, printers, scanners, facsimile machines, electronic mail. He learns how to use microcomputer software packages such as word processing, database, spreadsheet, and graphics. He learns how to select, implement, and manage local area networks and about issues relevant to connectivity (data communications and telecommunications).
>
> OIS is designed to provide the education and skills for a student to follow a career in:
>
>> microcomputer hardware and software acquisition, training and support (the student will have the expertise required to help microcomputer users select the appropriate hardware and software to solve their business problems), or office information systems analysis and design.
>
> Courses suggested for this area of study (in addition to the required courses of COBOL, Fundamentals of Systems Analysis and Design, and File Design and Data Base Management) include:
>
>> Data Communications
>> Automated Office Systems
>> Micro Based Software
>> LANS and WANS
>> Advanced Data Base Design
>
> We believe this new emphasis fulfills a **largely unmet need for office information systems graduates.** We invite your comments and suggestions on our implementation of this area of study.
>
> **REFERENCES**
>
> Disney, Christine. "Towards the Electronic Office," Further Education Unit, London (September 1983).
>
> Everett, Donna R. "Competencies for Information Systems Workers." Ph.D. diss., University of Houston, 1988.
>
> Graves, Charlotte K. "Concepts Needed by Managerial Personnel in Automated Offices as Perceived by Office Systems Consultants and Collegiate Business Faculty," The Delta Pi Epsilon Journal XXVIII (Fall/Winter 1985): 93-99.
>
> Hosler, Mary Margaret. "Revising our Curriculum for the Secretary's New Role," Business Education Forum 43 (December 1988): 16-18.
>
> Khosrowpour, Mehdi. "Office Automation As a Managerial Tool: The Underlying Importance of Education," Journal of Educational Technology Systems (1988-89): 79-87.
>
> Mulder, Martin. "New Office Technology," Beroepsgerichte Volwasseneneducatie in de Kantoorautomatisering: 19-27. Research project from April 1986-July 1987.
>
> Regan, Elizabeth A. "Behavioral and Organizational Issues of Office Automation Technology," Delta Pi Epsilon Journal (1984): 77-100.
>
> -4-

Figure 15-7
Page 4

TextArt image, first place the insertion point where you want the image to appear in your document.

- Choose <u>G</u>raphics ⇒ Te<u>x</u>tArt.
- Type the text.
- Click on the text shape.
- Change the justification and attributes.
- Choose OK.

When the TextArt image is inserted in the document, you can resize and move it as you would any other graphic image.

In the following exercise you will use one of WordPerfect's ExpressDocs to fill out an expense statement for the costs one of Bookworm's authors incurred while on a business trip.

1. Choose <u>F</u>ile ⇒ <u>T</u>emplate

✓ Press (Ctrl) + (T)

The Templates dialog box appears as in Figure 15-8.

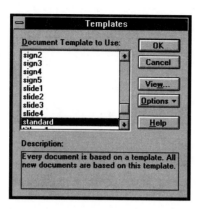

Figure 15-8

2. Scroll through the list of templates in the <u>D</u>ocument Template to Use window until "expense" is highlighted

3. Click on OK

The Personalize Your Templates dialog box appears. The insertion point should be in the Name window.

NOTE: This dialog box appears only the first time you open an ExpressDoc. The information you include in this dialog box may appear in subsequent ExpressDocs, even though a different student opens it.

4. Type your name

5. In the Title window, type `Acquisitions Editor`

This information will not appear on the expense document.

6. After Company, type `Bookworm Computer Publishing Company`

7. Move the insertion point to Address and City, State, and Zip windows, and type

`2568 Montgomery`

`Albuquerque, NM 87109`

8. In the Telephone and Fax boxes, respectively, type:

`505-837-1932;`
`505-837-3968`

Your screen should look similar to Figure 15-9.

9. Press (Enter)

Figure 15-9

The Template Information dialog box appears as shown in Figure 15-10. You want to fill in the author's name and the week she traveled.

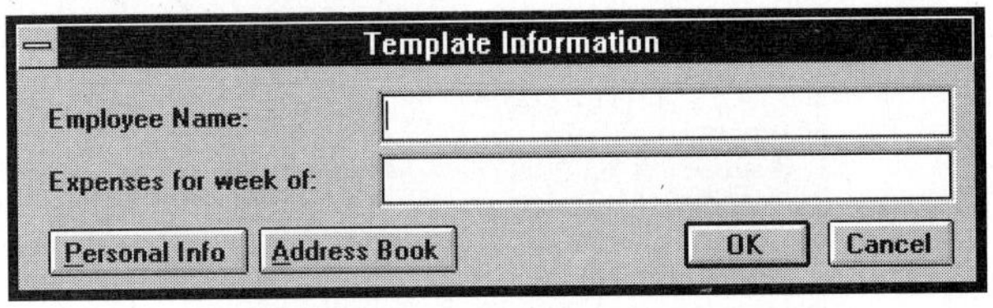

Figure 15-10

10. In the Employee Name window, type **Susan Franz**

11. Move to the next window, and type today's date

12. Click on OK

    After a moment, the expense sheet reappears with the company's name, address, author's name, and date filled in. You are now ready to fill in the author's expenses and calculate the totals.

13. Move the insertion point to the Monday column and the cell representing Breakfast

14. Type **5.39**

15. Move the insertion point to the cell for Lunch on the same day and type **12.21**

16. Fill in the other expenses as follows:

    Monday: Dinner **28.50**
    Lodging **85.00**
    Car rental **99.00**
    Airfare **558.00**

    Tuesday: Breakfast **4.49**
    Lunch **6.78**
    Dinner **25.58**
    Lodging **85.00**

    Wednesday: Breakfast **5.29**
    Lunch **8.88**
    Dinner **31.27**
    Lodging **85.00**

17. Click on Calc Doc on the button bar

The total for each of the rows and columns is filled in automatically. The final total at the bottom right of the document should read $1,041.38. If your total is not correct, reenter any erroneous numbers and click on Calc Doc again to recalculate.

18. Save the document as franzexp.wpd

19. Print the document and close it

Your document should look similar to that in Figure 15-11.

Expenses

Bookworm Computer
Publishing Company
2568 Montgomery
Albuquerque, NM 87109
505-837-1932
Fax: 505-837-3968

Employee Name: Susan Franz
Date: (today's date)

DAILY EXPENSES FOR WEEK OF: (today's date)

ITEM	SUN	MON	TUE	WED	THU	FRI	SAT	TOTAL
Breakfast		5.39	4.49	5.29				15.17
Lunch		12.21	6.78	8.88				27.87
Dinner		28.50	25.58	31.27				85.35
Lodging		85.00	85.00	85.00				255.00
Telephone								0.00
Car rental, taxi, bus		99.00						99.00
Parking or towing								0.00
Tips								0.00
Airfare		558.00						558.00
								0.00
								0.00
Daily Total	$0.00	$788.10	$121.85	$130.44	$0.00	$0.00	$0.00	
							TOTAL	$1,040.39

ENTERTAINMENT

DATE	WHO	PLACE	BUSINESS	AMOUNT
			TOTAL	$0.00

OTHER EXPENSES

DATE	DESCRIPTION	AMOUNT
	TOTAL	$0.00

TOTALS

TOTAL FROM ABOVE	$1,040.39
MINUS ADVANCE	
TOTAL DUE EMPLOYEE	$1,040.39

_____   _____
Employee Signature   Approved By

Figure 15-11

In the following exercise, you will customize a template with TextArt and use it to create a memorandum.

1. Choose File ⇒ Template

   ✓ Press (Ctrl) + (T)

2. Select Memo3 and click on Options ⇒ Edit Template

   Most of the memo template is acceptable to you. However, you want to remove the horizontal lines and add TextArt to the top of the document.

3. Turn on Reveal Codes

4. Press (Ctrl) + (Home) five or six times until the red cursor bar is to the right of Open Style: Initial Style code

5. Search for and remove the two graphic line codes contained in the document ((F2) ⇒ Match ⇒ Codes ⇒ Graph Line ⇒ Insert ⇒ Close ⇒ Find Next)

6. Again, move to the top of the document to the right of the Initial Style code box

7. Press (Enter) eight times

8. Press (Ctrl) + (Home) to move to the top of the document

9. Click on Graphics ⇒ TextArt

The TextArt window appears with the insertion point in the Enter Text window as shown in Figure 15-12.

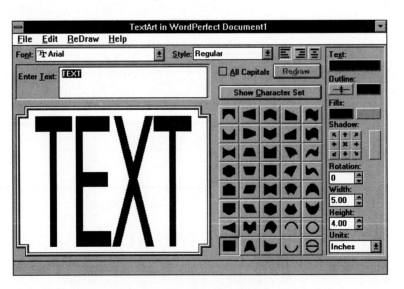

Figure 15-12

10. Type the following:

    Bookworm Computer (Enter)
    Publishing Company

11. In the Width box, enter 3.5" and in the Height box, enter 1"

12. Select the wave shape at the far right side of the first row of text shapes

    The text in the window takes the shape of a wave (sort of a symbolic worm).

13. Select <u>F</u>ile ⇒ Exit & Return to WordPerfect

    A box appears with a prompt asking if you wish to update embedded objects in WordPerfect.

14. Click on <u>Y</u>es

    After a short wait, the template reappears with the TextArt image at the top.

15. Click on the TextArt image

    The small, black sizing points appear.

16. Place the mouse pointer in the image until it takes the shape of a four-headed arrow

17. Drag the image until it is centered above "MEMORANDUM"

18. Click outside the image to remove the sizing points

19. Click on <u>F</u>ile ⇒ Save <u>A</u>s

    ✓ (F3)

    The Save Document Template dialog box appears.

20. Type `wpwin60\template\memobkwm.wpt`

21. Press (Enter)

22. Click on E<u>x</u>it Template on the feature bar

    This will save the template as is for future memos. You are returned to a clear screen.

Now that you have created your personalized template, you will use it to send a memorandum. In the following exercise you will select your template and type in the information needed to request a sales seminar for the sales representatives at Bookworm.

1. Click on <u>F</u>ile ⇒ <u>T</u>emplate

2. Select memobkwm and choose OK

   The Template Information dialog box appears with the insertion point in the Name of Recipient window as shown in Figure 15-13.

Figure 15-13

3. Type `Monroe Stuart`

4. Tab to CC: and type `Jim Ackerman`

5. Tab to Subject and type `Sales Representative`

6. Click on the <u>P</u>ersonal Info button

   The Edit Your Personal Information dialog box appears.

7. In the Name window, type your name

8. Click on OK

   You are returned to the Template Information dialog box.

9. Click on OK

   The document reappears with all the headings filled in and the insertion point placed for you to type the body of the text.

10. Type the following text:

    ```
    Sales representatives from Bookworm will be visiting
    schools during the month of February. It is time to set
    up the information seminars about our products for our
    representatives.

    Please set up a time and place for these seminars and
    attend to all the pertinent details as you have in the
    past. Send me a schedule when you complete it.
    ```

11. Print and close the document

    Do not save it; it takes more than 330,000 bytes because of the graphic image and all the interactive codes. Your document should look similar to the one in Figure 15-14.

On Your Own

Review of Commands

Description	Menu Commands	Function Keys
Create a style	_____	_____
Save a style document	_____	_____
Retrieve a style document	_____	_____
Edit a style	_____	_____
Use QuickCreate	_____	_____
Create a template	_____	_____
Customize a template	_____	_____
Use TextArt	_____	_____

Lesson Review

1. What are styles?

2. What is the advantage of using styles?

3. Where are styles stored?

Bookworm Computer Publishing Company

Memorandum

To:	Monroe Stuart
CC:	Jim Ackerman
From:	Your name
Date:	(today's date)
Subject:	Sales Representative

Sales representatives from Bookworm will be visiting schools during the month of February. It is time to set up the information seminars about our products for our representatives.

Please set up a time and place for these seminars and attend to all the pertinent details as you have in the past. Send me a schedule when you complete it.

Figure 15-14

4. What is a character style?

5. What is a document style?

6. What is a paragraph style?

7. How do you apply a style to existing text?

8. How do you edit a style?

9. How do you save styles in a style document?

10. How do you retrieve a style and attach it to another document?

11. What is the difference between a paired style and an open style?

12. What is a template?

13. What is the name of WordPerfect's interactive templates?

14. What is TextArt?

15. What happens when a style attached to a document is edited?

▌Assignments

15-1   Directions

1. Open a new document.

2. Create the following styles:

   DocFormat: document, left justification, Widow/Orphan on

   MainHeading: Paragraph, Enter key chains to None, centered, large, bold

   MainHeading2: Paragraph, Enter key chains to None, centered, bold

   Subheading: Paragraph, Enter key chains to None, centered, italic

   Sideheading: Paragraph, Enter key chains to None, left justification, underlined

3. Save the styles as a style document called newlan.sty.

4. Close, but do not save the document.

15-2   Directions

1. Open a new document.

2. Retrieve the style document newlan.sty that you created in the previous exercise.

3. Retrieve the document from your data disk named newlan.wpd.

4. Turn on the MainHeading style, and in all caps, type `A LAN IN-STALLATION`.

5. Press `Enter` three times, turn on the MainHeading2 style, and type `A Case Study`.

6. Apply the Subheading style to the following headings: "Abstract," "Introduction," "Background," "Future Objectives," "Conclusion," and "Solutions."

7. Apply the Sideheading style to the following headings: "Reasons for LAN Installation," "Hardware," "Topology," "Operating System Software," "Printers," "LAN Personnel," "Software Training," and "Help Center."

8. Scroll through the document to see if all page endings are acceptable. If not, apply the necessary formatting commands.

9. Save the document as lan15.wpd, print it, and close it.

15-3 Directions

1. Open the lan15.wpd document and save it as lan15a.wpd.

2. With your pointer at the beginning of the document, edit the Sub-heading style to change the text to small caps (leaving it in italics and centered). Check to see if the style has changed all the subheadings.

3. Save, print, and close the document.

15-4 Directions

1. You are going to create a template. Make sure a new document is open.

2. Choose File ⇒ Template ⇒ Create.

3. Name the template Todo and base it on the None template.

4. When the blank screen appears, create the template as follows.

TO DO LIST

Your name   Date Code

1. (Tab)
2. (Tab)
3. (Tab)
4. (Tab)
5. (Tab)
6. (Tab)
7. (Tab)
8. (Tab)
9. (Tab)
10. (Tab)

---

5. Exit the template from the template feature bar. Check the list of templates to make sure Todo is listed.

15-5 Directions

1. Make sure a new document is open.

2. Select the Todo template created in Exercise 15-4. Save the document as todo1.wpd.

3. Add the following seven items:

Call Jerry about course information for CMS 101

Fill out grade sheets

Call students about their final exam grades

Meet at 12:30 for faculty-student potluck

Wrap gifts for secretaries and put them on their desks before 2:30

Make sure exams are returned and locked in file cabinet

Pick up dry cleaning on the way home

---

4. Save, print and close the document.

15-6 Directions

1. Open a new document.
2. Center the insertion point at the top of the document.
3. Select TextArt from the button bar or menu.
4. Type the following text in the Enter text window: `Sign Up Sheet`.
5. Set the measurements: Horizontal 5"; Vertical, 4".
6. Select the shape in row one, column one.
7. Exit the TextArt screen and return to your document.
8. Center the graphic at the top of your page.
9. Print, but do not save the document.

A   Command Summary

APPENDIX

Topic or Feature	Menu Commands	Function Keys
Power Bar Commands		
Display power bar	View ⇒ Power Bar	
Edit power bar	File ⇒ Preferences ⇒ Power Bar ⇒ Edit	
Button Bar Commands		
Change location/ appearance of button bar	File ⇒ Preferences ⇒ Button Bar ⇒ Options	
Create new button bar	File ⇒ Preferences ⇒ Button Bar ⇒ Edit	
Display button bar	View ⇒ Button Bar	
Edit button bar	File ⇒ Preferences ⇒ Button Bar ⇒ Edit	
Select button bar	File ⇒ Preferences ⇒ Button Bar ⇒ Select	
Document Management Commands		
Display ruler	View ⇒ Ruler	(Alt) + (Shift) + (F3)
Document initial font	Layout ⇒ Document ⇒ Initial Font	
Close document	File ⇒ Close	
Document initial codes style	Layout ⇒ Document ⇒ Initial Codes Style	
Draft mode	View ⇒ Draft	(Ctrl) + (F5)
Exit WordPerfect	File ⇒ Exit	(Alt) + (F4)
Full Page	View ⇒ Zoom ⇒ Full Page	
Go to next document		(Ctrl) + (F6)
Go to previous document		(Ctrl) + (Shift) + (F6)
Open document	File ⇒ Open	(Ctrl) + (O)
Overlap windows	Window ⇒ Cascade	
Permanently display ruler	File ⇒ Preferences ⇒ Display ⇒ Ruler Bar	

349

Topic or Feature	Menu Commands	Function Keys

Document Management Commands

Topic or Feature	Menu Commands	Function Keys
Side by side pages	View ⇒ Two Page	
Print document	File ⇒ Print	(F5)
Retrieve file into document	Insert ⇒ File ⇒ Filename ⇒ Insert	
Save new document	File ⇒ Save As	(F3)
Save already named document	File ⇒ Save	(Ctrl) + (S)
Show all windows	Windows ⇒ Tile	
Spell check a document	Tools ⇒ Speller	(Ctrl) + (F1)
Switch document window	Window	
Thesaurus	Tools ⇒ Thesaurus	(Alt) + (F1)

Formatting Commands—Format Character

Topic or Feature	Menu Commands	Function Keys
Bold while typing	Layout ⇒ Font ⇒ Bold	(Ctrl) + (B)
Bold existing text	Select Text ⇒ Layout ⇒ Font ⇒ Bold	(Ctrl) + (B)
Case conversion	Edit ⇒ Convert Case ⇒ Lowercase/ Uppercase/Initial Capitals	
Initial font change	Layout ⇒ Document ⇒ Initial Font	
Font	Layout ⇒ Font	
Outline, shadow, small cap	Layout ⇒ Font ⇒ Outline/Shadow/Small Cap	
Special characters	Insert ⇒ Character	(Ctrl) + (W)
Underline existing text	Select text ⇒ Layout ⇒ Font ⇒ Underline	(Ctrl) + (U)
Underline while typing	Layout ⇒ Font ⇒ Underline	(Ctrl) + (U)

Format Document

Topic or Feature	Menu Commands	Function Keys
Align text at right margin	Layout ⇒ Line ⇒ Flush Right	(Alt) + (F7)
Center page vertically	Layout ⇒ Page ⇒ Center	
Center line of text	Layout ⇒ Line ⇒ Center	(Shift) + (F7)
Change tab settings	Layout ⇒ Line ⇒ Tab Set	
Columns off	Layout ⇒ Columns ⇒ Off	
Conditional end of page	Layout fi Page fi Keep Text Together fi Conditional End of Page	
Discontinue header/footer	Layout ⇒ Header/Footer ⇒ Discontinue	
Edit footnote	Insert ⇒ Footnote ⇒ Edit	
Edit header/footer	Layout ⇒ Header/Footer ⇒ Edit	
Enter current date	Insert ⇒ Date ⇒ Date Text	(Ctrl) + (D)
Enter current date each time file is used	Insert ⇒ Date ⇒ Date Code	(Ctrl) + (Shift) + (D)
Font for whole document	Layout ⇒ Document ⇒ Initial Font	
Footnote	Insert ⇒ Footnote ⇒ Create	
Hard page break	Layout ⇒ Page ⇒ Force Page	(Ctrl) + (Enter)
Headers/Footers	Layout ⇒ Header/Footer	
Indent text	Layout ⇒ Paragraph ⇒ Indent	(F7)

Topic or Feature	**Menu Commands**	**Function Keys**
Format Document		
Justification:	Layout ⇒ Justification	
Left		Ctrl + L
Right		Ctrl + R
Center		Ctrl + E
Full		Ctrl + J
Keep 2 words together (hard space)	Layout ⇒ Line ⇒ Other Codes ⇒ Hard Space ⇒ Insert	Ctrl + Spacebar
Margin changes	Layout ⇒ Margins	Ctrl + F8
New page number	Layout ⇒ Page ⇒ Numbering ⇒ Value	
Page size change	Layout ⇒ Page ⇒ Paper Size	
Paper size/type	Layout ⇒ Page ⇒ Paper Size	
Protect block of text	Layout ⇒ Page ⇒ Keep Text Together ⇒ Block Protect	
Replace text	Edit ⇒ Replace	Ctrl + F2
Reveal Codes	View ⇒ Reveal Codes	Alt + F3
Reverse last change	Edit ⇒ Undo	Ctrl + Z
Right align text	Layout ⇒ Line ⇒ Flush Right	Alt + F7
Set dot leaders	Layout ⇒ Line ⇒ Dot Leader Character	
Set up columns	Layout ⇒ Columns ⇒ Define	
Show document codes	View ⇒ Reveal Codes	Alt + F3
Suppress header/footer	Layout ⇒ Page ⇒ Suppress	
Undelete text	Edit ⇒ Undelete	Ctrl + Shift + Z
Widow/Orphan	Layout ⇒ Page ⇒ Keep Text Together	
Graphics Commands		
Create graphic line	Graphics ⇒ Horizontal Line	Ctrl + F11
	Graphics ⇒ Vertical Line	Ctrl + Shift + F11
Create figure box	Graphics ⇒ Figure	
Create text box	Graphics ⇒ Text	
Create user box	Graphics ⇒ Custom Box ⇒ User	
Macro Commands		
Create (record) macro	Tools ⇒ Macro ⇒ Record	Ctrl + F10
Edit macro	Tools ⇒ Macro ⇒ Edit	
Stop recording macro	Tools ⇒ Macro ⇒ Record	Ctrl + F10
Play macro	Tools ⇒ Macro ⇒ Play	Alt + F10
Merge Commands		
Create data file	Tools ⇒ Merge ⇒ Data	Shift + F9
Create form file	Tools ⇒ Merge ⇒ Form	Shift + F9
Perform merge	Tools ⇒ Merge ⇒ Merge	Shift + F9

Topic or Feature	Menu Commands	Function Keys
Search Commands		
Go to specific page	Edit ⇒ Go to	`Ctrl` + `G`
Word search	Edit ⇒ Find	`F2`
Next occurrence	Edit ⇒ Find ⇒ Find Next	`Shift` + `F2`
Previous occurrence	Edit ⇒ Find Previous	
Replace	Edit ⇒ Replace	`Ctrl` + `F2`
Table Commands		
Create table	Table ⇒ Create	`F12`
Delete row/column	Table ⇒ Delete ⇒ Rows/columns	
Insert row/column	Table ⇒ Insert ⇒ Rows/columns	
Join cells	Table ⇒ Join ⇒ Cell	
Lines	Table ⇒ Lines/Fill	`Shift` + `F12`
Format	Table ⇒ Format	`Ctrl` + `F12`
Split cells	Table ⇒ Split	

Text Insertion		Keystroke
Generally		
Beginning of a document		`Ctrl` + `Home`
Beginning of a document (before codes)		`Ctrl` + `Home`, `Ctrl` + `Home`
Beginning of a line		`Home`
Beginning of a line (before codes)		`Home`, `Home`
Bottom of the screen		`PgDn`
Top of the screen		`PgUp`
Next character		`→`
Previous character		`←`
Next line down		`↓`
Previous line up		`↑`
Previous word		`Ctrl` + `←`
Next word		`Ctrl` + `→`
Next page		`Alt` + `PgDn`
Previous page		`Alt` + `PgUp`
Specified page (Go to)		`Ctrl` + `G`
Next document		`Ctrl` + `F6`
Previous document		`Ctrl` + `Shift` + `F6`
Next window		`Ctrl` + `F6`
Previous window		`Ctrl` + `Shift` + `F6`
Next pane		`Ctrl` + `F6`
Previous Pane		`Ctrl` + `Shift` + `F6`
End of a document		`Ctrl` + `End`

Text Insertion	**Keystroke**

In a Column

Move 1 column to the right	Alt + →
Move 1 column to the left	Alt + ←

In a Table

Move up a cell	Alt + ↑
Move down a cell	Alt + ↓
Move right a cell	Alt + → (or Tab)
Move left a cell	Alt + ← (or Shift + Tab)
First cell in a row	Home, Home
Last cell in a row	End, End
Create	F12
Format	Ctrl + F12
Number Type	Alt + F12
Lines/Fill	Shift + F12
Data Fill	Ctrl + Shift + F12
Sum	Ctrl + = (equal sign)

In a Dialog Box

Next option	Tab
Previous option	Shift + Tab
Perform default action	Enter

Other Insertion Function

Back tab (margin release)	Shift + Tab
Hard return	Enter
Hyphen, hard	Ctrl + - (hyphen)
Hard space	Ctrl + Spacebar
Hard Page Break	Ctrl + Enter
WP Character	Ctrl + W

Text Deletion

Current character	Del
Character to the left	Backspace
Word	Ctrl + Backspace
Rest of a line	Ctrl + Del
Rest of a page	Ctrl + Shift + Del

File Management

New File	Ctrl + N
Open	Ctrl + O
Close	Ctrl + F4
Save	Ctrl + S
Save As	F3
Exit	Alt + F4

Text Insertion   Keystroke

Editing Functions
Copy text to the Clipboard	`Ctrl` + `C`
Cut text to the Clipboard	`Ctrl` + `X`
Typeover	`Ins`
Cancel	`Esc`
Undo	`Ctrl` + `Z`
Undelete	`Ctrl` + `Shift` + `Z`
Paste	`Ctrl` + `V`
Find	`F2`
Replace	`Ctrl` + `F2`
Go To	`Ctrl` + `G`
Speller	`Ctrl` + `F1`
Thesaurus	`Alt` + `F1`
Grammatik	`Alt` + `Shift` + `F1`
Edit Graphic Box	`Shift` + `F11`

Formatting Functions
Center	`Shift` + `F7`
Flush Right	`Alt` + `F7`
Font	`F9`
Margins	`Ctrl` + `F8`
Indent	`F7`
Hanging Indent	`Ctrl` + `F7`
Double Indent	`Ctrl` + `Shift` + `F7`
Justification	
Left	`Ctrl` + `L`
Right	`Ctrl` + `R`
Center	`Ctrl` + `E`
Full	`Ctrl` + `J`

Other Functions
Date Text	`Ctrl` + `D`
Date Code	`Ctrl` + `Shift` + `D`
Draft Mode	`Ctrl` + `F5`
Help	`F1`
Hide Bars	`Alt` + `Shift` + `F5`
Horizontal Line	`Ctrl` + `F11`
Macro Play	`Alt` + `F10`
Macro Record	`Ctrl` + `F10`
Merge	`Shift` + `F9`
Page Mode	`Alt` + `F5`
Print	`F5`
Reveal Codes	`Alt` + `F3`
Ruler Bar	`Alt` + `Shift` + `F3`

Text Insertion	Keystroke
Other Functions	
Show	Ctrl + Shift + F3
Sort	Alt + F9
Styles	Alt + F8
Template	Ctrl + T
Vertical Line	Ctrl + F11

Index